A Literary Anthology

Growing Up Gay/ Growing Up Lesbian

A Literary Anthology

Edited by Bennett L. Singer

NEW PRESS   NEW YORK

Published in the United States by The New Press, New York
Distributed by W. W. Norton & Company, Inc.,
500 Fifth Avenue, New York, NY 10110

ISBN 1–56584–103–4 (pb)
ISBN 1–56584–102–6 (hc)
LC 93–83622

Originally published under the title *Growing Up Gay*
by The New Press in 1993.

Permissions acknowledgments appear on pp. 313–317

Established in 1990 as a major alternative to the large,
commercial publishing houses, The New Press is the first
full-scale nonprofit American book publisher outside of the
university presses. The Press is operated editorially in the
public interest, rather than for private gain; it is committed
to publishing in innovative ways works of educational,
cultural, and community value that, despite their intellectual
merits, might not normally be "commercially" viable. The
New Press's editorial offices are located at the City University of New York.

Printed in the United States of America

94 95 96 97   9 8 7 6 5 4 3 2 1

Contents

III. Family

IV. Facing the World

Contents

Invisibility can be deadly.

—Don Clark, *Living Gay*

Preface

As I was growing up, I spent years searching for the answer to one simple but all-consuming question: *Am I the only one?* Am I the only person in my hometown who is gay?

My friends, teachers, and family members saw me as a diligent student and a hard-working editor of my high school newspaper. Invisible to them—but apparent to me for as long as I can remember—was my emotional, intellectual, and physical attraction to other men. For nearly twenty years, I never spoke about this attraction with anyone. I was terrified that people who saw behind my mask would reject me, and that everything I had achieved or might achieve would be negated by the truth about my sexual orientation. I knew that gay people existed somewhere, but I honestly believed that I was the only gay student among the 2,500 classmates at my high school.

Secretly, silently, I searched for clues that would help me understand myself and end my isolation. It was a difficult investigation. Gay characters seldom surfaced on television or in the movies; when they did appear, they were crude caricatures that seemed far removed from my world. There were no openly gay teachers or counselors at my high school, so I had no adult role models to consult. When the topic of homosexuality did come up at school, it was in the context of "fag jokes," which only reinforced my instinct to keep my feelings secret. Most of these jokes were told by students, but I can distinctly remember one teacher's comments upon seeing a newspaper photo of a men's swim team. "Those skimpy swimsuits should make the homos happy," he said, never imagining that I might be gay.

One of the key moments in my search for answers came unexpectedly, when I stumbled upon a "gay novel" at the public library. I was fifteen at the time; the year was 1979. I can still remember the book jacket—it was bright yellow and orange—and the book's title: *The Lord Won't Mind*. The novel, by Gordon Merrick, tells the story of the "forbidden love" that develops and ultimately triumphs between two dashing young men named Peter and Charlie. Peter and Charlie declare their love for one another on the very first day they meet; the book's last page finds them sharing their lives together thirty years later. The story's happy ending—and the book's very *existence*—provided comforting evidence that I was not alone and led me to consider the notion that two men or two women really could love one another. Unfortunately, however, the book left me with new and troubling questions: Is something wrong with gay people? Are they sick or diseased outcasts to be pitied? When Charlie tells his worldly grandmother that he is gay, she insists that his homosexuality is a form of "bestiality" caused by a "taint in the blood." "Do you wish me to believe that you have a warped and twisted nature?" she asks. Then she delivers an ultimatum to her once-beloved grandson: "If you give way once more to this disgusting sickness, I could never face you again."

Despite its mixed messages and depiction of brutal homophobia, *The Lord Won't Mind* was a lifeline for me, principally because it showed me that gay people should be true to themselves even if the world does not understand. Taking pride in one's sexual identity is one of several themes that runs through *Growing Up Gay/ Growing Up Lesbian*. The book's fifty-six selections are also intended to underscore the fact that *gay people are everywhere:* in every culture and ethnic group, in public schools and private academies, on football teams and yearbook staffs, in skyscrapers and on reservations, on army bases and navy ships.

And although they may be separated by differences in geography, racial background, and religion, lesbians and gay men often face remarkably similar questions in the course of growing up. How do I *know* I'm gay? Is there anyone that I can I discuss my feelings with? Will "coming out of the closet" and acknowledging that I am gay drive my friends away? Will my family understand? How will telling the truth about who I am change me?

These are important questions—and they have been answered in many ways by many writers. As a glance at the table of contents shows, there are a lot of different kinds of writing in this book. You'll find essays and short stories, poems and diary entries, rap lyrics and letters, and excerpts from novels and autobiographies. Throughout, reflections of adult writers are interspersed with writings by teenagers. Many of the selections are excerpted from previously published works, while others are printed here for the first time.

Although *Growing Up Gay/ Growing Up Lesbian* is not organized chronologically, the book does contain selections that reflect what is was like to grow up gay or lesbian in every decade since the 1920s. The book is divided into four parts; in each, male and female authors are represented in roughly equal numbers. The first section, "Self-Discovery," chronicles the process of finding one's sexual identity—a period of awakening, of exploration, and of looking for "the answers I needed," as Billie Tallmij puts it in her oral history about coming of age as a lesbian in the 1940s. Next comes a series of pieces that look at establishing friendships and relationships with other gay people, with selections by James Baldwin, Paula Gunn Allen, and David Leavitt. Section three, "Family," includes excerpts from a high school junior's journal about "coming out" to his mother, a poem by Essex Hemphill in which he speaks of the pain of being "the invisible son," and several pieces about having gay siblings. The book concludes with a section called "Facing the World," with selections on attending a high school prom with a same-sex date, responding to homophobia and anti-gay violence, and "coming out" in class.

A number of works in the collection address the transformation that took place in the gay and lesbian liberation movement following the Stonewall uprising in June of 1969, when gay and lesbian patrons of the Stonewall Inn fought back against New York City police who raided their bar. In addition, several authors write about the impact that AIDS has had on growing up gay in the 1980s and 1990s.

Given that the book spans almost the entire century, it's not surprising that writers use a variety of terms to describe themselves. Several authors refer to themselves by reclaiming terms that were once used disparagingly. For example, some female authors refer to themselves as "dykes"; some male authors refer to themselves as "fags" or "queens"; and some women and men refer to themselves as "queer." In the same vein, the pink triangle, which was used to identify homosexual prisoners in the Nazi concentration camps of World War II, is now worn by gay men and lesbians as a symbol of self-respect and pride.

While many of the contributors to this collection knew of their sexual orientation at an early age, others acknowledged their same-sex attractions later in life. It's important to remember, as the pioneering sex researcher Alfred Kinsey pointed out, that there is a wide range of sexual orientation and behavior: while some people are exclusively straight and others are exclusively gay, the majority of the population falls somewhere in the middle of this spectrum.

For that reason, I believe *Growing Up Gay/ Growing Up Lesbian* will be relevant to individuals growing up bisexual. Bisexual adolescents experience the same sense of isolation that gay and lesbian youth feel; indeed, bisexual youth face an additional challenge in that bisexual role models are even rarer that lesbian or gay ones. The experience of growing up bisexual certainly merits its own treatment. In the meantime, this book attempts to help serve part of that need by presenting a number of selection that address bisexual issues, and by underscoring the value of remaining true to one's sexual identity. In addition, an appendix contains state-by-state listings of support groups and services for bisexual, gay, and lesbian youth.

An unprecedented display of visibility, diversity, and solidarity occurred in April 1993, when an estimated one million people assembled for the National March on Washington for Lesbian, Gay, and Bi Equal

Rights and Liberation. One of the undisputed highlights of the march came when Martina Navratilova delivered a rousing speech on the importance of coming out and on the need to be open and honest about one's sexual identity. As I stood among the vast crowd and listened to Ms. Navratilova speak, I thought back to my days in high school and reflected that it would have been immensely valuable to have heard such an affirming and unapologetic declaration from such a highly respected public figure. It also occurred to me that young people who did not attend the march would benefit from hearing the speech, and I approached Ms. Navratilova about including her remarks in this book. She graciously agreed, and her speech appears on page xv. As you read her remarks, I urge you to consider where you are in your own coming-out process, and to remember that coming out is a complex and intensely personal experience with many stages. Each of these stages—coming out to oneself, to one's friends and family members, and to the world at large—is addressed by contributors to the anthology.

Of the nearly sixty authors represented in this book, not one claims to have elected to be gay or lesbian. Rather, each suggests, directly or indirectly, that being gay is a natural and essential component of his or her identity. People do not choose their sexual orientation—but gay and lesbian people *can* choose to take pride in who they are, to respect themselves, and to end the isolation and solitude that come with invisibility. It is my hope that *Growing Up Gay/Growing Up Lesbian* will inspire gay and lesbian young people to make that choice.

BENNETT L. SINGER
San Francisco, July 1993

Foreword

I'd like to welcome you and to salute you for being here. What our movement for equality needs most, in my not-so-humble opinion, is for us to come out of the closet. We need to become visible to as many people as possible, so that we can finally shatter all those incredible myths that help keep us in the closet.

Let's come out and let all the people see what, for the most part, straight and square and normal and sometimes boring lives we lead. Let's come out and dispel the rumors and lies that are being spread about us. Let's come out and set everybody straight, so to speak.

Our goal is not to receive compassion, acceptance, or worse yet, tolerance, because that implies that we are inferior, we are to be tolerated, pitied, and endured. I don't want pity, do you? Of course not! Our goal must be equality across the board. We can settle for nothing less, because we deserve nothing less.

Labels, labels, labels. Now, I don't know about you, but I hate labels. Martina Navratilova, the lesbian tennis player. They don't say Joe Montana, the heterosexual football player.

One's sexuality should not be an issue, one way or another. One's sexuality should not become a label by which that human being should be identified. My sexuality is a very important part of my life, a very important part of my being, but it is still a very small part of my makeup, a very small part of what creates a whole human being. In any case being a lesbian is not an accomplishment. It is not something I had to learn, study for, or graduate in.

It is what I am. Nothing more and nothing less.

Now, I did not spend over thirty years of my life working my butt off trying to become the very best tennis player that I can be, to then be called Martina, the lesbian tennis player. Labels are for filing, labels are for bookkeeping, labels are for clothing. Labels are not for people.

Being homosexual, bisexual, or heterosexual is not good or bad. It simply is.

So now we are here today so that one day in the hopefully not-too-distant future, we will be referred to not by our sexuality, but by our accomplishments and abilities—Melissa Etheridge, the incredible rock 'n' roller; Barney Frank, the congressman from Massachusetts; Dave

---

This is a transcript of a speech delivered at the National March on Washington for Lesbian, Gay, and Bi Equal Rights, held on April 25, 1993.

Pallone, the baseball umpire; k. d. lang, the best pipes in the business, as Roy Orbison called her; Joe Zuniga, soldier, U.S. Army.

All these wonderful people and many more have come out of the closet. Each and every one had something to lose by that action, and each and every one could have made all kinds of excuses not to come out, but they didn't. So, now, I urge all of you who are still in the closet to throw away all the excuses.

Instead, find all the wonderful reasons why you too should be out. Believe me, in the long run, the good will far outweigh the bad, because if we want the world to accept us, we must first accept ourselves. If we want the world to give us respect, not to look at us with shame, we must first be willing to give ourselves respect. We must be proud of who we are and we cannot do that while we hide.

I believe the biggest, strongest weapon of our movement for equality is visibility, and the best way to get it is to come out. Yes, publicity of any kind—talk shows, articles, movies with positive gay characters—that all helps tremendously, but it is impersonal.

By coming out to our friends, family, employers, and employees, we make ourselves personal, touchable, real. We become human beings, and then we have the opportunity to show the world what we are all about—happy, intelligent, giving, loving people. We can show our moral strength, dignity, character. We can share our joy and sorrow, our happiness and pain. We can just be. I urge you to be out. Encourage your lovers and friends to come out. Come out, be proud, and be true to yourself. And as the song says, "Don't worry. Be gay."

MARTINA NAVRATILOVA

Acknowledgments

This book benefited in countless ways from the suggestions and involvement of many people.

Diane Wachtell of The New Press suggested that I undertake this project, and I am enormously grateful for her guidance, trust, and inspiration—and for her vision in recognizing the need for a book of this sort. I thank André Schiffrin for believing in this project, as well as Akiko Takano and the rest of the staff at The New Press for their support, patience, and unwavering professionalism.

Holly Adiele of the Harrison Middle School in Sunnyside, Washington, offered invaluable editorial advice during every phase of the project and provided numerous selections included in the book. This collection is infinitely richer and more diverse thanks to her.

I am indebted to Dan Kephart of the Department of English at Sunnyside High School in Sunnyside, Washington, and to Travis Wise, a high school junior, for reviewing the entire manuscript. I am also grateful to Ernest Hardy, Nancy Kates, Rochelle Kopp, Sean Mills, Steve Rohde, Julia Sullivan, and Don Yingling for suggesting material to include in this book. Kevin Jennings of Concord Academy provided practical editorial advice at key moments along the way, while Faith Adiele, Martin Anderson, Lawrence Eaton, Charles and Janice Feldstein, Sarah Flynn, Max Gordon, Adam Gwosdof, Bob Lavelle, Michael Melcher, Ellen Reeves, and Rachel Singer Sullivan provided much-needed support, editorial as well as moral.

I thank Richard Labonté of A Different Light bookstore in San Francisco for his generosity in loaning me books and for his valuable editorial suggestions, and Bill Stanton and the staff of San Francisco's Harvey Milk Branch Library for research expertise and encouragement.

I received helpful comments and editorial advice from Andy Humm of the Hetrick-Martin Institute; Dr. Virginia Uribe of Project Ten; Barbara Blinick of Bay Area Network of Gay and Lesbian Educators; Rick Aguirre of Bay Area Sexual Minority Youth Network; Tanya Domi and Heidi Scanlon of the National Gay and Lesbian Task Force; Bill Rubenstein of the American Civil Liberties Union; and Robin Tyler and Michelle Crone of the National March on Washington for Lesbian, Gay, and Bi Equal Rights.

Ed Cohen copyedited the manuscript with a remarkably keen eye, while Ann Sandhorst showed me the way through the thicket of permissions agreements and had answers to my every contract-related question.

I want to thank the authors, editors, agents, and permissions representatives who agreed to allow their material to be used in this book, and who in many cases altered their standard fees as a means of demonstrating their backing for this project.

My parents, Paul and Lynne Singer, taught me to respect myself and have taken a genuine interest in all of my work on gay issues, including this project. I deeply appreciate their involvement.

And finally, my partner, David Deschamps, was a sounding board, confidant, and constant source of emotional and editorial support throughout this project. I couldn't have done it without him.

I

Self-

Discovery

American Dreams

Kevin Jennings

A native of North Carolina, Kevin Jennings grew up believing that gay people are "twisted perverts destined for a lifetime of eternal damnation." In this essay, Kevin describes the long and painful process he went through to overcome this belief—and to discover his true dreams for himself as a gay man.

When I was little, I honestly thought I would grow up to be the President. After all, I lived in a land of opportunity where anyone, with enough determination and hard work, could aspire to the highest office in the land. I planned to live out the American Dream.

I realized, however, that something was amiss from an early age. I grew up in the rural community of Lewisville, North Carolina, just outside the city of Winston-Salem. As you might guess from the city's name, Winston-Salem makes its living from the tobacco industry: it was cigarettes that propelled local conglomerate RJR-Nabisco to its status as one of the world's largest multinational corporations. Somehow this rising tide of prosperity never lapped at our doors, and the Jennings family was a bitter family indeed. Poor whites descended from Confederate veterans, we eagerly sought out scapegoats for our inexplicable failure to "make it" in the land of opportunity. My uncles and cousins joined the Ku Klux Klan, while my father, a fundamentalist minister, used religion to excuse his prejudices—against blacks, against Jews, against Catholics, against Yankees, against Communists and liberals (basically the same thing, as far as he was concerned), and, of course, against gays. Somehow the golden rule of "Do unto others as you would have them do unto you" never made it into his gospel. Instead, I remember church services filled with outbursts of paranoia, as we were warned about the evils of those whom we (incorrectly) held responsible for our very real oppression. I grew up believing that there was a Communist plot undermining our nation, a Jewish conspiracy controlling the banks and the media, and that black men—whom I unselfconsciously referred to as "niggers"—spent their days plotting to rape white women. In case this seems like a history lesson on the Stone Age, please consider that I was born in 1963 and graduated from high school in 1981. Hardly the ancient past!

My father's profession as a traveling minister never left much money for luxuries like college tuition. Nevertheless, my mother was determined that I, her last chance, was going to make good on the Dream that had been denied to her and to my four older siblings. Not that it was going to be easy: my father died when I was eight, and my mother went to work at McDonald's (the only job she could get with her limited credentials). Every penny was watched carefully; dinner was often leftover Quarter-pounders that she didn't have to pay for. I'm the only person I know who sees the Golden Arches, takes a bite, and thinks, "Mmm, just like Mom used to make!"

Throughout high school, I was determined to make it, determined to show my mother—and myself—that the American Dream really could come true. I worked hard and got ahead, earning a scholarship to Harvard after I had remade myself into the image of what I was told a successful person was like. Little did I realize at that point the price I was paying to fit in.

The first thing to go was any sign of my Southern heritage. As I came into contact with mainstream America, through high school "gifted and talented" programs and, later, at college in Massachusetts, I began to realize that we Southerners were different. Our home-cooked meals—grits, turnip greens, red-eye gravy—never seemed to show up in frozen dinners, and if a character on television spoke with a Southern accent, that immediately identified him or her as stupid or as comic relief. As the lesbian writer Blanche Boyd put it: "When television programs appeared, a dreadful truth came clear to me: Southerners were not normal people. We did not sound like normal people . . . [and] what we chose to talk about seemed peculiarly different also. I began to realize we were hicks. Television took away my faith in my surroundings. I didn't want to be a hick. I decided to go North, where people talked fast, walked fast, and acted cool. I practiced talking like the people on television. . . . I became desperate to leave the South." Like Blanche Boyd, I deliberately erased my accent and aped the false monotone of television newscasters. I never invited college friends home to North Carolina for fear they might meet my family and realize they were worthless, ignorant hicks—which is how I'd come to view those whom I loved. I applied to colleges on the sole criterion that they not be in the South. I ran as far from Lewisville, North Carolina, as I could.

But there were some things about myself I could not escape from or change, no matter how hard I tried—among them the fact that I am gay.

I had always known I was gay, even before I had heard the word or knew what it meant. I remember that at age six or seven, the "adult" magazines that so fascinated my older brothers simply didn't interest me at all, and I somehow knew that I'd better hide this feeling from them. As I grew older and began to understand what my feelings meant, I recoiled in horror from myself. After all, my religious upbringing as a Southern Baptist had taught me that gay people were twisted perverts destined for a lifetime of eternal damnation.

Being as set as I was on achieving the American Dream, I was not about to accept the fact that I was gay. Here is where I paid the heaviest price for my Dream. I pursued what I thought was "normal" with a vengeance in high school, determined that, if the spirit was weak, the flesh would be more willing at the prospect of heterosexuality. I dated every girl I could literally get my hands on, earning a well-deserved reputation as a jerk who tried to see how far he could get on the first date. I attacked anyone who suggested that gay people might be entitled to some rights, too, and was the biggest teller of fag jokes at Radford High. But what I really hated was myself, and this I couldn't escape from, no matter how drunk or stoned I got, which I was doing on an almost daily basis by senior year.

That was also the year I fell in love for the first time, with another boy in my class. It turned out he was gay, too, and we made love one night in late May. I woke up the next morning and realized that it was true—I really was a fag after all. I spent that day trying to figure out how I was going to live the American Dream, which seemed impossible if I was homosexual. By night-fall I decided it *was* impossible, and without my Dream I couldn't see a reason why I'd want to be alive at all. I went to my family's medicine cabinet, took the new bottle of aspirin out, and pro-ceeded to wash down 140 pills with a glass of gin. I remember the exact number—140—because I figured I could only get down about ten at one swallow, so I carefully counted out fourteen little stacks before I began. Thanks to a friend who got to me in time, I didn't die that night. My story has a happy ending—but a lot of them don't. Those moments of desperation helped me understand why one out of every three gay teens tries to commit suicide.

At Harvard, the most important lessons I learned had little to do with Latin American or European history, which were my ma-jors. Instead, I learned the importance of taking control of my own destiny. I met a great professor who taught me that as long as I stayed in the closet, I was accepting the idea that there was something wrong with me, something that I needed to hide. After all, as my favorite bisexual, Eleanor Roosevelt, once said, "No one can make you feel inferior without your consent." By staying closeted, I was consenting to my own inferiority. I realized that for years, I had let a Dream—a beautiful, seductive, but ulti-mately false Dream—rule my life. I had agreed to pay its price, which was the rejection of my family, my culture, and eventually myself. I came to understand that the costs of the Dream far out-weighed its rewards. I learned that true freedom would be mine only when I was able to make my own decisions about what I wanted out of life instead of accepting those thrust upon me by the Dream. Since I made that realization, I have followed my own path instead of the one I had been taught was "right" all my life.

Once I started down this new path, I began to make some dis-coveries about the society in which I was raised, and about its notions of right and wrong. I began to ask many questions, and the answers to these questions were not always pleasant. Why, for example, did my mother always earn less than men who did the same exact work? Why did I learn as a child that to cheat someone was to "Jew" them? Why was my brother ostracized when he fell in love with and later married a black woman? Why did everyone in my family work so hard and yet have so little? I realized that these inequalities were part of the game, the rules of which were such that gays, blacks, poor people, women, and many others would always lose to the wealthy white heterosexual Christian men who have won the Presidency forty-two out of forty-two times. Those odds—100 percent—are pretty good ones to bet on. No, I discovered that true freedom could not be achieved by a Dream that calls on us to give up who we are in order to fit in and become "worthy" of power. Holding power means little if women have to become masculine "iron ladies" to get it, if Jews have to "Americanize" their names, if blacks have to learn to speak so-called Standard English (though we never acknowledge *whose* standard it is), or if gays and lesbians have to hide what everyone else gets to celebrate—the loves of their lives.

Real freedom will be ours when the people around us—and when we ourselves—accept that we, too, are "real" Americans, and that we shouldn't have to change to meet anyone else's standards. In 1924, at age twenty-two, the gay African-American poet Langston Hughes said it best, in his poem "I, Too":

> Tomorrow,
> I'll be at the table
> When company comes.
> Nobody'll dare
> Say to me,
> "Eat in the kitchen,"
> Then.

> Besides,
> They'll see how beautiful I am
> And be ashamed—

> I, too, am America.

By coming out as a gay man and demanding my freedom, I realize that I have done the most American thing of all. And while I have come a long way since the days when I dreamed of living in the White House, I have discovered that what I'm fighting for now is the very thing I thought I'd be fighting for if I ever became President—"liberty and justice for all."

It Happened on Main Street

Linda Heal

Linda Heal grew up in Kewanee, Illinois, the hog capital of the world. Going away to college allowed Linda to make a clean start in several ways: she recognized that she is a lesbian, began a relationship with another woman, and found the courage to "come out" to her mother. Linda now lives in Madison, Wisconsin.

Only a week before, we had done our first loads of college laundry together. Carefully following my mom's written instructions, we separated the whites and colors . . . and then, at fifty cents per load, decided to consolidate everything into one machine and hit the "cold" button. We'd deal with laundry that didn't win awards.

We were eighteen and freshmen at a small liberal arts college in an Illinois town of about 100,000. The first class I went to was called Social Problems, where I sat behind a short, controlled, but intense woman in beat-up running shoes. In high school, I had sweat out a lot of energy on the basketball and volleyball teams, so as an ex-jock, I'm always looking at the quality of people's footwear to see how seriously they take themselves. The person in the well-worn Adidas turned out to be Kay, and on an October evening, we decided to get together to study for our first college exam. Since Kay was constantly in motion, we opted to study while walking on Main Street. We'd barely touched the material in Section One when she screeched to halt and sat down in a flower box in front of a tanning spa.

"Can I trust you?" she blurted out into the traffic noise and lingering scent of ultraviolet-induced tans. "And can you trust me?"

I nodded to both of those, hearing in the rhythm of Kay's voice that if she slowed down for a moment, she would never get her words out. "Are you gay or straight? Me, I'm as queer as a three-dollar bill."

And there it was in a chill over Main Street—the question I had avoided thinking about for the past five years. But there was something new, too: a good reason to say, "Yeah. Maybe." This was the first time someone had come out to me. This was the first person my age even to *hint* at the kind of self-knowledge that had been chewing at my own edges. This was also as scared as I'd ever been in my entire life.

So I said it. "Yeah. Maybe. I mean, I've always thought I probably was, but I've never had the chance to, umm, I've never checked it out." And I hadn't. I grew up in a midwestern town of 10,000 that acted even smaller. Openly gay men and women were as hard to find as tasteful radio stations, so I hadn't dared to talk about what I thought was happening to me. But quietly I knew.

The word *homosexual* first turned up in my life when I was eleven. I was watching an episode of "Family" when one of Willie's friends came out to him. Later in the show, mother Kate asked daughter Buddy, "Do you know what a homosexual is?"

"Yeah," said Kristy McNichol (perhaps a little too fast, now that I think about it). "A guy who likes a guy or a girl who likes a girl." Oddly enough, that show never made it into reruns, but I filed away that concise definition—and the knowledge that different feelings and ways of living were possible.

I had just turned thirteen when I noticed that my attachments to my new friends seemed *incredibly* strong. I hesitantly admitted it a year later in my journal, after fifteen pages of confiding how close I felt to Michelle and Julie, and how much I respected them because they ignored the other kids who kept asking me if I was going to have a husband or a wife, or if transsexual tennis star Renee Richards was my hero. I knew that my feelings didn't want to stay within the ordinary boundaries of friendship. And looking around in my junior high homeroom, it seemed that nobody else felt as passionate about members of their own gender as I felt about Julie and Michelle.

"I think I'm gay," I wrote in my early teen handwriting that vacillated between the large loopy way everybody else wrote and my own tight pointy letters. "It isn't from other people calling me that—I just have what adults would call 'very confusing feelings.' Damn right they're confusing. I'm not attracted to boys at all. I want to be with Julie and I want to do with her the things I'm supposed to want to with boys. Dammit, what's going on? I think I love her. What's the matter with me?"

In lots of ways, I was different from the other eighth graders. I never had urges to adopt "feminine" manners, for one thing. I spent time skateboarding and decorating my shins with bruises and scabs while my friends were begging to get their ears pierced. I dreaded the onset of bras and eye shadow, and tried to figure out ways to avoid them. I never looked forward to lipstick, uncomfortable shoes, learning to carry a purse. Barbie had always given me the creeps; my heroes were women who had short hair, athletic ability, and feet that could stand flat on the ground. From the first time I realized it was possible, in first grade, I'd sneak on pairs of shorts under the dresses I resented so. Even for church. You never know when you'll accidentally fall upside down during the benediction. So in this adolescent part of my life, when conformity was queen, I stood out quite a bit.

And the other eighth graders had noticed. It was okay, though, because I'd carved out a niche. Early on, I found that humor, used well, can focus people's observations exactly where you want them to be. Or away from where you don't want them to be. So being weird was okay with most of the kids, because I was also funny. I could handle anything. I could see potential jokes lying around everywhere, and I made sure to tell them. Being a clown kept people from looking too hard at me, kept them from seeing what was painful and lay beyond the jokes.

Frankly, I was frightened. Although I'd become somewhat comfortable with my label as "the weird one," lesbianism was *too* weird. For the next four years, I never acted on my feelings for women, hoping that eventually they would evolve into heterosexual feelings. Every now and then, on the pages of our newspaper, Ann Landers promised that they would. So I waited. I could even be spotted at high school dances, waiting patiently, being a good sport about the death-by-pantyhose I was suffering underneath the dressy costumes you had to wear to get into those events.

All the while, I knew that I was shushing a major part of myself. I stopped writing journals, because introspection was dangerous. I stopped reading contemporary books, because I never knew when a teenage character would strike some nerve and remind me of the beautiful fullness of life that I was disallowing myself. Instead, I poured myself into being busy—I participated in varsity sports, wrote for the yearbook, played jazz trombone, and fell in love with early American literature, which seemed safely removed. Those stories never talked about love, not outright at least, only solitary men freezing to death on tundras.

All those years of painstaking squelching had brought me here, to a flower box on Main Street where I finally decided that what I had been trying to overlook, to wait out, might have some positive force. Kay could hardly keep still. It's a personal trait of hers, but that night her wiggling seemed to disturb the cells of every living thing around us.

Kay and I kept walking and talking, and my confusion and pain of hiding began to leak out . . . into the ears of someone who knew what it felt like. Kay had come out about a year before, read voraciously, and was not shy about quizzing people about what they had learned. So I was able to ask her questions I'd been stewing about. It was Kay, for instance, who made me realize that maybe it just doesn't matter *how* we got to be gay in the first place. "That's all history," she said. "What we need to deal with is now. We can choose to accept the fact that things work out differently for us than for most people. Or we can choose to ignore it."

She laid it out just like that, like there was no stigma there at all. Suddenly I was one hundred miles away from my hometown, my family, anyone who had a picture of me suffering through a high school dance waiting for my hormones to notice someone, anyone, as long as he was wearing a suit. The sun had gone down, motorists' headlights had come on. Possibilities were unfolding. Goose bumps were starting to show.

Kay said she found me attractive. So whenever I felt ready, she said, she wondered if we could consider dating. Right there, in a haze of one-way traffic on Main Street, we embarked on a relationship that lasted nearly two years, and on a friendship that has spanned a decade.

When we first started dating, there were a lot of knowing smiles—it felt like a secret affair, and the sparks I felt with Kay were something new, coming surprisingly easily after all those years of trying to force some sort of fleshly interest in the guy I was dating. When she and I slept together three weeks later, there was an undeniable feeling that this was how things are best for me: I was meant to love a woman's softness.

Coming out to myself, as much as it was a relief, was still a stressful time for me. My roommate, a petite prom queen with a tiny voice (but the housing computer had said we were compatible!) found out that Kay and I were more than friends. She freaked out and moved out: evidence that coming out wasn't all goose bumps and grins. I also noticed an increasing distance when I talked with my mom, with whom I'd always had a very warm, open, friendly relationship. Every time I picked up the phone, I tried to become who I'd been in high school, and the fast transitions between the worlds made my ears ring.

As I became more comfortable with the idea of gayness itself, with myself, and with other gay students at a nearby larger university's gay student support group, I realized that I needed to come out to my mom. There was too much trust between us, and she had been so supportive during those gawky years of long limbs and bad jokes and endless band concerts. And I thought that Mom, who had shown me what love looked like by loving me so unconditionally, would want to know that I was in love with someone for the first time. As I headed downstairs to help Mom with the dishes during a weekend visit home, I told myself that she probably already knew I had lesbian leanings. She's probably been waiting patiently for me to find the courage to voice them.

Wrong.

To my surprise, I caught my mom completely off balance. She hadn't made anything of my lack of kinship with the high school guys I had dated or wondered why I'd never had any trouble coming home by ten o' clock. She hadn't made any assumptions about my intense connections with my women friends. When I told her I was a lesbian, she thought I was joking. She thought it had something to do with a class she knew I was taking called "Social Problems."

It was a long dishwashing session. And for the next year or so, it was a long period of unraveling. There was disbelief, there was blaming. Mom blamed Kay for manipulating me into saying I was a lesbian. "Maybe you just want the bond of her friendship so much you'll do whatever she tells you—even act like a lover." When I reiterated that I'd had these feelings for women long before I met Kay, Mom started blaming herself. "I guess Dad and I don't show enough affection for each other, and you haven't seen how strong male-female love can be."

During that time, my whole body and soul felt like one big scraped knuckle. I felt like Mom was knocking my strength as a human being, the strength she'd praised so much when it kept me from getting into trouble or when it preserved my self-esteem in the face of tough times. I was angry that she'd even *dare* to assert that I could be made into a puppet by anyone, including Kay. Even more painful was that she seemed to be ignoring my ability to love, something she'd nurtured in me. I had trusted my mother to trust my judgment, and she had let me down for the first time. I didn't want my relationship with Mom to get stuck at this point, but I wasn't sure I knew how to get us through all this.

The two of us had always done a lot of talking, but talking about something this powerful was new and halting. We both had to keep remembering to look up from our own pain to know what the other was feeling. Mom needed to see that I was the same person as before, that I wasn't rebelling against every value that she'd ever taught me. Instead, I was just taking that value scheme with me in the process of discovering myself. She needed to see that being lesbian was a whole way of living and loving, not just a string of sexual encounters. I needed to listen to her go through some of the same things I'd gone through myself, just not out loud: first she hoped it was a phase, then that I could just be quiet about it, and later that I could just forget about the whole thing. Sometimes it was really frustrating. Sometimes it seemed like we'd never both be relaxed at the same time. Sometimes it seemed like were *always* going to have that same tense eyebrow when we looked at each other.

But you know what? It all worked out. I'm writing this ten years later, and in that time I've become relaxed and energetic and happy. My lesbianism is important to me—it always colors my way of seeing the world—but it's not *all* of me. For a while, after making the decision to live with my lesbianism, "Being a Lesbian" rushed to the foreground and dictated everything. Then it quietly became a part of me. It was that integrating process that helped my mom see I hadn't completely lost my sense of perspective. Now she looks at me, at my confidence and sheer joy of living, and she is proud of the woman that she raised. She is proud of my strength, proud that I had the guts to live the life that I knew was mine. She and I live 200 miles apart now, but we visit frequently. She knows my friends. She loves my lover. And she is absolutely swept away by her granddaughter, born by choice into my relationship with an esteemed scientist named Amy. Amy and I are very "out" lesbians in a supportive town, where wearing a T-shirt with huge letters proclaiming "Big Dyke" causes strangers to giggle and point out that we're really not that big. Our daughter, Dory, was conceived through donor insemination, and Amy was the mom brave enough to give birth. My mom shows piles of pictures to anyone who will hold still, making clear that she raised a lesbian daughter who is now happily raising a child of her own. "Whenever anybody asks about you, the first thing I say is, 'Linda is very happy.' Because that's the first thing that comes to my mind when I think of you," my mom said to me about six months ago.

My mom has seen in me, after all those years, the integrity and joy of living a full, honest life. And she and I share the confidence that comes with that, the self-esteem that leads *both* of us to come out: she as the mom of a lesbian, and me as a lesbian mom.

I feel so much more genuine for having accepted my lesbianism, and for sharing the strength and warmth that comes with having done that. All the coming-out scrapes and bruises seem a bargain to me now. I know now how it feels to have my sexuality out in the open, and how it feels to enjoy the acceptance of the people I love the most—including myself.

My Image of Myself: An Interview with Dennis

In the following interview, Dennis, a young Chinese-American man, speaks of the alienation and isolation he felt as he was growing up, and of the challenges he faced in forging an image of himself that he could feel comfortable with. Dennis's oral history appears in a book called Word is Out: Stories of Some of Our Lives. *The book, which is based on a documentary film made in 1977, features extensive conversations with twenty-six men and women talking frankly about their lives and about what it means to be gay or lesbian in America.* Word is Out, *recently released on video by New Yorker Video, can be found in many video stores.*

Q: Let's talk a little about gay Asians and how you feel—what you have to deal with in this country being a gay Asian.

A: When you're a kid, you have John Wayne, you have Steve McQueen, and if you're a slant-eyed Chinese kid, and if you happen to be slightly effeminate—really, it drives knives into your stomach! It's really scary standing in isolation from everybody else—and that's what I feared most of my life; the fact that I wasn't part of a group. . . . I think there's such a societal instinct to try to act white, to act straight, or to act gay. And it's really infuriating to see people settling for second best. Gay Asians tend to mimic a whole lot of white gay values which I think are really detrimental to the emergence of selves which are free to create. I think there are a lot of gay images that emphasize the whiteness, the blue-eyedness, the blond-

ness. I'm angry about that. I think the only way not to
be second best is to start gaining support from being one's
self—no matter how tacky, no matter how unfamiliar one
finds oneself. I'm never going to gain an inch by trying
to imitate other people. Dishonesty hurts more than the
truth ever would.

I think it's a whole social consciousness. It starts with
individuals saying, "Yeah. I'm gay, but how do I feel
about being gay?" That question, in itself, makes you
appear more human to yourself. In terms of coming out
for gay Asians, I think that one can come out when one
can come out as an Asian. And I think that if Asian parents accept themselves as having yellow faces, they can
truly accept their children as having different sexual in-
clinations. I think that's the gist of it. That's one thing
that gay Asians have in favor of themselves that white
gay people don't: every Asian knows deep down somewhere that it is rough to be an Asian.

It's a hard point. I think gay Chinese people have to
deal with the fact that they are of a different color. It
doesn't separate people forever, but it's something that
they have to come to terms with. Being white gives you
a kind of security in a sense that I don't have. I cannot
fall back on white impersonations. At a certain point,
people start throwing all these labels on you. You start
to realize, "Yes, I do have a brown or a yellow face, and
the way I act is characteristically feminine or masculine,
and it's wrong to do these things." For me, it's a question
of somehow getting through this whole thicket of confusion: "You should be this way; you shouldn't be that way."
I know a lot of Asians disregard this whole thing and say,
"I feel like an American. My yellowness doesn't have
anything to do with my relating to other white people."
But where I'm coming from is the fact that I do feel
unique. I do feel different things. . . . I think to really
be yourself—no matter what that might be—is an asset.
Just believing enough in myself to be what I can be. I
think that if you can relate to one other person—gay,

straight, male, female, white, black, yellow—you know that's where it really starts to count. In that sense, I'm really afraid of limiting my experience to people of one kind. I think I have a lot to learn, really, and I think a lot of it has to do with giving up the fact that growing up was really painful for me.

You go through a lot of hurt when someone calls you a "Chinaman." And so, in one sense, you're more able to deal with someone calling you a "fag." And you can spring back more easily and say, "I'm a person. I am me."

Johnnieruth

Becky Birtha

*In this short story, a teenager named Johnnieruth recalls several women
who made a strong impression on her as she was growing up. Each
of these women was "different"—and each contributed to Johnnieruth's realization that there were "different ways to be, from the way
people be around my way." The story is told from Johnnieruth's point
of view and the style is conversational, as if Johnnieruth were speaking directly to the reader. Becky Birtha was born in Virginia and
now lives in Philadelphia. Her books include* Lovers' Choice *and*
For Nights Like This One, *both collections of short fiction that
feature African-American women.*

There was one Sunday when I musta
been around eight. I remember it was before my sister Corletta
was born, cause right around then was when I put my foot down
about that whole sanctimonious routine. Anyway, I was dragging
my feet along Twenty-fifth Street in back of Mama and Vincent
and them, when I spied this lady. I only seen her that one time,
but I still remember just how she look. She don't look like nobody
I ever seen before. I *know* she don't live around here. She real
skinny. But she ain't no real young woman, neither. She could be
old as my mama. She ain't nobody's mama—I'm sure. And she
ain't wearing Sunday clothes. She got on blue jeans and a man's
blue working shirt, with the tail hanging out. She got patches on
her blue jeans, and she still got her chin stuck out like she some
kinda African royalty. She ain't carrying no shiny pocketbook. It
don't look like she care if she got any money or not, or who know
it, if she don't. She ain't wearing no house-shoes, or stockings or
high heels neither.

Mama always speak to everybody, but when she pass by this lady she make like she ain't even seen her. But I get me a real good look, and the lady stare right back at me. She got a funny look on her face, almost like she think she know me from some place. After she pass on by, I had to turn around to get another look, even though Mama say that ain't polite. And you know what? She was turning around, too, looking back at me. And she give me a great big smile.

I didn't know much in them days, but that's when I first got to thinking about how it's got to be different ways to be, from the way people be around my way. It's got to be places where it don't matter to nobody if you all dressed up on Sunday morning or you ain't. That's how come I started saving money. So, when I got enough, I could go away to some place like that.

Afterwhile I begun to see there wasn't no point in waiting around for handouts, and I started thinking of ways to earn my own money. I used to be running errands all the time—mailing letters for old Grandma Whittaker and picking up cigarettes and newspapers up the corner for everybody. After I got bigger, I started washing cars in the summer, and shoveling people sidewalk in the wintertime. Now I got me a newspaper route. Ain't never been no girl around here with no paper route, but I guess everybody got it figured out by now that I ain't gonna be like nobody else.

The reason I got me my Peugeot was so I could start to explore. I figured I better start looking around right now, so when I'm grown, I'll know exactly where I wanna go. So I ride around every chance I get.

Last summer, I used to ride with the boys a lot. Sometimes eight or ten of us'd just go cruising around the streets together. All of a sudden my mama decide she don't want me to do that no more. She say I'm too old to be spending so much time with boys. (That's what they tell you half the time, and the other half the time they worried cause you ain't interested in spending more time with boys. Don't make much sense.) She want me to have some girl friends, but I never seem to fit in with none of the things the girls doing. I used to think I fit in more with the boys.

But I seen how Mama might be right, for once. I didn't like the way the boys was starting to talk about girls sometimes. Talking about what some girl be like from the neck on down, and talking all up underneath somebody clothes and all. Even though I wasn't really friends with none of the girls, I still didn't like it. So now I mostly just ride around by myself. And Mama don't like that neither—you just can't please her.

This boy that live around the corner on North Street, Kenny Henderson, started asking me one time if I don't ever be lonely, cause he always see me by myself. He say don't I ever think I'd like to have me somebody special to go places with and stuff. Like I'd pick him if I did! Made me wanna laugh in his face. I do be lonely, a lotta times, but I don't tell nobody. And I ain't met nobody yet that I'd really rather be with than be by myself. But I will someday. When I find that special place where everybody different, I'm gonna find somebody there I can be friends with. And it ain't gonna be no dumb boy.

I found me one place already, that I like to go to a whole lot. It ain't even really that far—by bike—but it's on the other side of the Avenue. So I don't tell Mama and them I go there, cause they like to think I'm right around the neighborhood someplace. But this neighborhood too dull for me. All the houses look just the same—no porches, no yards, no trees—not even no parks around here. Every block look so much like every other block it hurt your eyes to look at, afterwhile. So I ride across Summit Avenue and go down that big steep hill there, and then make a sharp right at the bottom and cross the bridge over the train tracks. Then I head on out the boulevard—that's the nicest part, with all them big trees making a tunnel over the top, and lightning bugs shining in the bushes. At the end of the boulevard you get to this place call the Plaza.

It's something like a little park—the sidewalks is all bricks and they got flowers planted all over the place. The same kind my mama grow in that painted-up tire she got out front masquerading like a garden decoration—only seem like they smell sweeter here. It's a big high fountain right in the middle, and all the streetlights is the real old-fashion kind. That Plaza is about the prettiest place I ever been.

Sometimes something going on there. Like a orchestra playing music or some man or lady singing. One time they had a show with some girls doing some kinda foreign dances. They look like they were around my age. They all had on these fancy costumes, with different color ribbons all down they back. I wouldn't wear nothing like that, but it looked real pretty when they was dancing.

I got me a special bench in one corner where I like to sit, cause I can see just about everything, but wouldn't nobody know I was there. I like to sit still and think, and I like to watch people. A lotta people be coming there at night—to look at the shows and stuff, or just to hang out and cool off. All different kinda people.

This one night when I was sitting over in that corner where I always be at, there was this lady standing right near my bench. She mostly had her back turned to me and she didn't know I was there, but I could see her real good. She had on this shiny purple shirt and about a million silver bracelets. I kinda liked the way she look. Sorta exotic, like she maybe come from California or one of the islands. I mean she had class—standing there posing with her arms folded. She walk away a little bit. Then turn around and walk back again. Like she waiting for somebody.

Then I spotted this dude coming over. I spied him all the way cross the Plaza. Looking real fine. Got on a three-piece suit. One of them little caps sitting on a angle. Look like leather. He coming straight over to this lady I'm watching and then she seen him too and she start to smile, but she don't move till he get right up next to her. And then I'm gonna look away, cause I can't stand to watch nobody hugging and kissing on each other, but all of a sudden I see it ain't no dude at all. It's another lady.

Now I can't stop looking. They smile at each other like they ain't seen one another in ten years. Then the one in the purple shirt look around real quick—but she don't look just behind her—and sorta pull the other one right back into the corner where I'm sitting at, and then they put they arms around each other and kiss—for a whole long time. Now I really know I oughtta turn away, but I can't. And I know they gonna see me when they finally open they eyes. And they do.

They both kinda gasp and back up, like I'm the monster that just rose up outta the deep. And then I guess they can see I'm only a girl, and they look at one another—and start to laugh! Then they just turn around and start to walk away like it wasn't nothing at all. But right before they gone, they both look around again, and see I still ain't got my eye muscles and my jaw muscles working right again yet. And the one lady wink at me. And the other one say, "Catch you later."

I can't stop staring at they backs, all the way across the Plaza. And then, all of a sudden, I feel like I got to be doing something, got to be moving.

I wheel on outta the Plaza and I'm just concentrating on getting up my speed. Cause I can't figure out what to think. Them two women kissing and then, when they get caught, just laughing about it. And here I'm laughing too, for no reason at all. I'm sailing down the boulevard laughing like a lunatic, and then I'm singing at the top of my lungs. And climbing that big old hill up to Summit Avenue is just as easy as being on a escalator.

Martina

Martina Navratilova

*Born in Czechoslovakia in 1957, Martina Navratilova is among the
world's greatest athletes. In 1978, she defeated Chris Evert at Wimbledon to become the top-ranked female tennis player in the world;
she went on to win the Wimbledon championship eight more times.
"I felt I was on top of the world," she writes in her 1985 autobiography,* Martina, *"and that I'd stay there forever." Earlier in her
autobiography,* Martina *discusses the different kinds of freedom she
found upon defecting to the United States at age nineteen—including
the freedom to explore her "social, emotional, professional, intellectual, [and] sexual" attractions to other women.*

My green card was just one of the
big changes in my life that took place around my nineteenth birthday. Another change was discovering that my childhood crushes
on some of my female teachers had not been "just a phase."

Once I started traveling to the States, I realized I felt more
comfortable around women than men. It wasn't disillusionment
over my love affair with the boy back home, or any generalized
resentment toward men. Maybe I felt uncomfortable around men
because I wasn't as pretty as some other girls; but on the other
hand, I'd always hung around boys when I was young because I
could do the things they could do. I still liked men; I just liked
the company of women better.

A lot of it has to do with freedom. Once I became a regular on
the circuit, I saw a lot of women doing what they wanted to do.
I saw them making business decisions for themselves, tennis decisions, and smaller decisions about where they wanted to live,
how they wanted to eat and dress, what movies they wanted to

see. They were professionals, their lives not always defined by men.

That sounds like a political statement when I say it, yet it really wasn't a matter of dogma. I just perceived some women doing what they wanted to do, and felt comfortable in their society. Of course, not all the professionals I admired were so-called gay. Nothing so simple. But I came to realize my attractions—social, emotional, professional, intellectual, sexual—were toward women.

I guess I'd known that for a long time, going back to childhood, when I had urges to be with some of the teachers, wanted to know everything about them, their secrets, the way they did things. I had much less curiosity about men.

As I grew up through my teens, I never had any relationship with a woman, and I don't think anybody ever treated me as different. I had a family, I had a tennis life, I had a boyfriend. But I was also aware of gay people, particularly after I started traveling, and reading magazines, and looking around me in the big cities. You'd see couples you knew were gay, or meet somebody and know she or he was gay.

I never thought there was anything strange about being gay. Other people would make jokes, but I couldn't figure out why these people were "sick." I knew it was more tolerated in the West than in Czechoslovakia. There, they would put you in the sanatorium for crazy people, literally. You'd read about it sometimes in the paper, and it was considered being sick.

I knew homosexuality wasn't such a crime in the States. Even when I thought about it, I never panicked and thought, Oh, I'm strange, I'm weird, what do I do now? It was just a matter of time for me. I had to get other parts of my life in order first. Plus, my first sexual experience hadn't made me all that eager for a second one.

Looking back to when I was sixteen or seventeen, I can see I had some crushes on some women players and didn't really know it. I just liked being with them. By the time I was eighteen I knew I always had these feelings.

When it finally happened, it was with somebody older than me, a woman I met in the States, and it seemed so natural. I was pretty much a rookie with women, and I'm shy anyway, so it took forever for me to get the hints she was throwing at me. Finally, the way she put it, I was invited over to snuggle, and it went on from there. She knew what she was doing. I don't remember any flowers and candlelight, but I do remember feeling relaxed and happy being with her, waiting for the next step.

When it finally happened, I said, This is easy and right. And the next morning—-*volià*—I had an outright, head-over-heels case of infatuation with her. When will I see you again? What will we do with our time together? I was in love, just like in the story-books, and everything felt great.

At the time, although a few people knew, I never felt I would have any image problem. I was one of the up-and-coming female tennis players in the world, and I didn't imagine my sexuality would become a major issue to anybody. It seemed like *my* business somehow.

I had no idea what it was like to be a public figure. Whether I was seeing a man or a woman, I wouldn't want pictures of us in the papers. It would be nice to be able to put your arm around somebody while you're out at a restaurant, and I've tried to be guarded about my private life, but it always gets out. Look what Chris had to go through when she and John were separated for a while. Reporters gain an interview by claiming to be interested in tennis, but you know they're going to ask about your love life. People do stakeouts on your house, ring your doorbell at three in the morning.

I remember one time when Rita Mae Brown and I took an apartment near Sloane Square during Wimbledon and one of those high-caliber British journals stationed a photographer across from our building. The only picture he got was Rita Mae walking out of a grocery store. The headline was something like: "Writer Shops for Martina Love Nest." I thought it was funny because actually I did most of the shopping.

Right from my first affair in the States, I wanted privacy but I was also uncomfortable about pretending to be something I wasn't. Somebody once said to me, "Society isn't ready for it." And I told her, "Hey, we're society, too."

The David Kopay Story

David Kopay and
Perry Deane Young

In 1975, David Kopay—a veteran running back who had played football with the San Francisco Forty-Niners, the Washington Red-skins, the New Orleans Saints, the Detroit Lions, and the Green Bay Packers—startled the country when he became the first professional athlete to "come out" and state publicly that he is gay. In The David Kopay Story: An Extraordinary Self-Revelation, *Kopay writes movingly about discovering his sexual identity. He recalls being in the ninth grade (before he even knew the words* homosexual *or* gay*) and feeling an attraction to a classmate who was the best athlete at his school. Kopay and his friend were attending high school at a junior seminary in Los Angeles, where both were preparing for the priesthood. (Kopay later left the seminary and attended the University of Washington.)*

For many months I was very happy at the seminary. I even loved the strict routine—the outward sense of order eased my guilt, helped me forget the inner confusions about sex. At that time this had little to do with my being attracted to my own sex—I wasn't even aware that kind of sex was possible. It was simply my occasional indulgence in masturbation that bothered me—I enjoyed it; the church said it was evil.

Our days at the seminary began before dawn and we lived by rigid schedules, every minute accounted for. We slept in common dormitory rooms of about fifty beds each. We dressed in khaki military uniforms during the week and blue suits on Sundays. We marched—eyes straight ahead—to and from all classes, study halls, and meals. We lived under a code of behavior spelled out in a little gray handbook called *The Mirror* and in solemn weekly lectures on morality given by the head prefect. We were not allowed to run, laugh, or shout. Silence was enforced in the refectory, the lavatory, and especially in the dormitory.

According to *The Mirror:* "The Claretian postulant shall ardently love and cultivate the beautiful lily of purity with the greatest care; thus, he will please his Heavenly Mother. Let him respect and even revere himself as a living temple of the Holy Spirit; thus, he will shun impure and dangerous imaginations as if they were flames from hell; will keep perfect modesty, especially in public; will flee particular friendships; and will never be idle . . . if any one should hear any word offensive to holy purity, notice any indecent action, or that someone is the object of too much familiarity on the part of any of his companions, the entire affair should be manifested to Father Prefect as soon as possible."

Physical contact was specifically forbidden and we were often lectured on keeping "modesty of the eyes." This meant that we could not look at each other. We never saw each other naked. The showers were inside stalls with doors, and we had to go in and out of them fully clothed. During recreation periods we were not allowed to lie back on the grass or around the swimming pool, presumably because this was a suggestive pose that might provide an "occasion for sin."

Even with every kind of sex forbidden, the brothers and priests were still visibly concerned about appearances and masculine manners. The best student in the grade ahead of mine was also one of the most serious and devout postulants, but he was never allowed to become a novitiate. The reason had to be his effeminate manners. His devotion was such that he eventually went to Europe, where he was able to join another order and become a priest.

In spite of the rules it seemed that everybody was paired off with a special friend. I was separated from most of my own class because I had made the varsity athletic teams even as a freshman.

I never felt I had a best friend, but I did have two special relationships—one with a boy who was by far the best athlete in the school, the other with Father Ernest Hyman, the head prefect.

The athlete was two years older and a captain of the basketball team. He had blond hair, blue eyes, sharp features, and stood six feet three. He moved with a real swagger. He wore taps on his shoes and kept his pants just a bit lower on his hips than the rest of us. We were like the two friends in *A Separate Peace* except that our competition was more evenly matched. If we were on opposite teams in a basketball game, it became a vicious struggle between the two of us. We competed so hard we would fight over the least infraction, and Father Hyman and the other students would often have to pull us apart. And yet, somewhere within all this outward violence there was a deep feeling between us. I wanted a sweater with a letter and captain's star just like his. If there was a movie, we maneuvered so that we could sit next to each other. If we had to move the irrigation sprinklers in the pastures, I would get myself assigned to his crew. In the refectory I always sat at his table, even though we weren't allowed to speak. When one of the brothers would pronounce the Latin phrase breaking the silence, we would cheer and talk together. When we took our summer vacations at the retreat in Malibu Canyon, he and I were always in the same group swimming or hiking. I didn't recognize this as a sexual attraction then, but what I felt for him certainly was sexual. I knew the word *homosexual*, but I had no idea how it was acted out. I was also sure that I was not one of the "queers" and "fags" my brother and his buddies talked about beating up down at Coffee Dan's in Hollywood. When I masturbated I didn't think of my friend because I didn't think sex with him was possible. I just did everything I could to be close to him. When we would line up for showers, for example, I saw to it that I was in the stall next to him so that I could see his body reflected in the water on the floor under the partition between us. . . .

This idea of competition as an expression of sexual feeling may be difficult for anyone to understand who has not been as committed to athletics as I have been. In an article published in the Sunday, May 21, 1972, *Washington Star*, George Sauer, then twenty-eight and just resigned as an all-pro wide receiver with the New

York Jets, wrote: "The literal meaning of the word *competition* is to seek together, to strive together. The implication is that while opponents are set against each other, they are still doing something together with a common purpose. . . . If competition is so deeply significant, it may be because it can bring opponents close, spiritually as well as physically, each providing the other with a challenge that will force them to call on all their reserves of skill and perseverance to seek beyond previous limits." Sauer also quoted from the scene in D. H. Lawrence's *Women in Love* in which two male friends respond to the sexual tension in their relationship by taking off their clothes and wrestling in naked embrace: "They became accustomed to each other, to each other's rhythm. They got a kind of mutual physical understanding. And then they had a real struggle. They seemed to drive their white flesh deeper and deeper against each other, as if they would break into a oneness . . . rapturously, intent and mindless at last, two essential white figures working into a tighter, closer oneness of struggle. . . ."

For many years this kind of struggle represented the only sexual outlet I had except for masturbation. Many people have described this feeling we had for each other in the game, but they're all terrified that it might also include physical love. Coach Lombardi was always talking about love, but he would say he didn't mean physical love, he meant love in the sense of respect and loyalty for your teammates. . . .

I wonder now why the coaches—or anybody else—are so afraid of physical love with another man. Their fear of it only makes it more a monster—inside and outside their heads—than it really is. This fear of physical love kept me from a healthy, happy life for a long time. It's also the reason, I think, that few real friendships develop among football players. On the field we can get away with all kinds of physical affection men wouldn't risk showing anywhere else. We aren't ashamed to reach out and hug our teammates. After a touchdown you will see men embracing on the field like heterosexual lovers in the movies. We were able to hold hands in the huddle and to pat each other on the ass if we felt like it. I think these are healthy expressions of affection. What is unhealthy, I think, is that we are so afraid of expressing ourselves in the same way anywhere outside of the stadium, out of uniform.

The Answers I Needed

Billie Tallmij

Though growing up as a gay man or lesbian in the 1990s can be difficult, life for gay and lesbian young people in the 1940s was infinitely harder. There were no national organizations, no local support groups, few role models, and limited reading material. Moreover, the medical establishment viewed homosexuality as a sickness, meaning that gay men and lesbians could be sent to medical institutions to be "cured" of their "disease." Dozens of accounts of how it felt to grow up during these years are recorded in the oral history collection Making History: The Struggle for Gay and Lesbian Equal Rights, 1945–1990, *by Eric Marcus. Billie Tallmij, now in her early sixties, told Marcus how she learned about homosexuality. (Billie Tallmij is a pseudonym.)*

I was seventeen, and in my first year of college in Kansas in the late 1940s, when a high school friend wrote me a letter from school and described how she had gotten involved with another girl. It blew me away. I could not accept that Joanna could have done this. So I went to my dean of women, who was marvelous, and I said, "I've got to talk to you." I said, "A friend of mine is a homosexual. I don't know what it means. Tell me what it's about." So she gave me a whole bunch of books to read, including *The Well of Loneliness*.

The Well opened the door for a lot of people, including me. I read that book and found that I was coming home. I recognized myself in the characters, and I also recognized the emotions that were so beautifully written there. I was always a tomboy and I had crushes on girls. I tried things with boys, but they were simply not my cup of tea. I was uncomfortable. This was an answer that I had sought for a long time.

After reading *The Well* I decided that if this was what I was, then I needed to know what one was supposed to do in this sort of business. The problem was finding information. Beyond *The Well*, which was the Bible for me, there were certainly no books that I could have read. There was nothing that existed for a total tyro like me. The only thing that you could get was Krafft-Ebing,* which is not something to teethe your newfound identity on. The particular cases in his book were so abnormal and so beyond the pale of who I felt I was.

Of course, there was no organization to call for information, so I had to find someone to talk to who could give me the answers I needed. I had heard from other students about this big dyke on campus. I didn't even really know what *big dyke* meant, but I just knew that she was someone who I wanted to talk to. So I followed her, followed her for days. Finally, I saw her coming out of a café just off campus. She was going to her car, and I went up to her and I asked her if she was Esther. And she said, "Yes." And I said, "I want to talk to you." I'm sure I came off just that strong. She sort of looked at me and said, "Okay, get in the car."

We got in her car, and she started driving. She said, "What is it you want to talk to me about?" I said, "I just found out I'm a homosexual and I want to know what this is all about." She looked at me and she said, "What do you want to know?" I said, "I want to know how to make love to a woman. I never have and I think I'd better know." She kind of chuckled and said, "Well, the only way, really, is to show you." And I said, "No, don't show me, tell me."

We drove out to a park, and I asked her every question I could think of: What is this? What causes this? Where does it start? Why is it? How *do* you make love to a woman? What do you do? She could have blown me out of the water. She could have been

---

*Richard von Krafft-Ebing was a late-nineteenth-century psychiatrist and medical writer who argued that homosexuality violated the hidden laws of nature.

brusque and bitter, but she wasn't. She was just as gentle as she could have been and answered to the best of her ability anything that I put to her. When I look back on that particular scene, I think I knew then that everybody was asking questions like that and that somewhere, somehow, there should be people who could answer these questions as honestly as they could.

After college, I discovered firsthand what could happen if you were found out. I was working in the acoustics division at Boeing Aircraft in Seattle. Boeing was one of the early companies that made rockets. Because I handled important material, I had to have top-secret clearance, which meant I was investigated. I was followed by an FBI agent for about three weeks before I discovered the FBI had begun the investigation process. Naturally, I wasn't told. But I found out one evening when the agent followed me right into a gay bar, right along with me! The bar was on my way home from work, and I sometimes stopped in there at about six o'clock for a Coke. I didn't go to the bar for any long length of time except on the weekends. Shorty, my lover at the time, and I would go there on Friday and Saturday nights.

So the agent sat down on the bar stool next to me. He was in his late twenties. He introduced himself and said, "By the way, I'm checking on your security clearance." I said, "For what?" He said, "Your work at Boeing." He had my name, my address, and my lover's name. Everything! He said, "You're just lucky." And I asked, "Why?" He said, "Because I'm gay myself, otherwise you would have been out of your job immediately." I was flabbergasted. I couldn't believe it.

I saw him in there one other time. He told me he wasn't there on business. We sat and chatted, and I asked him, "How do you get away with this?" And he said, "I'm open. They know it. I'm chosen often to do this kind of work." His immediate boss knew that he could send this guy into a gay bar and that he wouldn't stick out like a sore thumb. He wasn't swish or anything. He was very nice. We didn't discuss it any further. I don't know if they knew up the ladder at the FBI that he was gay.

The agent knew I was going to quit my job at Boeing within a few months. Shorty and I had planned to move to California. She was working with the telephone company at the time, and we were waiting for her transfer down to the San Francisco area. I told him that. I assume that's why he didn't say anything. I never did know exactly why. It's funny, just before I quit, I finally got my top-secret clearance.

from

The Well of Loneliness

Radclyffe Hall

Published in 1928, Radclyffe Hall's The Well of Loneliness *was one of the earliest literary works to demand equality for lesbians and gay men. Banned in England in 1928 and censored in certain parts of the United States, the novel tells the story of Stephen Gordon, a lesbian, and of her love affairs with women. In this excerpt, Stephen's mother confronts her daughter about "this unspeakable outrage that you call love." Stephen replies with a passionate plea for acceptance.*

"Mother—you don't know what you're saying—you're my mother—"

"Yes, I am your mother, but for all that, you seem to me like a scourge. I ask myself what I have ever done to be dragged down into the depths by my daughter. And your father—what had he ever done? And you have presumed to use the word love in connection with this—with these lusts of your body; these unnatural cravings of your unbalanced mind and undisciplined body—you have used that word. I have loved—do you hear? I have loved your father, and your father loved me. That was *love*."

Then, suddenly, Stephen knew that unless she could, indeed, drop dead at the feet of this woman in whose womb she had quickened, there was one thing that she dared not let pass unchallenged, and that was this terrible slur upon her love. And all that was in her rose up to refute it; to protect her love from such unbearable soiling. It was part of herself, and unless she could save it, she could not save herself any more. She must stand or fall by the courage of that love to proclaim its right to toleration.

She held up her hand, commanding silence; commanding that slow, quiet voice to cease speaking, and she said: "As my father loved you, I loved. As a man loves a woman, that was how I loved—protectively, like my father. I wanted to give all I had in me to give. It made me feel terribly strong . . . and gentle. It was good, good, *good*—I'd have laid down my life a thousand times over for Angela Crossby. If I could have, I'd have married her and brought her home—I wanted to bring her home here to Morton. If I loved her the way a man loves a woman, it's because I can't feel that I am a woman. All my life I've never felt like a woman, and you know it—you say you've always disliked me, that you've always felt a strange physical repulsion. . . . I don't know what I am; no one's ever told me that I'm different and yet I know that I'm different—that's why, I suppose, you've felt as you have done. And for that I forgive you, though whatever it is, it was you and my father who made this body—but what I will never forgive is your daring to try and make me ashamed of my love. I'm not ashamed of it, there's no shame in me." And now she was stammering a little wildly, "Good and—and fine it was," she stammered, "the best part of myself—I gave all and I asked nothing in return—I just went on hopelessly loving—" she broke off, she was shaking from head to foot, and Anna's cold voice fell like icy water on that angry and sorely tormented spirit.

"You have spoken, Stephen. I don't think there's much more that needs to be said between us except this, we two cannot live together at Morton—not now, because I might grow to hate you. Yes, although you're my child, I might grow to hate you. The same roof mustn't shelter us both any more; one of us must go— which of us shall it be?" And she looked at Stephen and waited.

from

The Naked Civil Servant

Quentin Crisp

Born in 1908, Quentin Crisp shocked London society by "coming out" publicly in 1931, when even the mention of homosexuality was greeted with contempt. In his autobiography, The Naked Civil Servant, *Crisp tells how he discovered that he was not the only homosexual in England—and how he set about to educate straight society by becoming "not merely a self-confessed homosexual but a self-evident one." By stressing, rather than downplaying, his flamboyant and effeminate manner, Crisp succeeded in demonstrating that he was not afraid to be himself. Full of wit and humor, Crisp's 1968 autobiography was adapted into a television program in 1975. Crisp has lived in New York City since 1977.*

I was now eighteen and beginning to feel really uneasy about the future—openly on the grounds that I was so inadequate to earn a living, and secretly because I suspected that sexually I was quite unlike anyone else in the world. Friends were starting to ask me questions about my private life. Their intention was not unkind, but I was filled with misgiving.

"Are you keen on this girl you talk so much about?" a friend of my mother asked. "Good God, no," I replied, putting on a face as though I had just stepped in something. Then I hastily embarked upon a cynical diatribe against all human sentiments. This was the kind of conversation that my mother's friend loved, but I now think that I wasted a rather wonderful woman. If I could simply have told her that, to my bewilderment, I did not think that I was ever going to be able to take a sexual interest in any girl, I'm sure she would have listened. This would have been at least a thin rope flung from my tiny island toward the mainland.

She would not have believed me, because in those far-off days a homosexual person was never anyone that you actually knew and seldom anyone that you had met. She would have thought that I had chosen at random a peculiarity that would make me more interesting, but she would not have been shocked. She was my first glimpse of the *vie de bohème*.

Her name was Mrs. Longhurst, a big striding strident person of about forty ("I'm longing for one of those bonnets with jet beads on them"). By profession she was a stewardess and sometimes a portrait model ("Who cares as long as it brings in some money?"). She lived in Charlotte Street ("I adore all foreigners") in a room whose walls were covered with African knives. Her other room she had let to a nurse who has attended my mother during her four years in various nursing homes. After a while this nurse came to dislike Mrs. Longhurst, but at first she thought her a "real character." She introduced her as such to my mother and me. Mrs. Longhurst took to me at once and allowed me to visit her constantly to play pontoon and talk about myself. Her mode of speech was the most exaggerated that I had ever heard. These are the words with which she warned my mother (who longed to leave Battersea) not to try Hampstead: "Don't live in Hampstead. That's where the parents lived and they were crippled with rheumatism—bed-ridden. They moved and what happened? Within a week they were dancing in the streets of Maida Vale." This woman did not fly to extremes; she lived there. I also soon became an adept at this mode of talk and, with the passing of the years, came to speak in this way unconsciously.

Mrs. Longhurst's attitude to homosexuality, as to most things, was a mocking curiosity but she was never savage. The rest of the world in which I lived was still stumbling about in search of a weapon with which to exterminate this monster whose shape and size were not yet known or even guessed at. It was thought to be Greek in origin, smaller than socialism but more deadly—especially to children. At about this time *The Well of Loneliness* was banned. The widely reported court case, together with the extraordinary reputation that Tallulah Bankhead was painstakingly building up for herself as a delinquent, brought Lesbianism, if not into the light of day, at least into the twilight, but I do not remember ever hearing anyone discuss the subject except Mrs. Longhurst and my mother. If one is not going to take the necessary precautions to avoid having parents, one must undertake to bring them up. This was what, very cautiously, I was beginning to do with my mother. My father remained invincibly ignorant.

When I left King's College, London (needless to say without a diploma in journalism), I could at first find no better occupation than sitting at home getting on my parents' nerves. I became so listless that my mother thought it only polite to regard me as ill. She sent me to her doctor. Without making even the most cursory examination of me he declared that all I needed was a lesson in life. My father was very annoyed. He realized that he would have to pay a consultation fee for these few glib words. He was lucky that psychology had not yet reached the middle classes. He might have had to pay much more for less. At the time, my own reaction to the doctor's remark was blank incomprehension. Later when, to vary the monotony of my existence, I took to wandering about the streets of the West End, I stumbled on the very truth that was just what the doctor had ordered. I learned that I was not alone.

As I wandered along Piccadilly or Shaftesbury Avenue, I passed young men standing at the street corners who said, "Isn't it terrible tonight, dear? No men about. The Dilly's not what it used to be." Though the Indian boy at school had once amazed us all with the information that in Birmingham there were male prostitutes, I had never believed that I would actually see one. Here they were for all the world to recognize—or almost all the world. A passer-by would have to be very innocent indeed not to catch the meaning of the mannequin walk and the stance in which the hip was only prevented from total dislocation by the hand placed upon it. . . .

My outlook was so limited that I assumed that all deviates were openly despised and rejected. Their grief and their fear drew my melancholy nature strongly. At first I only wanted to wallow in their misery, but, as time went by, I longed to reach its very essence. Finally I desired to represent it. By this process I managed to shift homosexuality from being a burden to being a cause. The weight lifted and some of the guilt evaporated.

It seemed to me that there were few homosexuals in the world. I felt that the entire strength of the club must be prepared to show its membership card at any time, and, to a nature as dramatic as mine, not to deny rapidly became to protest. By the time I was twenty-three I had made myself into a test case. I realized that it did no good to be seen to be homosexual in the West End where sin reigned supreme or in Soho which was inhabited exclusively by other outcasts of various kinds, but the rest of England was straightforward missionary country. It was densely populated by aborigines who had never heard of homosexuality and who, when first they did, became frightened and angry. I went to work on them.

The message I wished to propagate was that effeminacy existed in people who were in all other respects just like home. I went about the routine of daily living looking undeniably like a homosexual person. I had had a lot of practice at school in being the one against the many but, even so, I was not prepared for the effect my appearance had on the great British public. I had to begin cautiously.

I was from birth an object of mild ridicule because of my movements—especially the perpetual flutter of my hands—and my voice. Like the voices of a number of homosexuals, this is an insinuating blend of eagerness and caution in which even such words as "hello" and "goodbye" seem not so much uttered as divulged. But these natural outward and visible signs of inward and spiritual disgrace were not enough. People could say that I was ignorant of them or was trying without success to hide them. I wanted it to be known that I was not ashamed and therefore had to display symptoms that could not be thought to be accidental.

I began to wear make-up. For a while I still went on as before at home and never mentioned to my mother anything about the life I lived in the outer world. She once protested that I never brought home any of my friends. I explained, quite truthfully, that she would hate them if I did. She never mentioned the matter again, which I took to be a sign that the protest was formal and that secretly she would be glad to hear no more on that subject.

Zami

Audre Lorde

Born in New York City, Audre Lorde (1934–1992) described herself as a "Black, Lesbian, Feminist, Warrior, Mother, lover, woman, poet." In her poetry, she celebrated the spirit and courage of ancestral women and spoke out powerfully against racial and sexual oppression. Lorde's 1982 autobiography, Zami: A New Spelling of My Name, *contains frank and honest passages on growing up as a lesbian in the 1950s. In the selection that follows, Lorde talks about being "young and Black and gay and lonely" in Greenwich Village, a largely gay and lesbian neighborhood in New York City.*

I remember how being young and Black and gay and lonely felt. A lot of it was fine, feeling I had the truth and the light and the key, but a lot of it was purely hell.

There were no mothers, no sisters, no heroes. We had to do it alone, like our sister Amazons, the riders on the loneliest outposts of the kingdom of Dahomey. We, young and Black and fine and gay, sweated out our first heartbreaks with no school nor office chums to share that confidence over lunch hour. Just as there were no rings to make tangible the reason for our happy secret smiles, there were no names nor reason given or shared for the tears that messed up the lab reports or the library bills.

We were good listeners, and never asked for double dates, *but didn't we know the rules?* Why did we always seem to think friendships between women were important enough to *care* about? Always we moved in a necessary remoteness that made "What did you do this weekend?" seem like an impertinent question. We discovered and explored our attention to women alone, sometimes in secret, sometimes in defiance, sometimes in little pockets that almost touched ("Why are those little Black girls always either whispering together or fighting?") but always alone, against a greater aloneness. We did it cold turkey, and although it resulted in some pretty imaginative tough women when we survived, too many of us did not survive at all.

I remember Muff, who sat on the same seat in the same dark corner of the Pony Stable Bar drinking the same gin year after year. One day she slipped off onto the floor and died of a stroke right there between the stools. We found out later her real name was Josephine.

During the fifties in the Village, I didn't know the few other Black women who were visibly gay at all well. Too often we found ourselves sleeping with the same white women. We recognized ourselves as exotic sister-outsiders who might gain little from banding together. Perhaps our strength/might lay in our fewness, our rarity. That was the way it was Downtown. And Uptown, meaning the land of Black people, seemed very far away and hostile territory. . . .

In a paradoxical sense, once I accepted my position as different from the larger society as well as from any single sub-society— Black or gay—I felt I didn't have to try so hard. To be accepted. To look femme. To be straight. To look straight. To be proper. To look "nice." To be liked. To be loved. To be approved. What I didn't realize was how much harder I had to try merely to stay alive, or rather, to stay human. How much stronger a person I became in that trying.

But in this plastic, anti-human society in which we live, there have never been too many people buying fat Black girls born almost blind and ambidextrous, gay or straight. Unattractive, too, or so the ads in *Ebony* and *Jet* seemed to tell me. Yet I read them anyway, in the bathroom, on the newsstand, at my sister's house, whenever I got a chance. It was a furtive reading, but it was an affirmation of some part of me, however frustrating.

If nobody's going to dig you too tough anyway, it really doesn't matter so much what you dare to explore. I had already begun to learn that when I left my parents' house.

Like when your Black sisters on the job think you're crazy and collect money between themselves to buy you a hot comb and straightening iron on their lunch hour and stick it anonymously into your locker in the staff room, so that later when you come down for a coffee break and open your locker the damn things fall out on the floor with a clatter and all ninety-five percent of your library co-workers who are very very white want to know what it's all about.

Like when your Black brother calls you a ball-buster and tricks you up into his apartment and tries to do it to you against the kitchen cabinets just, as he says, to take you down a peg or two, when all the time you'd only gone up there to begin with fully intending to get a little in the first place (because all the girls I knew who were possibilities were too damn complicating, and I was plain and simply horny as hell). I finally got out of being raped although not mauled by leaving behind a ring and a batch of lies and it was the first time in my life since I'd left my parents' house that I was in a physical situation which I couldn't handle physically—in other words, the bastard was stronger than I was. It was an instantaneous consciousness-raiser.

As I say, when the sisters think you're crazy and embarrassing; and the brothers want to break you open to see what makes you work inside; and the white girls look at you like some exotic morsel that has just crawled out of the walls onto their plate (but don't they love to rub their straight skirts up against the edge of your desk in the college literary magazine office after class); and the white boys all talk either money or revolution but can never quite get it up—then it doesn't really matter too much if you have an Afro long before the word even existed.

Pearl Primus, the African-American dancer, had come to my high school one day and talked about African women after class, and how beautiful and natural their hair looked curling out into the sun, and as I sat there listening (one of fourteen Black girls in Hunter High School) I thought, that's the way god's mother must have looked and I want to look like that too so help me god. In those days I called it a natural, and kept calling it natural when everybody else called it crazy. It was a strictly homemade job done by a Sufi Muslim on 125th Street, trimmed with the office scissors and looking pretty raggedy. When I came home from school that day my mother beat my behind and cried for a week.

Even for years afterward white people would stop me on the street or particularly in Central Park and ask if I was Odetta, a Black folksinger whom I did not resemble at all except that we were both big Black beautiful women with natural heads.

A Diet of Green Salads: An Interview with Whitey

Whitey is one of the twenty-six men and women whose stories appear in the book and film Word is Out: Stories of Some of Our Lives. *She grew up in New York during the 1950s, when homosexuality was viewed by most doctors, teachers, and members of the clergy as a sickness. At age thirteen, Whitey ran away to Greenwich Village, in New York City. She was later found by her father and sent to a state hospital to be "treated" for homosexuality. (In 1973, following national protests against the medical establishment's attempts to "cure" and "correct" homosexuality, the American Psychiatric Association removed homosexuality from its list of mental disorders. With that momentous change, lesbians and gay men no longer had to contend with being officially classified as "sick.")*

Q: Tell me about your childhood.

A: "God will punish you!" was my mother's favorite saying to me. She—and my father, too, I guess—were very church oriented, very Lutheran. I remember going to Sunday school at a very early age—it was a must. Sunday school can be heavy for a child. You are taught to believe strongly in a kind of heaven-and-hell thing—and in the wrath of God. You tend to think that every little thing you might do is wrong, or that every little thing you think about that's not right is punishable in some way; so you are always fearful. If you do *anything* that isn't right, you are terrified you'll be struck by lightning or go to hell. It caused a lot of fear. You never knew exactly what form the punishment would take, so you were always anticipating that something terrible would happen to you. It's a pretty heavy trip to put on a kid.

Q: Do you remember when you stopped believing in that stuff?

A: I was pretty well brainwashed, so it was quite a while before I didn't believe it completely. I realized I could never live up to all the things you were supposed to do, and that caused me a great deal of guilt and fear. As I grew older—and mostly on an unconscious level, I guess, because I couldn't have survived had it been on a conscious level—for a long time I believed God would take pity on me and change me, or help me out. I prayed a lot because I believed if I had enough faith I would get over this . . . this sickness. I remember those years of confusion—trying to do what was right but not quite knowing what that was; being made to carry around guilt for something that was quite natural to me.

As I developed as a human being, I felt I was somehow stunted because I spent all that time grappling with that problem when I could have been learning how to live.

Q: When were you first conscious of being gay?

A: In grammar school—even though I didn't know what being gay was. I didn't know it was anything strange at the time. I was enjoying crushes, until I found out they were considered abnormal. I was about twelve, and at that age girls were getting interested in boys. I heard someone remarking once that "so-and-so was acting like a lesbian," and I wondered what that was, and so I asked and everybody laughed. "That's a woman—or a girl—who likes other girls instead of boys." I thought, "Oh-oh, that sounds like me." It scared me a little because that was the name for what I felt, but I didn't know whether it was bad. I thought about it and started to get a little worried. I read a pocket book that was going around school about homosexuals—males—so I realized it could happen to a boy too.

Q: Why weren't you into boys?

A: I have no idea. I just liked girls.

Q: Did you talk to anyone about it?

A: I was still very naïve about the whole thing, so I decided to ask my mother just what a homosexual was. My God!—her reaction was so violent that it really scared me. She screamed. "Where did you hear that word?" and I said, "In this book." She took the book, tore it up, threw it down the incinerator, and said, "I don't ever want to hear you repeat that"—*without telling me what it was.* So I thought it must be really horrible—and I didn't push it.

My mother told my father about it, and he just laughed. That made me more confused. I didn't really have a good grasp on what the whole thing meant in terms of my life. About a year later I did learn what it meant and thought, "I really am a homosexual—*for real.*" But I thought it was some kind of disease that could maybe be cured. So again, I mentioned this to my parents. My mother didn't want to believe it and my father, again, didn't take it very seriously. But my mother was so terrified she talked my father into taking me to see a psychiatrist who was connected with the Church. I was full of expectations that going to a psychiatrist was going to solve all my problems; I would be fine, and my mother would be happy. The psychiatrist put me on a diet of green salads.

Q: A diet of *what?*

A: Two green salads a day. What this had to do with anything I don't know, but I figured she knew what she was doing. I had a schedule of green salads interspersed with prayer, but obviously it didn't do any good. I blamed myself for its not working. I was made to feel I was disgracing my family—that it was a reflection on them. My father wasn't around much at that time, but my mother would look at me strangely; all of a sudden it was like a wall had dropped, and I was some kind of freak thing that wasn't supposed to have happened.

Q: Did it have to do only with your homosexual tendencies?

A: Well, that's when all this change took place in people's attitudes towards me. I realized I could not say to somebody, "I am a homosexual," because they then no longer related to me as they had before—which made me think it was something to be ashamed of and to hide.

Q: How old were you?

A: Thirteen. Eventually the pressure got to be so great that I decided I could no longer talk to anyone about it—my mother or anybody—because they had such a negative reaction to me and to the whole thing. There was no point in discussing it. I decided the best thing I could do would be to leave so as not to disgrace my family, and they wouldn't have to deal with it. At this point I felt I was doomed to this life. It was like my whole life was just turned around. I didn't know what in the world to do—it was such a drastic thing. I resigned myself to the fact that I guessed I should find people like me and live my life shut off from everyone else. I had no idea what type of life homosexuals led. I just knew my parents' reaction to me and the psychiatrist's . . . people's reaction just to the *word*. The word *pervert* was always attached to it, and this meant something horrible for me.

The whole thing was devastating. All of a sudden I had sunk to the depths. I had heard about the Village by then—not much, just that that's where homosexuals were. So I left, got on the train, and went down to the Village determined to find other homosexuals and learn to live however they lived. I didn't feel like I had any other choice. There was the trip—sleeping on roofs, rooftops, and under stairwells. You have to know New York . . . you could do that. I was actually glad to be found, because I knew, by that time, I would—could never survive like that.

Q: So your father found you in the Village?

A: Yeah, I was walking by the westside subway entrance when who should come up but my father. He grabbed me by the neck, and all of a sudden police cars were pulling up. I don't know how they got there so fast, I was in such shock seeing him. My father was more sympathetic; to him these people were perverts, but I don't think he really thought I was—he just thought I was sick and he wanted me someplace where I could "get well again"—which meant hospitals and doctors.

Q: Then what happened?

A: I was put in a police car and whisked off to Kings County Hospital, which is like Bellevue, only in Brooklyn—for observation. At the end of thirty days, they sent me home. It was strange because nothing was settled one way or the other. I was in limbo. It was unbearable living at home. It would have been unbearable in the Village too. I was just too young. I wouldn't have known where to get a job. Consequently I went back and forth to Kings County. If I had been smart enough, I would have played their game and pretended I was okay, but I was too upset and miserable, and I couldn't lie to my mother. She kept trying to get me to do things that everyone else did—to have the normal relationships that kids have at that age, the whole trip. I got dragged to church and to talk to the minister periodically. We all had to get down and pray for my affliction.

Finally they considered me incorrigible, and I was sent to a state hospital, which was an entirely different number. I went willingly, thinking that there I'd get intensive care—which, in retrospect, is really funny since I saw a doctor maybe two or three times the whole time I was there, which was four years. Being in there at that age and being as naïve as I was, I had a really rough time.

I saw mostly other patients and attendants. Later I was on tranquilizers; they almost killed me with them. You were given no other treatment of any kind, so I don't know how they expected you to get any better. There were lots of other homosexuals; that's where I actually learned the facts of life. I was completely changed from what I was when I went in there. I was full of hate, angry at the world. I was a totally different person, mainly because of the kinds of things you had to do in there in order to survive. It was a totally different way of living. It was a shock—something you either adapted to or you went crazy. It was a horrible, horrible experience. I saw things in there that no one who hadn't been in a state hospital in the fifties could have allowed themselves to believe was happening in this country. But it was like a horror movie.

Blueberry Man

David Bergman

Born in Fitchburg, Massachusetts, David Bergman is a poet, theater critic, and college professor. In this poem, Bergman reflects on the feelings of isolation he experienced as a young boy, and the connection he felt to the outcast who delivered blueberries to his family's house. "Blueberry Man" appears in Cracking the Code, *a collection of Bergman's poems published in 1985.*

I was never the one to spot him walking
slowly up the street, pulling his yellow
wagon. It was always a brother or sister
who'd race home with the news. Then everything
spun into action like gulls at low tide.

Mother would shoo the children from the yard
and hide us out of danger in the living room,
warning with harsh whispers not to peek
from the windows and knowing we would anyway,
tracking the blueberry man across the porch
to where he knocked at the kitchen door.

Grandfather greeted him. Mother said
she was afraid. But I think she was jealous.
For though I was five or six, I knew I'd
never see such beautiful hair again. Hair
like a storybook princess. Great golden skeins,
falling halfway down his back. And such eyes,
freaked like a robin's egg and bobbing
beneath mascara waves of lashes. I remember

the Victory Red lips unfurling like a flag
when he spoke and the frilly shirt.

My brothers
giggled nervously. But I wasn't scared.
I wanted to pull the chiffon curtains back
and speak. But what would I say? That I knew
what it was to be alone? That I had heard
my own family scamper with trepidation
from my door when I was quarantined with
scarlet fever and no one but my mother was
allowed into my room?
I could have said:
I'm only a child but certain to end an outcast too.
Still, I said nothing, except once, a weak
goodby for which I was roundly scolded.
I used to ride my bike to his house, a tiny
cabin covered with angry brambles and
the hiss of intriguing bees, hoping we'd meet.
But he stayed inside during the day when he
wasn't peddling the wares he gathered at night.

One sleepless dawn I saw him coming home
with a kerosene lantern in one hand
and a silvery pail in the other.
Mother washed his berries twice to cleanse
them of his memory, as if he communicated
with his touch the fearful urge to dress
in women's clothing. For dessert she'd douse
the fruit with milk or pile them on peaks of
sour cream, chubby mountain climbers in the snow.
My brothers ate them greedily. But I
when everyone had left the table, would
still be seated, savoring the sweet juice
and the delicate flesh he had brought me.

A World of Possibilities

Steven Saylor

Steven Saylor grew up outside of Austin, Texas—in a town so small that his high school senior class contained just twenty-five students. Saylor's memoir about growing up comes from a 1992 book entitled Hometowns: Gay Men Write about Where They Belong. *(In his essay, Saylor refers to his hometown as "Amethyst, Texas," but adds that he has chosen to give the town a pseudonym out of respect for the privacy of certain people he mentions.)*

I first discovered the existence of homosexuality when I read an article in one of my mother's *Cosmopolitans* titled, "I Married a Homosexual." This must have been around 1966, when I was ten years old. It was a typically lurid (and I imagine completely fictitious) first-person confession, with little redeeming educational or literary value, but I can still recount the finer points all these years later, especially the part where the neglected bride discovers her husband and his "best friend" in the living room. The description was intentionally pathetic rather than pornographic, but it electrified me nonetheless: best friend wrapped in the wife's silk robe, lying on the sofa while the naked husband knelt beside him stroking his face.

Cosmo set me searching for more tawdry glimpses into a world of possibilities that seemed very remote from Amethyst. The information I could get from books was fragmentary, contradictory, and always tainted with condescension and squeamishness—clinical disdain in something called *A Marriage Manual* among my mother's books, vicious jokes in Dr. Reuben's *Everything You Always Wanted to Know about Sex*, the lurid cover painting of two nude men on a paperback edition of Mishima's *Forbidden Colors* in a catalogue of paperbacks.

Then, from a convenience store in a town thirty miles away that sold liquor to underage customers as well as porn paperbacks, I acquired a copy of a novel called *Pretty Boys Must Die*. It satisfied my curiosity about what homosexuals did in a way that the *Britannica* had not. I was excited out of my mind. Next came *The Corporal's Boy*, and then *Military Chicken*. As a sophisticated reader, I knew there must be a difference between pornography and real life, just as there was a difference between Middle Earth and Dallas, but I also knew that somewhere out there, beyond Amethyst, someone had to be doing something remotely like what leather hustler Riley Jacks did to naïve young David (the "Pretty Boy") for it to have ended up in a book. I was ready.

But I had to wait. To have sex with another boy in Amethyst simply seemed impossible. Beginning at about age ten, Amethyst boys learned to use the word "cocksucker" as the worst imaginable epithet, and fear of being called a cocksucker kept everyone in line; to actually *be* a cocksucker was too scary to think about.

Meanwhile I was a perfect student. I played trumpet in band. I worked as a sack boy at the grocery store. I dated girls, and even did a passable amount of making out. I holed up in my room or escaped to the ancient oak tree on my grandparents' land and read for hours and hours—fantasy (Tolkien, Heinlein, Cabell, Dunsany), Russian novelists (Tolstoy, Dostoyevsky, the then-fashionable Solzhenitsyn), best-selling "trash" (my mother's word for Arthur Hailey and Leon Uris), and everything ever written by Larry McMurtry. I gorged on new porn when I could get it, and otherwise reread *Pretty Boys Must Die* until I had all the sex scenes memorized.

Mostly I bided my time, waiting to get out of Amethyst, putting life (which for a teenage boy means the hunt for sex) on hold. When I was a junior I visited my brother in the marijuana haze of his student apartment in Austin, and I saw the future. Until it arrived, I was content to read for hours, and masturbate for hours, and imagine a life beyond the wildest dreams of Amethyst.

The World Outside

Julia Sullivan

Julia Sullivan grew up in a small Massachusetts town, from which she later escaped. She is currently a writer and book editor.

I grew up in a small town surrounded by hills, and much of my childhood was devoted to planning my escape. This was not considered unusual; the town seemed to decide early on which young people would stay and which would go. There was some kind of sign, invisible to me, but as apparent to those who cared to look for it as the difference between good eggs and bad was to the chicken farmers I knew in those days.

No one was surprised when I left, but then we were not from the small town surrounded by hills. We had moved there, when I was still very young, from a small town almost surrounded by water. We came for a number of reasons, most of them mythical, but mainly because it was cheaper to live there and my father would have more time to write poetry and plays. Hardly anybody new ever moved to the town in those days, and most of the new people didn't stay. The life there suited the people who led it, and if it didn't suit others, well, there were plenty of other places for them to live. There was a ham and bean supper or a turkey raffle almost every night for some charitable purpose; when the Town Hall burned down, everybody came and stood around the Common to watch. It was almost like a different planet, with a heavy atmosphere and its own gravitational pull.

I knew it would be important to plan a good escape. I had seen others try it, and get caught in the town's field of gravity, drawn inexorably back into the round of lodge meetings and bingo nights. I watched carefully, making note of the dangerous areas and planning how to avoid them. Like most escapees, I kept my best ideas to myself. I might talk big with the big talkers about how I was going to be an astronaut, or a throat surgeon, or a Hollywood screenwriter, but that was just talk, and talk was the cheapest thing there was. The important thing—the only thing—was to stay as far as possible from the town's gravitational pull until I had left its orbit and was heading for the world outside.

The power of the town lay in three strong attractors: Comfort, Family, and Sex. I was pretty much immune to any comforts the town had to offer: our standards at home were different enough from the ones around me that I knew I would never fit in, although I could see, sometimes with envy, just how reassuring that would be. My family was small, and lived far away from the town, and was never the kind of family that made demands on your time. I was safe from two of the force-fields, then . . . I just had to be sure not to get trapped by Sex.

I had had a preview of what it could do. At one point in my childhood, my mother was a town official, and her duties included issuing marriage licenses. One night (it seemed to be very late), a couple still in their teens came to her, begging for a license, the girl in tears. They were underage, and her parents had thrown her out of the house; you could probably write the rest of the story yourself. The thing that frightened me most was the desperate exhaustion on their faces, a look I had only seen before in trapped animals' eyes. My mother took charge of the situation, gave them coffee and cookies, called their parents and reasoned them into submission, convinced the girl to go home, and told them both to come around to her office the next day. After she closed the door behind them, my mother came to me under the dining room table where I was hiding and said, "I hope you've learned something tonight." I had, of course, but it took a few years for the lesson to be of much use, since I had the young child's contempt for adults who were ensnared by sex. How could something fit only for the lowest campfire jokes have dominion over people old enough to drive a car and stay up as late as they liked? It seemed ridiculous.

Not too many years later, I realized what all the fuss was about. It was the seventh grade, on the day before Thanksgiving. Some expert or other was telling our teachers how to teach us every-thing while spending no money and tricking us into enjoying it, so the students were all sitting in the multipurpose room watching the movie *Oliver!* The bare-chested lout who played Bill Sykes was snarling some stereotyped defiance into the camera, and I dis-covered that my stomach felt funny, the way it did when I jumped my bike over a pothole. I sank lower into my multipurpose chair and took stock of the situation. It was definitely a bad sign. Two days later, I was watching the Rolling Stones on "Don Kirshner's Rock Concert," and my worst suspicions were confirmed. A good look at Keith Richards produced the same feelings; I would have to be very careful, or my escape would be doomed.

I thought about it a lot, and decided that it would be safe to have sexual feelings about people who didn't really exist, or who existed somewhere else, in towns that weren't surrounded by hills. I stayed up late into the nights, watching old black-and-white movies on our battered nine-inch set. I saw *The Philadelphia Story* over and over, dizzy with love for everyone in it. Bette Davis moved me to tears; I saw *The Thin Man* and didn't know whether I wanted to be Nick or Nora. The world that flickered in the den at night seemed closer to me than the one I lived in by day. Nobody ever sold Joan Crawford a ticket for a ham and bean supper. She went to opening nights in black silk and sequins and exchanged longing glances with broad-shouldered men in white tie and tails. How could you settle for less than that?

Then there were books. The movies might be a window, but books were letters from the outside world. Somebody else, some-where else, was having feelings like yours. Somebody else, some-where else, was really living their life, and taking the time to write to you about it. They were in love, they were out of love, they were moving around, free of the heavy gravity of the small town. It could be done, if you could watch and wait and work to get out.

It was clearly going to be imperative to keep my sexuality to myself. I was already pretty good at keeping things to myself; my mother had died the previous year, and I had built up a hard shell of pride to keep from accepting help from the kind people around me. If I was going to keep my mind on my escape, I would have to stay free. I would have to keep silent. I would have to work things out on my own.

Anyway, I didn't think much of sex as it appeared in the small hill town. For one thing, it was all tied up with babies and marriage and settling down and all the things I was fighting so desperately to stay clear of. Sex in the movies was different; it was like a dance, where partners moved together until a tune ended, then found another and began again. This seemed as profoundly right to me as the other seemed wrong, but I was smart enough not to mention it. My family were the kind of educated, polite people who were "open-minded" about sexuality. They saw it as something like diabetes—an unfortunate physical defect, best not mentioned, that could be controlled with the right kind of treatment. I doubted they'd have much patience with my ideas.

Since sex, for me, was so intensely private, it seemed logical to me that I would be as attracted to Katharine Hepburn as I was to Cary Grant. I knew that I was different, and this was just another difference nobody had to know about. I could talk with the girls at lunch about how cute Peter was on *The Brady Bunch* and just not mention that I really preferred Jan. If I just kept my silence, nothing would ever get out, since my basketball teammates were just as safe from me as the boys who raked the Common with their shirts off. No one I grew up with seemed at all a sexual object. I had an incest taboo that stretched for miles in all directions. Like an athlete in training, my energies were completely focused. Anything that didn't help me to get out was a distraction. All I had to do was keep quiet and wait for my escape.

Still, the silence frightened me sometimes. What if I was wrong? What if I never got away to a place where people would understand me? As I got older, my friends talked endlessly about sex and love. Most of their sex lives began as mostly hypothetical, and grew more and more actual, as they began to put their fantasies into action. *My* fantasies seemed to have no connection with my unsatisfactory real-life encounters, but it seemed impossible to speak of my disappointments, even with men. As for my dreams about women, I could never, never tell them to anyone. I thought that I might always be alone, that the love that I dreamed of was just as make-believe as the movies I paid more attention to than life.

Then I came across the word *bisexual* in a biography of Marlene Dietrich, one of my favorite Hollywood stars. The author obviously didn't think much of Marlene's lifestyle, but I was riveted to the page. There was a word for it; it wasn't just me. Marlene loved men sometimes and women sometimes, and she was one of a number of people who did that, and that was *one of the things you could do.* It would be all right in the world outside. The book went on to say that this was one of the reasons for her great popularity with gay men. It seemed right to me that people who said no to the walls around their sexuality would band together. There had to be a community of people who saw love as something that made you free, not something that tied you down.

It was as though I had found something I didn't know I had lost. I felt a tremendous sense of relief, and proceeded to read everything about homosexuality, lesbianism, and bisexuality that I could find. I scoured the pages of history for bisexual men and women, and took comfort in thinking that Julius Caesar, Colette, Cary Grant, Shakespeare, Eleanor Roosevelt, and Greta Garbo were *just like me.* Anything about people who were "different" was of interest: I became an expert on the handkerchief signals men used in leather bars, and the latest lesbian folk albums from Olivia Records. It was easier, somehow, to keep my sexuality to myself now that I knew there were people outside with whom I could share it one day.

This story doesn't really have an ending. I went to college, graduated, found a job and a life in the city, and never went back to the small town surrounded by hills. Sometimes the simplest escapes are the best ones. My love life became less hypothetical and more actual, but I still go to the movies a lot more than I should. I have friends of all flavors, gay, bi, lesbian, and straight. They talk to me about the people they love and desire and I talk to them about the people I love and desire. That seems so simple now, but I remember how completely impossible it seemed back then. Sometimes I am sorry I kept these things inside for so many years; I had to make a lot of mistakes as an adult that most straight people make in their teens. If I could go back in time, though, I don't think I could make anything different. I don't know what I could say to the girl who watched her little television like it was a window onto life. I don't think I could give her the courage to speak, and I don't think anybody would hear her if she did.

Sometimes I regret the silence in my past, but I was silent then about so many things. I was only waiting for the time when I would be free to speak, when I had finally made my way to the world outside.

Different Is Not Bad

Michael

Michael wrote this essay in 1992, when he was sixteen. He lives in Oregon.

Each day, as I skim through the newspaper and read the articles concerning homosexuals, and as I look at the editorials, I wonder what the big deal is. Why does it matter that I like members of my own sex?

There are a lot of answers to that question. We, as a sexual minority, face a lot of discrimination in everyday life. Probably the most prevalent source of this stems from the simple reason that we are different. Anything that is not mainstream and "generally accepted" is different, and therefore hated by many people. Most people have trouble adjusting to something that they're not used to. The other side of this is religion. Most religions deem homosexual and bisexual behavior as void of love, damaging to society, and wholly unacceptable.

Through all of this hate, disgust, and lack of knowledge, people are not really facing the issues at hand. Why does it really matter that I'm gay? I like other guys; I find companionship with another male very pleasurable. I do not harm other people in the process; quite the opposite. I can bring love and happiness to someone's life, and does it really matter that that person may be another male? Different is not bad, and such a relationship is most certainly filled with love.

What is damaging to society is the refusal to deal with current issues. Religion teaches that all people are created equally, yet it discriminates on the basis of sexual orientation. Which is more damaging to society—persecuting people because they like members of their own sex and forcing them to feel isolated, guilty, and less than human (which directly affects society), or allowing people to be as they are, and accepting them for who they are? Not a very difficult question to answer.

In the process of dealing with my sexuality, I have discovered more about myself, and about other people. I look at the world and remark about its awesome beauty, and I laugh with other people and have fun spending time with them. I am no different from anyone else. I did not choose to be gay, but I don't want to change (assuming that I could). True, being straight in today's world is much easier than being gay. Yet, at the same time, I have learned much through my struggle to accept myself as I am, and I refuse to cover up my feelings, which are just as wonderful as those of heterosexuals. The bottom line is that it doesn't matter that I'm gay. It doesn't matter that someone else is gay. People are all equally capable of sharing love and friendship, regardless of who they share those feelings with. The ability of one person to bring happiness to someone else is truly amazing. Does it matter if both of them are male or female? As my best friend says, "So I like other guys; big deal."

Exactly.

Friendships /

Relationships

Annie on My Mind

Nancy Garden

Annie on My Mind *tells the story of two high school students, Liza
and Annie, who live in New York City. The novel, told from Liza's
point of view, portrays the beginning of their love affair in simple,
direct language. In the excerpt that follows, Liza visits Annie at her
house, and the two young women discuss their growing feelings for
one another.*

It was cold and very damp outside, as
if it were going to snow, but it was warm in Annie's room. She
had some quiet music on her rickety old-fashioned phonograph,
and her hair was in two braids, which by now I knew usually
meant she hadn't had time to wash it or that she'd been doing
something active or messy, like helping her mother clean.

We just looked at each other for a minute there in the doorway
of her room, as if neither of us knew what to say or how to act
with each other. But I felt myself leave Sally and school and the
fund-raising drive behind me, the way a cicada leaves its shell
when it turns from an immature grub into its almost grown-up
self.

Annie took my hand, shyly, pulled me into her room, and shut
the door. "Hi," she said.

I felt myself smiling, wanting to laugh with pleasure at seeing
her, but also needing to laugh, out of nervousness, I guess. "Hi."

Then we both did laugh, like a couple of idiots, standing there
awkwardly looking at each other.

And we both moved at the same time into each other's arms,
hugging. It was just a friendly hug at first, an I'm-so-glad-to-see-
you hug. But then I began to be very aware of Annie's body pressed

against mine and of feeling her heart beat against my breast, so I moved away.

"Sorry," she said, turning away also.

I touched her shoulder; it was rigid. "No—no, don't be."

"You moved away so fast."

"I—Annie, please."

"Please what?"

"Please—I don't know. Can't we just be . . ."

"Friends?" she said, whirling around. "Just friends—wonderful stock phrase, isn't it? Only what you said on the beach was—was . . ." She turned away again, covering her face with her hands.

"Annie," I said miserably, "Annie, Annie. I—I do love you, Annie." There, I thought. That's the second time I've said it.

Annie groped on her desk-table and handed me an envelope. "I'm sorry," she said. "I didn't get any sleep last night and—well, I couldn't tell you a single thing anyone said in school today, even at rehearsal. I'm going to wash my face."

I nodded, trying to smile at her as if everything was all right—there's no reason, I remember thinking, why it shouldn't be—and I sat down on the edge of Annie's bed and opened the letter.

Dear Liza,

It's three-thirty in the morning and this is the fifth time I've tried to write this to you. Someone said something about three o'clock in the morning being the dark night of the soul—something like that. That's true, at least for this three o'clock and this soul.

Look, I have to be honest—I want to try to be, anyhow. I told you about Beverly because I knew at that point that I loved you. I was trying to warn you, I guess. As I said, I've wondered for a long time if I was gay. I even tried to prove I wasn't, last summer with a boy, but it was ridiculous.

I know you said on the beach that you think you love me, and I've been trying to hold on to that, but I'm still scared that if I told you everything about how I feel, you might not be ready for it. Maybe you've already felt pressured into thinking you have to feel the same way, out of politeness, sort of, because you like me and don't want to hurt my feelings. The thing is, since you haven't thought about it—about being gay—I'm trying to tell myself very firmly that it wouldn't be fair of me to—I don't know, influence you, try to push you into something you don't want, or don't want yet, or something.

Liza, I think what I'm saying is that, really, if you don't want us to see each other anymore, it's okay.

Love,
Annie

I stood there holding the letter and looking at the word "Love" at the end of it, knowing that I was jealous of the boy Annie'd mentioned, and that my not seeing Annie anymore would be as ridiculous for me as she said her experiment with the boy had been for her.

Could I even begin an experiment like that, I wondered, startled; would I?

It was true I'd never consciously thought about being gay. But it also seemed true that if I were, that might pull together not only what had been happening between me and Annie all along and how I felt about her, but also a lot of things in my life before I'd known her—things I'd never let myself think about much. Even when I was little, I'd often felt as if I didn't quite fit in with most of the people around me; I'd felt isolated in some way that I never understood. And as I got older—well, in the last two or three years, I'd wondered why I'd rather go to the movies with Sally or some other girl than with a boy, and why, when I imagined living with someone someday, permanently I mean, that person was always female.

I read Annie's letter again, and again felt how ridiculous not seeing her anymore would be—how much I'd miss her, too.

When Annie came back from the bathroom, she stood across the room watching me for a few minutes. I could tell she was trying very hard to pretend her letter didn't matter, but her eyes were so bright that I was pretty sure they were wet.

"I'd tear this up," I said finally, "if it weren't for the fact that it's the first letter you've ever written me, and so I want to keep it."

"Oh, Liza!" she said softly, not moving. "Are you sure?"

I felt my face getting hot and my heart speeding up again. Annie's eyes were so intent on mine, it was as if we were standing with no distance between us—but there was the whole room.

I think I nodded, and I know I held out my hand. I felt about three years old.

She took my hand, and then she touched my face. "I still don't want to rush you," she said softly. "I—it scares me, too, Liza. I—I just recognize it more, maybe."

"Right now I just want to feel you close to me," I said, or something like it, and in a few minutes we were lying down on Annie's bed, holding each other and sometimes kissing, but not really touching. Mostly just being happy.

Still scared, though, too.

That winter, all Annie had to do was walk into a room or appear at a bus stop or a corner where we were meeting and I didn't even have to think about smiling; I could feel my face smiling all on its own. We saw each other every afternoon that we could, on weekends, and called each other just about every night, and even that didn't seem enough; sometimes we even arranged to call each other from pay phones at lunchtime. It was a good thing I'd never had much trouble with schoolwork, because I floated through classes, writing letters to Annie or daydreaming. The fund-raising campaign went on around me without my paying much attention to it. I did pledge some money; I listened to Sally and Walt make speeches; I even helped them collect pledges from some of the other kids—but I was never really there, because Annie filled my mind. Songs I heard on the radio suddenly seemed to fit Annie and me; poems I read seemed written especially for us—we began sending each other poems that we liked. I would have gone broke buying Annie plants if I hadn't known how much it bothered her that I often had money and she usually didn't.

We kept finding new things about New York to show each other; it was as if we were both seeing the city for the first time. One afternoon I suddenly noticed, and then showed Annie, how the sunlight dripped over the ugly face of her building, softening it and making it glow almost as if there were a mysterious light source hidden inside its drab walls. And Annie showed me how ailanthus trees grow under subway and sewer gratings, stretching toward the sun, making shelter in the summer, she said, laughing, for the small dragons that live under the streets. Much of that winter was—magical is the only word again—and a big part of that magic was that no matter how much of ourselves we found to give each other, there was always more we wanted to give. . . .

We didn't always use words when we were together; we didn't need to. That was uncanny, but maybe the best thing of all, although I don't think we thought about it much; it just happened. There's a Greek legend—no, it's in something Plato wrote—about how true lovers are really two halves of the same person. It says that people wander around searching for their other half, and when they find him or her, they are finally whole and perfect. The thing that gets me is that the story says that originally all people were really pairs of people, joined back to back, and that some of the pairs were man and man, some woman and woman, and others man and woman. What happened was that all of these double people went to war with the gods, and the gods, to punish them, split them all in two. That's why some lovers are heterosexual and some are homosexual, female and female, or male and male.

I loved that story when I first heard it—in junior year, I think it was—because it seemed fair, and right, and sensible. But that winter I really began to believe it was true, because the more Annie and I learned about each other, the more I felt she was the other half of me.

We Two Boys Together Clinging

Walt Whitman

Born in New York, Walt Whitman (1819–1892) left school at age eleven to enter the printing trade. In 1855, he published Leaves of Grass, *a volume of poems about equality, democracy, immortality, and the self that has since become an American classic. Whitman also wrote about "the love of comrades"—men he knew, admired, or yearned for. Later, when* Leaves of Grass *became more popular, Whitman was fired from his government job in the Department of the Interior for having written an immoral book. In "We Two Boys Together Clinging," Whitman evokes the bond of friendship that existed between two boys and suggests that "loving" was a natural element of the relationship between these two boys.*

We two boys together clinging,
One the other never leaving,
Up and down the roads going, North and South excursions mak-
    ing,
Power enjoying, elbows stretching, fingers clutching,
Armed and fearless, eating, drinking, sleeping, loving,
No law less than ourselves owning, sailing, soldiering, thieving,
    threatening,
Misers, menials, priests alarming, air breathing, water drinking,
    on the turf or the sea-beach dancing,
Cities wrenching, ease scorning, statues mocking, feebleness chasing,
Fulfilling our foray.

My Archenemy

Jill Frushtick

A native of New York, Jill Frushtick writes about the pain, both emotional and physical, of her first crush on another young woman. Frushtick now lives in Florida with her partner of more than fifteen years.

One day when I was thirteen years old and a student at Harry B. Thompson Junior High School on Long Island, New York, I passed my archenemy, Diane Terz, on the stairway in the crush between classes. I was headed upstairs to social studies, and she was headed downstairs. Normally, I had a mild-mannered, subdued, and even "wimpy" personality; however, this young woman lathered me up into a frenzy of hatred. With all of my might, I smashed into Diane, knocking her books and notebooks to the floor, where they were swept away in the sea of feet descending the staircase. Aha! Victory! With flushed cheeks, an ecstatic gleam in my eye, and an extra hop in my tomboy gait, I celebrated silently until after school, when I scrambled to tell my best friend, Cliff, the great news.

Back then, I had no clue as to why I hated Diane. It wasn't until ten years later, talking to a straight male friend, that I realized my behavior was the same as that of some little boys who chase and trip little girls they have crushes on. I was madly, passionately in love with Diane Terz.

I was twelve when Diane moved into the house seven doors down. I met her at our bus stop on the first day of seventh grade—the first day of junior high. I had never known anyone like her. She was physically very mature, with huge breasts, and she was fresh out of Catholic school. She was very feminine and giggly. I was Jewish and had mostly hung out with Jewish boys, by choice, until then. Getting to know this new kid on the block was exciting, and I planned to show her the ropes in our close-knit neighborhood.

I don't think Diane had ever known kids like us, either. We were a fairly vulgar bunch: the kind that threw snowballs at passing cars in the winter and told dirty jokes (really gross ones) all summer. This left the fall for throwing crab apples, especially at the Wygoda house. (We occasionally broke windows, but this was ordinary hatred here, not the romantic variety.)

I remember wanting to be near Diane a lot, even though she did goofy stuff like spending hours putting on the little bit of makeup her mother would allow her to wear. She did other boring things, too, like talk endlessly about the boy next door, David, who already had big muscles and a broad chest. I had known David since our early baby-carriage days, so this was truly dull.

One sunny afternoon, I remember sitting out with Diane on the lawn in front of my house. She had brought one of those *Teen Beat* magazines and was drooling over these movie-star guys for hours. I just really liked being close to her (though there were a couple of cute pictures that I liked, too).

By the next spring there was a lot of excitement in the neighborhood as we planned for the bar mitzvah parties of our friends. We also got into having secret clubs, with even more secret boy-girl make-out parties. I was a complete failure here. I needed a lot of practice and I wasn't getting much. After one of the longer sessions in Cliff's basement, Diane took me aside, squealing that David had kissed her "here and here and here"—on the cheek, on the neck, and even on the shoulders. She was delirious. Big deal, I thought. Then I came up with a plan. I decided that Cliffy, my best friend in the whole world, should go steady with Diane. This became my quest. Why, you may ask? So that I could be closer to her, of course—so that I could vicariously go steady with her too. I even told Cliffy this. He was decidedly disinterested in anything female, but he agreed to give her his new I.D. bracelet.

Sometime after that, things deteriorated. Diane's mother was understandably fed up with these wild, foul-mouthed boys (and with me, the tomboy) clamoring at her daughter's window, and she eventually got more strict. We concluded she despised us. This prompted Cliff and me to muster our genius with art to create "The Terz Family Album." It was a thing of rare beauty. Each Terz got their own individual page. My best piece was "The Grandmother," a drawing with exaggerated features and warts, much like *Mad* magazine, only naked and disgusting!

Unfortunately for us, Mrs. Terz accidentally got a glimpse of our drawings. Cliff soon had his I.D. bracelet back, and Diane began to avoid me. It was clear that she no longer wanted to be friends. Now, twenty-five years later, I can see that what I really wanted from Diane was hugs and kisses, attention and adoration. But in the world I grew up in, I never even imagined anything like an actual relationship with Diane, or with any other girls, for that matter. Unfortunately, Diane paid the price—or more specifically, Diane's shins paid the price. For a while there, I lived for kicking them.

The Best Little Boy in the World

John Reid

The Best Little Boy in the World *is the 1973 autobiography of an overachieving young man who is viewed as the perfect son and the perfect student—by those who do not know that he is gay. In this passage, the author, John Reid, talks about the charade he went through as a high school student, pretending to be interested in girls when in fact he was interested in boys.*

In high school it had been enough to learn to check out attractive girls on the street—look them up and down, leer a little, nudge my companion (naturally I only bothered with this nonsense when there was someone else around), maybe sigh or pant a little, or mutter something dirty—and then go back to noticing the boys.

Noticing attractive girls was not as easy to learn as it sounds. There was no department in my subconscious responsible for spotting pretty girls out of the corners of my eyes, as there was in the subconsciouses of my friends. I had to remind myself consciously to look or else suffer the embarrassment of being reminded by a friend's poke to *catch those legs—oooo WEEEEE!* But I ran a significant risk in leering and nudging: As I was attracted to boys, not girls, I had to use the most mechanical techniques in deciding which girls were "attractive." (If I knew instinctively, I was afraid to trust my instincts.) While others would have a simple groin reaction, I would nervously rush through a little checklist. I knew girls in laced shoes or combat boots were out. I knew legs were important and had heard someone talk scornfully about a girl with "piano legs," so I tried to avoid those. I would ignore any girls whose heads did not at least come up even with the parking meters as they walked by, as well as those whose heads brushed the bus stop signs. Frizzy redheads, for some reason, were out. Girls who looked like boys except with ponytails were out. The hardest part, especially under winter coats, was to determine whether a girl was "built" or just fat. There was nothing whatever to be gained by leering and chortling over a dog. One slip like that and my cover would be blown: *You're not really attracted to girls!* YOU'RE FAKING IT!

My back-up defense in such situations was myopia. I purposely kept my glasses off—they weren't very strong anyway—so that any omitted or mistaken leers and nudges could be blamed on my ophthalmologist.

In college you had to do more than just leer and chortle. You had to date. Maybe you didn't have to if you were ugly, and maybe you didn't have to if you weren't worried about your normality. But if you were me, you had to date.

Not counting high school parties and camp dances, where everyone had to go by the busload—more like holding a special dancing lesson than a date—I can remember having had three dates prior to entering Yale. . . .

My third date was . . . when I was about fifteen, my last summer in camp, and Tommy Roth's. Tommy was dating a counselor at our sister camp. Who was I dating? I had to be dating somebody, so I was dating Hilda Goldbaum, from Queens. Hilda's chin was in proper proportion to the rest of her face and body, which in total couldn't have weighed thirty pounds more than mine. She was particularly weighed down by two of the most enormous, terrifying boobs I could imagine. But that's how things happened to pair up the first night they took a busload of us seniors out to the sister camp for a dance, so it was Hilda and me for the summer.

Brother-sister camp dances, as you may know, are very risky affairs that send camp directors' hearts aflutter. Once, in 1932, a girl got pregnant possibly as a result of one of these dances, and the sister camp went out of business then and there. Since 1932, the state militia had been called out to guard the exits at all of our brother-sister camp dances, and the only way you could possibly hold your head up in the bus on the way back to camp was if you had been *missed*—that is, if you and your girl had been missed at some point during the course of the evening. Maximum points were scored by the couple who could turn up under the yellow circle of flashlight—down at the rifle range. Where they have mattresses.

"This bus ain't leavin' till we find Tommy. And when we *do* find him, he's gonna catch hell, lemme tellya."

Five minutes later Tommy and Kathy are discovered down at the rifle range. The bus pulls off with all kinds of adulation being showered on Tommy. Hey, Tommy! What were you shooting down there anyway? Har, har, har. The camp director would find out about it the next morning, telephone Tommy's parents, and threaten to have Tommy sent home. Tommy's proud father, who had been caught down on the same rifle range in his day, would mention Tommy's three younger brothers, nearing camp age at $1,000 apiece—and the matter would be dropped.

So Hilda and I *had* to be missed. Yet this was one test of my manhood I was just going to have to fail. I couldn't bring myself to seduce Hilda into the dark piney woods. I would just have to blame it on the security guards and change the subject when people asked me.

As it happened, Hilda had different ideas. She led me through a maze of piled tables and chairs, through the kitchen and the dishwashing apparatus, to an unguarded ratty old warped sinful-looking screen door, and out into the dark piney woods. She was hot, she said, why not go for a walk? I stopped after a few yards to try to marshal my resources for some kind of brilliant excuse. When I got older I planned to use the one about having had my thing shot off in the war, but Hilda, I knew, would not have accepted this from a fifteen-year-old. Maybe I could say it was shot off at the archery range. I started to open my mouth, in a hesitating sort of way because I was not too sure of what I would say, and Hilda grabbed me as though she were an alcoholic and I were the last bottle left on earth. She pressed her lips hard against mine. I gritted my teeth and held my breath.

It was awful. The kiss itself, my first on the lips, could have been worse. It was just like pressing your lips against something squishy. Nothing more, nothing less. But knowing that it was nothing more, when it should have been, and, far worse, knowing that when this kiss was over (it was dragging on and on) Hilda and the world would have discovered that I didn't know how to kiss—that was awful.

Finally she loosened her grip and moved her face away, and I prepared for the worst. I had just stood there, after all. Whatever kissing is, however they do it in the movies, I had just stood there. My major achievement had been to repress the natural impulse I had to wrinkle up my nose. But do you know what she said? She said, "Oooow, that was *wonn*derful. It's been a *month* since I had a man!" That line sent me a lot of conflicting signals. Of course, I was tremendously relieved to know I could pass for a lover just by standing in the woods letting her squish her lips against mine. I felt like remarking in amazement, crying with relief, laughing at the ridiculous thing she had said, gloating at having pulled it off. And now she was doing it again.

I had heard of French kissing, but I didn't think we were doing it. Before she decided to get into *that*, I figured I would take a gamble, newly self-confident as I was, and when she backed away, I said in my deepest, most leadership kind of voice, "I think we'd better get back before they miss us." Apparently, I noted, she had gotten her rocks off, as she dutifully followed her man back to the dance.

The following week, Hilda and Kathy somehow contrived to get over to our camp to see Tommy and me. Tommy was delighted, and after lunch (I remember it was ravioli) he commandeered an empty tent for us. He put the flaps down. I kept trying to protest about the grave risk we were taking, but Tommy had had the flaps down before. He started making out with Kathy, lying on top of her, kissing her, putting his hands all over her. I made some very awkward attempts, with more help from Hilda than I wanted, to do roughly the same things, hoping against hope that some counselor would come along and break it up. Even being sent home would be better than this. And by now, all things considered, it might not have been altogether bad for my image at home to be sent back for this. My parents weren't pushing, but they let me know I would be more than welcome to start bringing girls home, to start dating under proper circumstances, to go to more dances—and who was I planning to take to the Junior Prom?

But no counselor came along. Hilda, meanwhile, was getting ready to go all the way. It was time to French kiss. She pried open my mouth with her crowbar tongue and stuck it in. Agh! *Germs!* Germs, hell: *ravioli!* I don't mean to be vulgar; but her breath smelled like ravioli, and I felt like puking. Or running, or passing out. But there was Tommy, whose respect meant more to me than anything, making out gleefully with Kathy. *Please* stop. *Please* don't look at how awkward I am. *Please*, Great Phonifier, at least don't make me puke.

End-of-rest-hour was bugled out over the loudspeaker, which, thank God, was the call for retreat. It was over. The girls had to go back with the counselor who had brought them over. If anything, Tommy thought I was more normal than ever. Kathy was happy, Hilda was happy. I went for a gargle in the lake.

My Best Friend Is Gay?!

Shawn

Shawn wrote this essay in 1992, when she was sixteen. She lives in Oakland, California.

I recently found out that my best friend is gay. We've been friends since I was two and I never really thought that he'd one day tell me, "I'm gay." When he told me, I wasn't threatened or surprised. In fact, I kind of knew. My reaction was that of typical understanding—"Really? I kind of knew, but I'm glad you told me." The funny thing is, it doesn't matter. It hasn't changed one thing. I even think that it has brought us closer.

Before I found out that my friend was gay I looked down on "those people," possibly because my home life expresses an intense rejection towards the homosexual population. I now feel that my best friend has opened my eyes and helped me realize that my discrimination was just plain ignorance. We reject that which we do not understand because we are uneducated or ignorant. I understand my friend more and I have more in common with him than I ever had. I think that my acceptance was so easy because I'm a girl, he's a boy, and I didn't feel threatened. If it were a girl opening up to me I think that I would feel my sexuality was being threatened.

The weirdest thing is that we have similar likes in guys. It's the same with my girlfriends; we end up liking the same people. I have heard that gay people are much more sensitive than heterosexuals. I feel the "stereotype" is true in this case. I can tell my friend anything and he is in tune with everything that I say; more so than my best girlfriend.

What really pisses me off is when the remarks come streaming in about us. "Gross, you're friends with a gay guy? Are you really friends? I mean can you still have that same relationship?" And my favorite—"Does he make passes at your brother?" Frankly, I think that being a friend with "a gay guy" is the best thing that has happened to my over-hormonal mind, and we couldn't be better friends than we are, just to answer the first two questions. In response to the latter question—that's just how Grandma subtly asks her granddaughter if she's started her period yet—at the dinner table. It just doesn't come out like it should. You can't just flat out ask someone something like that! But, no, he doesn't make passes at my brother.

Basically, I love my friends—straight or gay—and who they choose to love does not affect the way that I feel about them.

It's Too Hot

David J. Deschamps

David J. Deschamps grew up in Salem, Massachusetts, and studied piano performance at the University of Lowell in Massachusetts. Adapted from a journal David kept during his college years, "It's Too Hot" tells of a life-changing trip to New York and of the support and love David received from his friends.

Saturday, April 19, 1980

I can't get John out of my mind. Copper skin . . . sky-blue eyes . . . perfect white teeth . . . tight Calvins hugging his oh-so-sexy body . . . curly brown hair reminiscent of a Greek statue. . . . Mmm, mmm. Celeste certainly has excellent taste in high school crushes—though it must be frustrating for her to keep falling in love with gay men. First John, then the two in college, now me. She and John have remained close friends; I really hope the same thing will happen with us now that Celeste knows I am gay. Our love has been very important to me, bringing me the confidence to finally accept myself. How ironic and sad that her passion *for* me brings out the passion *in* me for men.

We've been in New York for less than twelve hours and already I feel more relaxed. I'm glad I skipped counterpoint class to come on this weekend trip with Celeste and Leslie, and I'm relieved that I won't be sleeping two feet away from my roommate Andy, desperately wanting just to hold him but knowing nothing will ever happen between us because he's straight. He knows I'm gay; in fact he was the first person I ever told. And he knows I'm in love with him; we talk about it all the time. Christ, I wish he wouldn't be so understanding—it makes me care even more about him.

Last night, I told my friend Leslie that I am gay—after I had sex with her. She just laughed and said, "What a surprise." I guess she already knew. It's amazing that there is no awkwardness between us today. I wonder, though, why it happened. Were we both just horny and alone? Was I trying to make it easier to tell her? How would that make it easier? I can't say for certain, but I do know that the physical and emotional intimacy has brought us closer together.

Sunday, April 20, 1980

After seeing *Sweeney Todd* last night, Celeste and I went to meet her friend John at the Eighth Street Playhouse, where he works. We were early, so I got a chance to take my first walk down Christopher Street in Greenwich Village. How can a few blocks of seamy city concrete stir such emotions in me? A smattering of bars, lots of men in tight designer jeans and T-shirts, a newsstand. The Erotic Bakery was fun but not really cause for celebrating. Is it being in a place where no one knows me, where I can imagine my life any way I want? Is it just the sexual titillation of imagining myself with the men I passed? Maybe it's finding a place where I fit in, one of the crowd, no secrets. I'm not sure, but I feel elated, as if I were a new person. My past is gone. That day when I was eleven and realized I wasn't quite like the other boys and cried myself to sleep—gone. The ten years of self-loathing and sleeping with women to prove to myself that I was a real man—gone. The period when I tried to hide my being gay by becoming a born-again Christian and physically stopped myself from looking at men—gone. The hidden collection of *Playgirl* magazines that it took me months to work up courage to go in and buy—forgotten. Even the pain of being in love with straight old Andy seems miles away, back at school. I feel free. But there is still this deep yearning, a longing for the unknown, a need to start living honestly.

After my drug-like experience on Christopher Street, John was waiting for us, looking cuter than ever. We headed back to Brooklyn and he told us about his first apartment, which just happened to be on Christopher Street. How perfect! Listening to him, I felt like a little boy devouring candy. I think it can safely be said that I'm smitten.

Later that night

   I don't have much time to write. We're about to leave to go to a Thai restaurant on 50th and Broadway. But I need to put my thoughts on paper. We went shopping on the Lower East Side this morning. I felt as if I was walking onto the set of *Funny Girl*—people hanging out of windows, tiny little shops, an incredible kosher dairy bar where I had my first blintzes. We were riding on the subway and I mentioned in passing how I would love to live in New York. Leslie turned to me and said ever so casually. "Well, why don't you?" And as Bugs Bunny would say: *Koing!* It hit me. *Why not, indeed?* Could I really leave school and move to New York? Leslie said there was nothing keeping her in Boston and that she'd consider moving with me. It feels so right, or am I just being blinded with emotion? Am I just running away? No. The thought of going back to my old self, my old self-loathing self, can't be right. What have I got to lose?
   Leslie and I then went to meet John and Celeste. John had gotten us free tickets to see *Strider*, a bizarre musical with horse-like choreography. It was enjoyable if slightly incoherent. More enjoyable was sitting next to John. Our knees would touch occasionally, sending sparks through my body. At intermission I excused myself to go to the men's room. John said, "I think I'll go with you." I panicked. The old "fear-of-getting-an-erection-at-the-urinal" syndrome strikes again. Would I be relegated to a stall, or would I stand man-to-man at the urinal? As we were maneuvering our way through the crowd, my hand accidentally brushed against John's thigh. That was it—defeat. Why is it that the more I try not to become excited, the more difficult it is to control myself? I could feel my crotch start to stir and my face begin to color. Time to camouflage. Hands in pocket. We walked into the men's room. Disaster. Floor-length urinals with no dividers. No hiding anything here. I immediately headed to the first stall and tried to calm

myself. I wonder if John noticed my predicament. How humiliating. I feel enough like a child around him.

Tuesday night, April 22, 1980

I was in the back seat of Celeste's car, half asleep as we were driving back to school, and the song "Too Hot" by Kool & the Gang came on the radio. As the singer told of running for shelter and shade to escape from the heat, silent tears filled my eyes. Yet I felt calm and peaceful. All the emotions and changes I had experienced over the weekend seemed to be flowing out of those chords, those lyrics; it was as if my body was being rinsed clean. It didn't matter that the words were trite and the music simple. Maybe I sensed too much had happened this weekend and I identified with the need to run and hide and digest it all. My life has always seemed so planned. Now I can see all these variations that never seemed possible before.

Celeste and I stayed at her mother's house last night and drove to school this morning. The campus was a different place to me. Everything seemed to be brighter, glossier, with a sheen I never noticed before. Every person I met seemed friendlier, more sincere. I felt as if I was in one of those early Warner Bros. cartoons with all the dancing and singing flowers. It was a beautiful spring day—but it was more than that. It was me. Instead of being all wrapped up in feeling ashamed of myself, I could see clearly the people and things around me. For the first time in my life, I was truly happy and confident. I wonder if you can really know as it's happening that a certain day is going to be the happiest day of your life. Even going to rehearsal for *The Marriage of Figaro*, usually a drag, seemed fun. Andy was there. We had a great talk about my weekend. I felt such a strong bond with him. What's even better is I didn't feel that pain, that futile longing for something I couldn't have. Now I realized there are thousands of gay men that I could love and maybe even would love me.

Which leads me to John. Maybe my attraction to him is so intense because for the first time, there is the chance that my feelings might actually be returned. Celeste and I stayed up all last night talking about the weekend. She seems to think there's a possibility that he might be interested in me. It's incredible, given her intense feelings for me, how supportive she is being of my crush. Maybe she understands my attraction to John, given her own. Or maybe she feels that John is part of her—and therefore that my feelings are directed towards her. Maybe they are.

Right now I feel closer to Celeste, Andy, and Leslie than seems humanly possible. Without their love and support, I never would have had the courage to even dream about starting a new life. It's becoming clear to me that my friends have been my shelter, have been my shade.

Giovanni's Room

James Baldwin

*James Baldwin (1924–1987) is recognized as one of the most impor-
tant American writers of the twentieth century. Born and raised in
New York City, Baldwin spoke out against discrimination and in-
equality through fiction* (Go Tell It on the Mountain) *as well as
nonfiction* (Notes of a Native Son). *Although Baldwin, an African-
American, is best known for his writings on racial issues, he also
wrote one of the first American novels to deal frankly with homosexuality,* Giovanni's Room, *published in 1956. The story is told from
the point of view of David, a bisexual American man who has a
stormy romance in Paris with an Italian man named Giovanni. In
the excerpt below, David reflects on his relationship with a childhood
friend named Joey—a relationship David tried, but failed, to forget.*

I repent now—for all the good it does—
one particular lie among the many lies I've told, told, lived and
believed. This is the lie which I told to Giovanni but never succeeded in making him believe, that I had never slept with a boy
before. I had. I had decided that I never would again. There is
something fantastic in the spectacle I now present to myself of
having run so far, so hard, across the ocean even, only to find
myself brought up short once more before the bulldog in my own
backyard—the yard, in the meantime, having grown smaller and
the bulldog bigger.

I have not thought of that boy—Joey—for many years; but I
see him quite clearly tonight. It was several years ago. I was still
in my teens, he was about my age, give or take a year. He was a
very nice boy, too, very quick and dark, and always laughing. For

a while he was my best friend. Later, the idea that such a person *could* have been my best friend was proof of some horrifying taint in me. So I forgot him. But I see him very well tonight.

It was in the summer, there was no school. His parents had gone someplace for the weekend and I was spending the weekend at his house, which was near Coney Island, in Brooklyn. We lived in Brooklyn too, in those days, but in a better neighborhood than Joey's. I think we had been lying around the beach, swimming a little and watching the near-naked girls pass, whistling at them and laughing. I am sure that if any of the girls we whistled at that day had shown any signs of responding, the ocean would not have been deep enough to drown our shame and terror. But the girls, no doubt, had some intimation of this, possibly from the way we whistled, and they ignored us. As the sun was setting we started up the boardwalk towards his house, with our wet bathing trunks on under our trousers.

And I think it began in the shower. I know that I felt some-thing—as we were horsing around in that small, steamy room, stinging each other with wet towels—which I had not felt before, which mysteriously, and yet aimlessly, included him. I remember in myself a heavy reluctance to get dressed: I blamed it on the heat. But we did get dressed, sort of, and we ate cold things out of his icebox and drank a lot of beer. We must have gone to the movies. I can't think of any other reason for our going out and I remember walking down the dark, tropical Brooklyn streets with heat coming up from the pavements and banging from the walls of houses with enough force to kill a man, with all the world's grownups, it seemed, sitting shrill and disheveled on the stoops and all the world's children on the sidewalks or in the gutters or hanging from fire escapes, with my arm around Joey's shoulder. I was proud, I think, because his head came just below my ear. We were walking along and Joey was making dirty wisecracks and we were laughing. Odd to remember, for the first time in so long, how good I felt that night, how fond of Joey.

When we came back along those streets it was quiet; we were quiet too. We were very quiet in the apartment and sleepily got undressed in Joey's bedroom and went to bed. I fell asleep—for quite a while, I think. But I woke up to find the light on and Joey examining the pillow with great, ferocious care.

"What's the matter?"

"I think a bedbug bit me."

"You slob. You got bedbugs?"

"I think one bit me."

"You ever have a bedbug bite you before?"

"No."

"Well, go back to sleep. You're dreaming."

He looked at me with his mouth open and his dark eyes very big. It was as though he had just discovered that I was an expert on bedbugs. I laughed and grabbed his head as I had done God knows how many times before, when I was playing with him or when he had annoyed me. But this time when I touched him something happened in him and in me which made this touch different from any touch either of us had ever known. And he did not resist, as he usually did, but lay where I had pulled him, against my chest. And I realized that my heart was beating in an awful way and that Joey was trembling against me and the light in the room was very bright and hot. I started to move and to make some kind of joke but Joey mumbled something and I put my head down to hear. Joey raised his head as I lowered mine and we kissed, as it were, by accident. Then, for the first time in my life, I was really aware of another person's body, of another person's smell. We had our arms around each other. It was like holding in my hand some rare, exhausted, nearly doomed bird which I had miraculously happened to find. I was very frightened; I am sure he was frightened too, and we shut our eyes. To remember it so clearly, so painfully tonight tells me that I have never for an instant truly forgotten it. I feel in myself now a faint, a dreadful stirring of what so overwhelmingly stirred in me then, great thirsty heat, and trembling, and tenderness so painful I thought my heart would burst. But out of this astounding, intolerable pain came joy; we gave each other joy that night. It seemed, then, that a lifetime would not be long enough for me to act with Joey the act of love.

But that lifetime was short, was bounded by that night—it ended in the morning. I awoke while Joey was still sleeping, curled like a baby on his side, toward me. He looked like a baby, his mouth half open, his cheek flushed, his curly hair darkening the pillow and half hiding his damp round forehead and his long eyelashes glinting slightly in the summer sun. We were both naked and the sheet we had used as a cover was tangled around our feet. Joey's body was brown, was sweaty, the most beautiful creation I had ever seen till then. I would have touched him to wake him up but something stopped me. I was suddenly afraid. Perhaps it was because he looked so innocent lying there, with such perfect trust; perhaps it was because he was so much smaller than me; my own body suddenly seemed gross and crushing and the desire which was rising in me seemed monstrous. But, above all, I was suddenly afraid. It was borne in on me: *But Joey is a boy.* I saw suddenly the power in his thighs, in his arms, and in his loosely curled fists. The power and the promise and the mystery of that body made me suddenly afraid. That body suddenly seemed the black opening of a cavern in which I would be tortured till madness came, in which I would lose my manhood. Precisely, I wanted to know that mystery and feel that power and have that promise fulfilled through me. The sweat on my back grew cold. I was ashamed. The very bed, in its sweet disorder, testified to vileness. I wondered what Joey's mother would say when she saw the sheets. Then I thought of my father, who had no one in the world but me, my mother having died when I was little. A cavern opened in my mind, black, full of rumor, suggestion of half-heard, half-forgotten, half-understood stories, full of dirty words. I thought I saw my future in that cavern. I was afraid. I could have cried, cried for shame and terror, cried for not understanding how this could have happened to me, how this could have happened *in* me. And I made my decision. I got out of bed and took a shower and was dressed and had breakfast ready when Joey woke up.

I did not tell him my decision; that would have broken my will. I did not wait to have breakfast with him but only drank some coffee and made an excuse to go home. I knew the excuse did not fool Joey; but he did not know how to protest or insist; he did not know that this was all he needed to have done. Then I, who had seen him that summer nearly every day till then, no longer went to see him. He did not come to see me. I would have been very happy to see him if he had, but the manner of my leave-taking had begun a constriction, which neither of us knew how to arrest. When I finally did see him, more or less by accident, near the end of the summer, I made up a long and totally untrue story about a girl I was going with and when school began again I picked up with a rougher, older crowd and was very nasty to Joey. And the sadder this made him, the nastier I became. He moved away at last, out of the neighborhood, away from our school, and I never saw him again.

Life Line

Gloria E. Anzaldúa

In this piece of short fiction, Gloria Anzaldúa writes about the friendship between two women at the University of Texas. The women feel a strong connection to one another—until their relationship comes to a sudden end.

La Prieta* met Suel at the university during the summer session. They were both in graduate programs full of whites in a school full of whites. Both were floundering in the sea of white faces and they gravitated to each other as to life preservers. For hours they would sit in the air-conditioned commons buoying each other with iced drinks and talks about their courses, their families, movies, books, everything and anything. They would walk across the spacious lawns of the U.T. campus and then wind their way down a ravine to the creek where they would sit close together on the rocks and listen to the gurgle of the trickling water, fanning each other's hot faces with large green leaves while their feet, submerged in the water, cooled.

Suel never wore make-up. She was twelve years older than la Prieta and she wore her hair pulled back in a bun. When la Prieta asked her to wear it down, Suel said, "Don't be silly, it's too hot to wear down." As Suel looked at la Prieta, a brightness washed over her eyes and something in the depths of her eyes that seemed both naked and curtained refused to hold la Prieta's gaze. La Prieta had seen a similar look in children who were hungry and were

---

*La Prieta is a term of endearment for women; it means "the dark one."

ashamed of their hunger, children who knew that food was something they would never have enough of.

One day when the summer session was six days away from ending, they were lying on Suel's bed. They had been up all night working on papers and their heads were hollow from too much coffee and lack of sleep. In a few days they would return to the Valley to their respective hometowns. Their pueblos were sixty-nine miles apart. The more la Prieta thought about the sixty-nine miles, the further apart their towns seemed. She wondered if their families would think it strange if one drove to visit the other. It *would* look suspicious. It was peculiar, the closeness that had developed between them was different from the closeness she had with her sister or with her other girlfriends.

As they lay with arms and thighs touching, la Prieta wanted to say something about the recognition she'd glimpsed in Suel's eyes when they had first met, and that she had since then seen every time they looked at each other. She wanted to talk about the dense air that seemed to hang about them when they sat close to each other, the air that became progressively harder to breathe. The room was unbearably hot. "Do you want to talk about *it*?" la Prieta asked, touching the soft skin at the inside of Suel's elbow.

"Talk about what?" Suel responded in a low voice.

"I think we should figure out what to do about it."

"Do about what?" Suel's voice seemed sharper.

"*Tu sabes?* The feelings between us."

"What feelings?"

"You know, the lesbian feelings." Suel turned her head and stared at her. Slowly, she started backing away. Then, averting her face, she sat up, got up and walked out.

La Prieta waited for two more hours. Not wanting to fall asleep on Suel's bed in case Suel returned still angry at her, she returned to her place. The next day and the next and the next, la Prieta went to all their usual hangouts. She stopped and asked everyone who knew them, but no one had seen Suel. As a last resort, she went to the dean's office. She was told that Suel had had a family emergency and had left without finishing her course work.

A month later, when la Prieta had gotten her courage up, she called Suel's house. Suel's sister answered and yelled out to Suel to come to the phone. At the other end la Prieta heard Suel's voice say, "Tell her I'm not home, tell her I moved away and you don't know where I am."

Again la Prieta waited a few months before calling her again. The mother answered this time. She told la Prieta that Suel didn't live there anymore and hung up before la Prieta could say a word.

A year later at a conference la Prieta saw Suel sitting in the middle of the almost empty auditorium. Standing at the mouth of the auditorium she felt like she was falling and that Suel was the only life net that could catch her and break her fall. Smiling and with the lightest step she'd had in over a year, she made straight for the row where Suel sat. She saw Suel's thin neck under the familiar bun and felt something soften inside her. Then she saw Suel's head turn, saw her eyes register shock, saw her get up and, head bent, hurry down the row to the other side and circle back to the entrance. As she watched Suel leave, la Prieta felt the life line slipping through her fingers.

Take Off the Masks

Malcolm Boyd

With the autobiographical book Take Off the Masks, *Malcolm Boyd—a prolific author, civil rights activist, and Episcopal priest—came out of the closet and publicly acknowledged that he is gay. In the passage that follows, Boyd talks about a summer vacation he took as a boy and of the young men he met.*

One summer when I was about ten, my mother and I spent several weeks at a big resort hotel in the Adirondack Mountains in northern New York State. . . .

Up there in the Adirondacks was my first time among mountains. Later in Colorado and California I would see peaks far higher, crags and canyons more dramatic, but Mount Marcy—a mere five thousand feet—holds a mystery for me, a sense of wonder in its mass and presence that stays with me still. I wondered what it looked like, snowcapped in winter. Was it like Mount Olympus? Did strange Indian gods live up there? Would they descend, like Zeus and Aphrodite, Ares and Hermes, to mix their divinity with mere humans? Looking at Mount Marcy, I felt even less than mere human. I'd retreat into the nearby forests to find my scale.

My favorite place was a flat rock beside a stream. I was reading Howard Pyle's *Robin Hood* that summer, and all around me was Sherwood Forest. I'd leave the hotel after breakfast, clutching my book, and wend my way along the crunching forest floor and between the overhanging trees till I came to the flat rock, and the Merry Band. I could imagine, just up the stream, that bridge where Friar Tuck established the primacy of churchly virility.

But mostly who I waited for was Will Scarlet, sauntering through the woods, sniffing on a rose. I felt a surge of excitement, just reading about him and seeing Pyle's etching of him, princely and fastidious in hose and doublet—the power and mold of the legs, the bulge in the groin, chastely hidden—almost—by the doublet. I'd stroke my own puny bulge as my eyes stroked the illustration. Then I'd look up, searching through the tree trunks, hoping to catch a glimpse of him.

I had these fantasies that he'd come. And heart-stopping imaginings of what would happen if he came through the forest, and noticed me, walked to the flat rock, and sat down beside me. I could see the tilt of the eyebrow, hear the lilt of the voice: "Would ye like to smell my rose?"

But Will Scarlet did not come.

Instead, one afternoon, sitting with my back propped against the rock, reading, I heard a rustle in the underbrush. Turning, I saw three boys in their early teens standing there watching me. I recognized one of them as a guest at the hotel. The other two were strangers. Something about the way the three of them looked at me, the fixity of their eyes, made me suddenly fearful. I got to my feet.

They walked down the embankment and stepped up on the flat rock while I stood on the ground. They were bigger than I was and their standing on the rock made them bigger still. My eyes were on a level with their crotches, and the fear I felt was mingled with excitement. I didn't know what was going to happen, but secretly I wanted something strange and wonderful and gentle to happen. Maybe they'd take me away with them, camping, high in the mountains, away from everybody, and . . .

"Hi, kid." The boy had red, curly hair and a deep voice, and wore tight shorts. "Whatcha doin'?"

"Reading," I said.

The redhead exchanged impassive glances with his two companions. "Readin', huh? Watcha waitin' for?"

"I'm not waiting for anything. I'm just sitting here reading."

The redhead arched his eyebrows in mock surprise. "You weren't waitin' for nothin'? Aw, c'mon! You knew we was comin', didn't yuh?"

"No! I was just . . . sitting here . . . reading."

" 'Magine that. Just reading." He shook his head; then, with a bright grin: "Was you playin' with yourself while you read?"

"No." I felt a flush of guilt. "I wasn't playing with myself."

The redhead's hand dropped to his crotch, just a few feet away from my face. The hand had big freckles on it. "I bet you got a cute little pecker, huh?"

I stepped backward as I saw the redhead's two companions tense.

"An' how 'bout those little squirrel's nuts you're hidin' in them pants of yours?"

One of the boys, dark-haired and stocky, stepped off the rock and came close to me. The redhead slowly rubbed his crotch, his eyes on mine. "You're gonna show us that cute little pecker and them squirrel's nuts, ain't yuh?"

I shook my head, violently.

"Aw, sure you are! You're gonna drop them pants, and wiggle that little thing . . ." He leered at the other two boys. ". . . and then you're gonna bend over, yuh hear?" There was a commanding edge to his voice. "Are you a sissy or a real man? We're real men!"

The other boy, blond and lanky, the one I recognized from the hotel, now stepped down off the rock on the other side of me. I glanced at him in panic. He was from the hotel. We had something in common. Maybe he'd help. But his eyes were narrow-slitted and impassive. He grabbed my arm; his voice was barely above a whisper. "You heard what he said, didn't you?"

I felt the stocky boy's hand on my belt buckle.

There was a screaming inside my head. I wrenched away from their hands and lurched toward the stream. I knew that stream. I knew, rock-on-rock, how to jump across its width. But the boys didn't.

They chased me as I bounded across the water from one slippery rock to the next. First the blond boy slipped and fell into the water, crying as he twisted his leg. I didn't wait to find out what happened to the redhead, but when I reached the roadway on the other side of the stream, I was alone, panting and terrified.

I ran all the way back to the hotel.

That night I cried myself to sleep. Why had the boys done

that? Why had they scared me so? Why hadn't they just taken me camping with them, high in the mountains? I'd have done anything just to be with them.

The next evening at dinner, I caught sight of the blond boy at the other end of the hotel dining room. He was limping as he walked to his table. He saw me and turned his head away quickly. I sat at our table with my mother beside me and ate my fruit cup, and wondered what *his* pecker looked like. But I never found out. Two days later, he and his family finished their vacation at the hotel and left.

The incident by the stream left haunting echoes inside my head. It was so easy to drift along, cared for by my mother, warmed by other guests' attentions, peaceful in the ordered world of the hotel, the mountains there but distant, the fantasies of Sherwood Forest seen only through a scrim of imagination. So easy. So safe. So reassuring.

But the boys, on that flat rock, they were *real!*

Barely touching my body, they had raped my psyche, thrusting their presence into vitals of mine that both yearned for them and repelled their claims. Fearing them, I feared myself. Hoping for them, I feared myself even more. Who was I, anyway? What was happening to me? And why should it happen just to me?

I could look around the hotel dining room. The husbands. The wives. The grandparents. The children. The wealthy widows and maiden aunts. Even the resplendent bishop. All so properly dressed. All so genteel in their converse and gesture. All so related by blood or marriage. All held together by social sanction, and the politesse of a culture that I could later recognize as lingering colonial Victorian. Everybody had a place in it but me. How could I hide what I was? But was I? What was I? The blond kid, who was he? Did he know who he was? Yes, he had been right there in that dining room. With everybody else. Genteel. Related. Did his parents know how his eyes had slitted when he had grabbed my arm? What would he have done when they dropped my pants? I could feel the rape of him . . . that nice . . . well-bred . . . angelic . . . young man.

Who else?

I stared about the dining room in a kind of panic. No, it couldn't be! It was just us two. That was all. No one else. . . .

Strange how all foreboding vanished when I first caught sight of Jamie checking into the hotel with his mother and father. The desire I felt for him was sudden and electric. Maybe it was those eyes, big and watchful and direct, that answered my look at him and held steady for a long moment. I wanted to go over to him right then, but there was such a bustle of clerks and bellhops and luggage I held back. But I knew I'd know him and I wondered how long he would be staying at the hotel.

I watched him cross the lobby to the elevator. He was about my age, but slightly built, and he walked with a spring to his step. His hair was dark and he wore it somewhat longer than people did in those days. I wanted to tousle it. Just before he got onto the elevator, he looked at me again with a hesitant smile, and I smiled back.

At dinner that evening I watched for him in the dining room. By the time we were halfway through the main course, I was beginning to panic. He hadn't appeared. My eyes kept prowling the dining room, checking one familiar face after another. Why didn't he come? Maybe he was sick or something. Maybe they had gone someplace else to have dinner. Maybe . . . Maybe . . .

The waitress was clearing the main course at our table when Jamie and his mother and father came into the dining room and were directed to a table just two tables away from ours. I saw Jamie maneuver himself so that he could see me out of the corner of his eye.

I ate my dessert slowly and peacefully. Things, I felt, were going to be all right.

That night after dinner, I skipped being page boy to the hotel manager's royal progress to the veranda and ghosted around the lobby, listening to someone play the grand piano. The next thing I knew, Jamie was standing beside me, his eyes intent on the keyboard, his shoulder brushing, ever so lightly, against mine. I felt a lightheaded rush of excitement, my mouth went dry, and I couldn't think of anything to say. But in a few minutes, Jamie shifted on his feet. His voice was low and close to my ear. "C'mon, let's go down to the playground."

"Sure," I said, and we looked each other full in the eye.

It wasn't much of a playground. Just a slide, some swings, and a jungle gym. But we clambered up to the top of the jungle gym, sat there under the panoply of the evening sky, and talked about things, just like we'd been friends for years.

For the next week Jamie and I were inseparable. We went hiking in the woods and discovered caves. We swam in the hotel's outdoor swimming pool. We went fishing where the stream became a deep pool in a forested area just behind the hotel.

All the while, I was acutely conscious of Jamie's body. The wiry tension of his muscles. The bony structure of his face. At the same time, his cherubic lips and the gentle fleshiness of his buttocks. As we changed in the dressing room by the swimming pool, I glanced very quickly to find out what his genitals looked like, but his back was turned to me as he slipped on his trunks. Still I knew I'd find out, somehow.

At the end of the week, it happened. It was a warm day, and in the late afternoon we decided to go fishing at the stream, promising our parents we'd be home before supper. We got out our rods, lines, and hooks and settled down by an overhanging embankment by the pool to wait for a Big One. We waited and waited, but the Big One was not hungry. Not even the little ones were hungry. Overhead, the trees seemed heavy in the heat, and the silence surrounded us like a cloak. I felt us inexpressibly isolated, as if Jamie and I were the only two people in the world. We could share whispered secrets and no one would know. I wanted to tell him. . . . What did I want to tell him? I wanted to touch him. . . . Why did I want to touch him? And I didn't dare think of where I would touch him, or what would happen if I did. Yet he was sitting there, just inches away from me!

Jamie stirred, and pulled up his line. "There aren't any fish in the pool today. C'mon, let's take a swim."

"At the hotel?"

"No. Right here. It's deep enough."

"It's getting late."

"We got time."

I felt my pulse quicken. "We don't have trunks."

"Who needs trunks? There's nobody around." And he looked at me with those big eyes. Panic surged in me. The secret? Did he know? Could he tell? Would it show?

I tried to sound reluctant. "Okay. If you want."

His voice was soft. "C'mon, let's do it."

I remember the fright I felt when there was no more to take off but my underpants, the strange sense of relief when I stood naked by the shadowed pool, the throat-tightening excitement of seeing Jamie's slight lithe body, as naked as mine.

We tucked our clothes under the embankment. Then, with a whoop, Jamie dived into the pool. I stood on the pool's edge, watched Jamie's body squirming beneath the water's surface, and felt my penis begin to harden.

Jamie broke surface with a splash and looked at me. A quick grin crossed his face. "Dive in! It's great!"

I glanced down and saw that my cock was fully erected. I began to swim. The chill of the water mercifully shriveled me. But he'd seen me; I knew that. Was that why he'd grinned? And what was he thinking when he grinned? Or was he just enjoying the swim?

We swam around for a while. Jamie would do surface dives in the deep parts of the pool, his buttocks rearing above the water as he plunged down and then disappearing beneath the shimmer. I'd never know where he was going to come up. Once I felt a light touch on my leg and he came up right beside me, laughing in a burst of spume.

The chill of the water was beginning to get to me. I got out of the water and sat on a little patch of sand by the embankment.

"What's the matter?" Jamie asked.

"I'm cold."

Jamie swam over to where I was sitting and started out of the water. But he stumbled on a rock and fell sprawling across my knees. He looked up at me, his eyes mischievous. "C'mon, we'll wrestle. That'll warm you up." He grabbed me around the neck and pushed me back on the sand. The warmth of his body sent chills through mine. I struggled (although not very convincingly,

I'm afraid) against his grip as we rolled on the sand and I finally pinioned him on his back, astride him, my hands holding his arms.

He looked up at me. "Uncle," he whispered.

I released his arms. They glided around my neck, pulling my head down to his. I stretched full length on top of him, our heads touching. Our heavy breathing from the struggle gradually subsided. I felt my penis grow hard against his body, and, pressed against mine, I felt his grow hard too. I raised my head and looked at his face. He was looking at me. After a long moment I lowered my head till our lips touched. And held.

Then I moved over on my side next to him, and my hand reached down, slowly, until I touched the flesh of his cock. It stiffened still more and Jamie's hips stirred. I felt a wonder. I had caused this to happen in someone else. Someone else felt as I did. I wasn't alone. There was Jamie. And now we had *our* secret.

We shared the wonder of that secret, touching, exploring, responding, till we heard voices—adult voices—calling our names. We clutched each other, then scrambled to the hiding place of the overhanging embankment and lay absolutely still, pressed against each other, our heartbeats racing.

The voices passed into the distance.

"I guess it's late," I said. "We better get dressed."

"Yeah. I guess so."

We drew apart. We dressed in silence, not looking at each other, gathered up our fishing gear, and trudged back to the hotel. We didn't say much of anything to each other. All I could think of were those voices, the voices that had wrenched us apart as surely as those adult hands might have done. What we had done was wrong—to them—and if they ever found out . . . ?

I glanced at Jamie, staring straight ahead as we walked. Would he tell? What if his parents made him tell or tricked him into admitting what we had done? Would his mother tell my mother? And would one of them tell the hotel manager?

Suddenly that slender body walking shoulder to shoulder beside me was an ominous, dangerous thing.

As we walked up the steps of the hotel, I saw Jamie look at me, and there was fear in his eyes. "You're not going to tell, are you?"

I shook my head violently.

"I won't either," he said.

But we never hung around with each other much after that. When my mother and I left the hotel to go back to the city three days later, I said good-bye to Jamie. We shook hands, solemnly, and said we hoped we'd see each other again. But we both knew we never would. Our lost playful innocence was a grim specter of the complexity of the adult world that awaited us. How did we know even then as two small boys that it was considered very, very wrong to show natural affection to one another? But if we had been discovered playing a war game, it would likely have been accepted with approval.

The experience with Jamie is still vivid in my memory not just because it was one of the few sexual experiences of my childhood but also because it was one of the few times in those early years that I felt genuinely close to another boy. Yet male beauty left me shaken and breathless. I merely glanced at it, learned how to absorb its total eroticism in what appeared to be a casual turn of my eyes, and quickly looked away. Occasionally when I stood transfixed in sheer hunger and wonder before a godlike male apparition of utter beauty, my face burned in recognition that I had revealed what must remain a secret about my deepest feelings.

There were unmistakable implications of male same-sex love that leapt out of pages of books into my consciousness. When I was a youngster, David and Jonathan in the Bible could almost make me cry, because I yearned to share myself like that with another boy. Oh, to die for one's young male lover, a boy with shining, explosive dark eyes and a lithe body one held nakedly in a warm embrace of understanding and love.

At school I studied arithmetic, geography, *Silas Marner*, international relations, Latin, and biology. Out of all that education, couldn't someone have taught me about the place of gay experience in the history of the human race? I was given no gay role models. A few naturally dawned on me. Looking at Michelangelo's depiction of God's creation of man, and seeing the unabashedly physical and lusty man who served as the model, I grasped a deep truth that stayed with me. Michelangelo was, I knew, a brother.

One thing that I was taught in school was priorities. Success, recognition, and making money must always come first in a balanced life. This is, no doubt, why dozens of people whom I know make their life decisions—love, marriage or union, where they live, what kind of work they do—on the basis of money instead of their real needs and yearnings. But life is so short.

Thoreau said that a person who does not keep pace with companions perhaps hears a different drummer. Keep step to the music that you hear, however measured or far away, he urged. Society does not want people to listen to different drummers. It establishes common fantasies to be shared by all. These are fantasies concerning women, men, blacks, gays, success, failure, sexuality, death, and life. But even in high school I heard a different drummer. However, I could not keep step to the music that I heard. I stumbled and fell. I felt that I was torn apart.

The idea of two men making love, or two women embracing and coming to a climax, was too spaced out from everything I was taught for me to cope with it. Wasn't it terribly wrong? A sin against God and nature? Debauchery and decadence?

My Story

Dennis Cooper

A poet, novelist, and art critic, Dennis Cooper is the author of Closer *and* The Tenderness of Wolves. *"My story," from the collection* Idols, *describes the experimentation that takes place between two high school students.*

He's curious.
The word spreads,
and a senior
who's had his eyes
on the prince
takes him camping
in the closest bush.

They do the usual:
hike, trap dinner,
and grow a mean fire
to shiver around.

Den is wondering
how it begins
and then it has:
gloves in his hair,
they pop his jeans
and bring the long
gold zipper down.

When it's over
it's over; at sunrise

Den wakes alone
narrowing his eyes.

The older boy has
tried it and left it.
But Dennis slides
his hand down over
his well loved thighs.
Right then at sixteen
he's a homosexual.

Raven's Road

Paula Gunn Allen

Paula Gunn Allen, a Laguna Pueblo/Sioux Indian, has been writing and teaching about Native American life for more than twenty years. In this passage from the novel Raven's Road, *Allie, an Indian woman, reflects on her relationship with her first lover, a white woman named Bee. Allie had joined the U.S. Army in 1944 at the age of eighteen, "because she had heard a strange thing, because she was restless and full of angry vitality, because it was better than reform school, her alternative option." Bee was Allie's commanding officer (C.O.) in the army.*

After she had come down from the mountain, she had found a job in Seattle, settled into a life that was reasonably satisfactory. She worked at the university as a records clerk, though she had had some training as a technician in the army. The job was boring and tedious, and the salary wasn't much, but there were compensations. She believed that eventually the job would lead somewhere, given her special job in the army and her almost obsessive interest in postwar technology. She believed that Seattle was some kind of mystic center, both of the future and of the ancient earth of the tribal people. Her life there was free of the sense of oppression she had grown up with, and though she returned home as often as she could afford to, she returned to the Northwest like a magnetized needle to magnetic north. She felt a strange kinship to this place, its cool waters and pale sun, its seemingly endless rain. And there were other benefits. There was a community of lesbians, of sorts, that had grown up around their army days' bar, the Silver Slipper, a lesbian bar that was discreetly tucked away on the second floor of one of the downtown buildings.

She had been introduced to the bar by her first lover, a captain who was her C.O. Barbara—Bee they called her—had been military all the way. Correct and crisp, nearly brutal, she swaggered through her days and staggered through her nights. She was a heavy drinker, but then everyone was, and she held it well—at least until they got her back to her quarters, or until it was very late and her staggering and occasional bouts of terrifying rage would go unremarked by anyone with superior status or a desire to do her harm.

From the first time she saw Bee, shortly after arriving on base the spring of 1944, Allie had felt her stomach go weak with desire every time the woman had looked at her, her honey-colored hair, crisp and coldly shining under her cap. From the first time she saw her, Allie had wanted her. Bee was not the first woman Allie felt that erotic charge around, but Bee was the first who did much about it.

She called Allie to her quarters one night, late, and questioned her sharply about her work that day. Allie answered, feeling only mildly worried; she had faced frightening white authorities often in her life, so often that she was all but indifferent to their power. She knew it was only physical power in the end, and she was accustomed to beatings, solitary confinement, and social ostracism. Being deprived of white company was not much of a punishment, and branding her as socially unacceptable, deviant, unwanted, was the same as naming her Indian. And military prison might be rough, but so was her life. The way she saw it, the worst had already happened. There was little worse that they could threaten her with.

But Captain Brandon, after her interrogation, during which she had stared at Allie quite boldly, almost as though she was angry, abruptly, surprisingly, offered her some wine, invited her to stay and play a game of chess. Allie took the wine but refused the game, saying she didn't know how to play it. She wanted to stay but couldn't think how.

She needn't have worried. Bee thought of everything. She seemed to understand how Allie felt about her, and after a time she sat near her on the couch where she had directed her to be seated when she offered her wine. She refilled Allie's glass, turning her body in such a way that Allie could see the line of her throat as it blended toward the curve of her breast beneath her stiffly starched shirt. Allie had been ready for many kinds of trouble, for any kind, she had thought in her tough, youthful innocence.

But desire, now. Wanting. Seeing Captain Brandon's hair soft in the low light of her quarters. Seeing her neck gleaming as soft as polished turquoise stones, river rocks, agate, quartz, in the small vee her slightly opened blouse revealed. And why didn't she wear her tie? Well, it was evening. She wasn't on duty. And something else: the captain's face seemed softer, her eyes gray, receiving, not flat and hard as they were during the day. Now all this was of interest to Allie. Of interest and growing excitement.

This made Allie smile in herself, coil her muscles in another kind of tension, toss her head however slightly as she responded to Brandon's questions about her life, whether she liked the service, the work she did. Made her answer with less cynicism than she would have in another place, to another face, made her begin to notice her breath catching as it came in or out of her throat. Made her bold enough to look the captain directly in the eye, drink her wine without moving her gaze, like she saw them doing in the movies. Maybe white women thought a good stare was a sex signal. She decided to try it, hoping it would work, somewhat surprised at her daring but under it feeling somehow that what she was feeling and thinking about her C.O. was what was expected of her in any case.

Not that she wasn't afraid. This was something to be afraid of. Suppose they did something, whatever it was that two women did? Something like what she and a couple of girls in boarding school had done—kissing, playing with each other, shy and filled with laughter, bold and scared they'd be caught. She'd always wondered what they'd do if they found out, going so far sometimes as to imagine what she would say as one of the matrons was slapping her or locking her in the tiny closet they kept for uncooperative children, for those who thought they might defy a rule or who, not understanding enough English to obey a rule quickly, came under the punishing disapproval of their keepers.

Luckily, she had never found out. She'd had her share of run-ins with them, of course, but never over something so unthinkable as sex with a boy or a girl. She was pretty sure they'd come un-glued entirely if they knew about the girls' sex games in the dark, and truly, even to scare herself, she didn't like to spend much time thinking about what they might do to her if they found out. Maybe they'd just starve her. To death. She'd heard of that hap-pening to some boy, one she didn't know well but who suddenly disappeared from class and meals and never came back. She thought about her peril as she listened to the C.O. answering her queries in a quiet, Oklahoma drawl. She was sure that if this woman was putting the make on her, she'd be very, very happy to be made. And that also frightened her a little.

Suppose the woman there was only toying with her, testing her, trying to find her out? Suppose she wound up wanting the captain, the captain not wanting her? But then she'd look at the woman, at the pale skin lightly flushed, pearly, the strong square hands holding the wineglass, holding the bottle to pour more into their glasses. Allie put her thoughts behind her eyes, like putting her eyes behind dark glasses. She was barely eighteen, and while she had a lot of experience in war, and some experience in sex from hooking and cruising and hanging out, she didn't have any at all in loving women. She looked at her hands, wondered if they were weak.

She felt the burning in her crotch that knit it to her belly as though they were one organ, a limb or a heart, a head. And as she sat and answered to what was asked, and grew more and more tense, more and more languorous with her inward heat, dully pulsing with wine and desire, feeling her throat thickening, her voice deepening, hearing her breath wing its way past her nostrils, Captain Brandon leaned forward, took hold of Allie's wrist, looked for some time appraisingly into her eyes. Then nodded briskly, some question asked and answered in that moment. She stood, drawing Allie to her until their breasts touched, until their breasts fell into the softness of each other. Then slowly, deliberately, the captain kissed Allie, and that was all there was to it, and just like that, swiftly and silently as a deer pauses a moment then vanishes into the bush, Allie was taken by that twilight world, made a citizen of it, an outcast who forever would belong to wilderness, and there would be at home.

They had stories about it, the Indian people. Some of them, not her tribe, but her friends, had told her about Deer Woman, how she would come to a dance, so beautiful, so enchanting. She would choose you to dance with, circling the drum slowly, circling, circling in the light that blazed darkly from the tall fires that ringed the dance ground; she would dance with you, her elbow just touching yours, her shawl spread carefully around her shoulders and arms, held with breathtaking perfect precision over her cocked right arm, torso making just the right sideward bow, tiny steps perfect in their knowing of the drum. She would dance you, dance into you, holding your gaze with her eyes, for if your eyes looked down at her feet you would see her hooves and the spell would be broken. And after a time she would incline her head, say, perhaps, come, and you would follow. Away from the fire and the dancing, into the brush, into the night. And you would not return, or if you did, it would be as somebody else.

from

The Lost Language of Cranes

David Leavitt

Born in Pittsburgh, Pennsylvania, in 1961, David Leavitt is the author of Family Dancing *(a collection of short stories) and* Equal Affections *and* The Lost Language of Cranes *(both novels). In the passage below, from* The Lost Language of Cranes, *Philip Benjamin, the novel's central character, and his boyfriend, Eliot, are describing their respective experiences growing up gay. Eliot, who was raised by two gay men named Derek and Geoffrey, advises Philip to consider the costs as well as the benefits of telling his parents that he is gay.*

"How old were you when Derek and Geoffrey found out that you were gay?" Philip asked Eliot. It was four in the morning, and they were lying on the blue futon, nowhere near sleep.

"Oh, let's see," Eliot said, stretching his arms out behind his head. "I guess it must have been—but no." He smiled. "The thing is, with Derek and Geoffrey, I'd only have had to come out if I was straight. Come to think of it, I don't think I ever actually did come out to them. I just remember, when I was twelve or so, Derek walking into my room and finding me making out with Timmy Musseo. And he just said excuse me and closed the door."

Philip's jaw dropped. "You were making out with boys when you were twelve?"

"Eleven," Eliot said. "Geoffrey and Derek only found out when I was twelve."

"Then how old were you when you first had sex?"

Eliot shrugged. "I'm not sure," he said. "How do you define sex? If orgasm is the criterion, twelve. If anal or oral penetration is necessary, fifteen."

"And was that with Timmy Musseo?"

"No, no," Eliot said. "Timmy Musseo had a girlfriend by that time. My first experience was with a much older man, a friend of Derek's. He and Geoffrey never found out about it. Probably they still don't know."

"How old is older?"

"Oh, let's see," Eliot said. "When I was fifteen, he must have been twenty-nine, thirty. My age now. He came and stayed with me at the house whenever Derek and Geoffrey went away."

"Did he seduce you?"

"I seduced him," Eliot said, and laughed. "Oh, he wanted to for as long as I did. But I think he was afraid Derek would send him up for statutory rape or something. I was irresistible at fifteen. I kept asking him to give me massages, playing the little nubile waif. And finally—well, he couldn't hold back anymore." He sighed. "It was a wild night. We did everything."

Philip's mouth was dry. "When I was that age," he said, "—well, I never would have dreamed, no matter how much I might have wanted to—" But he knew enough about Eliot's childhood in that rambling brownstone on West Thirteenth Street to know that it was about as different from his own as you could get. Eliot had been raised not by normal parents, after all, but by two men, by Derek Moulthorp, the famous writer, and his lover, Geoffrey Bacon. When Philip imagined him as a child, he was lying in a brocaded canopied bed, having stories read to him by Colleen Dewhurst, but now the fantasy changed, and it was a young man with long brown hair, dressed in an unbuttoned tuxedo shirt, who sat leaning over Eliot in his bed, running his hand languidly through Eliot's hair.

"I just can't imagine," Philip said, "having that kind of self-knowledge, that kind of . . . wherewithal, at fifteen. At fifteen I was just discovering pornography. I didn't have sex until college."

"Everyone's different," Eliot said, "depending on their background." He was staring up at the ceiling, onto which he had pasted glowing constellations from a kit. At night, sometimes, he liked to name them: dog, dipper, hunter.

"One more question," Philip said. "If you don't mind."

"Not at all," said Eliot.

"How old were you when you had your first real lover?"

"Seventeen," Eliot said. "At Jasper Ridge. My roommate, Ben Hartley, and I were secret lovers for an entire year. He was wonderful. A hockey player. He must have been six foot five. We spent a semester together in Florence, and when we'd go to see the David, everyone would stare at Ben instead. He was the most amazing lover I ever had. But it was one of those secret things, so it didn't seem real."

"Was it always secret?"

"Unfortunately not," Eliot said. "One of the house monitors happened upon us one afternoon in the shower. Now this was Jasper Ridge, mind you, the hippie school to end all hippie schools, but homosexuality was still not exactly a thriving thing there. We had to talk to the Jaspers themselves, and Mr. Jasper, who was this old ex-Beat with a lot of money, he kept saying, 'Wow, that's really great. I can really relate to that.' He wanted Ben and me to go before the whole school and announce ourselves, because he thought it would be very consciousness-raising for the other kids." Eliot laughed. "Thank God we talked him out of it. Most of those kids were little thugs. They'd have killed us."

"Whatever happened to Ben Hartley?" Philip asked.

"He went to Colgate. We lost touch. Last I heard he was out in California, working as a carpenter or something."

Philip was silent for a moment. "My first love affair—if you can call it that—wasn't nearly so much fun," he said.

"You mean Dmitri?"

"Have I mentioned Dmitri?"

"Only in passing."

"Dmitri was a physics major," Philip said. "He was very dark, and he had these mad-scientist eyes that would kind of zero in on you and just not turn away. It was hard to resist. My first lover." He laughed. "You know," he said, "he hated the word 'lovers.' He preferred to say we were 'friends who had sex,' and of course only between us, because he was insistent that none of his friends or, god forbid, his professors ever find out he was gay. He made it clear from day one that if I mentioned our relationship to anyone, even to Sally, he wouldn't speak to me again. But even though he was so secretive, he was very promiscuous. He used to claim to be able to identify how much hair a man had on his ass by how much he had on his wrists. That kind of thing was very important to him."

"How long were you together?" Eliot asked.

"Six months, I guess, give or take a few weeks. The last semester of college. But he never loved me. He had an older brother, Alex, who was also gay, and also a physicist, and I think if he loved anyone it was him. Not sexually, of course, just in a sort of worshipful way." He smiled. "I remember at graduation I finally met Alex. He looked just like Dmitri, except he worked out, so he had muscles, and his boyfriend was a male model. They were there with their parents—the father was some sort of industrialist, and their mother was this very thin spacey woman from Texas—and also their grandmother. She was something. Maybe four foot eleven, and built like a tank. She had this little camera, and she was so proud she kept insisting on taking pictures of Dmitri, first alone, and then with Alex, and then with both of us. And standing there, it felt so strange to me, to think that this old woman worshipped them so much, and didn't have the slightest inkling, not the slightest idea about them. Of course, it must have been very hard, both of them being gay after all, and the only sons. I guess they really believed they'd be disowned if they told their parents, and probably they were right. But what amazed me was, it was as if they couldn't care less. They just made joke after joke about it. In fact, I thought I'd feel very nervous standing between them like that, I thought I'd be afraid every second the parents would see something. But somehow I felt safe, safer than I'd felt all that year. I think Dmitri and Alex protected each other, and it was as if their protection covered me as well—does that make sense?"

"Completely," Eliot said. His eyes were closed.

"After that," Philip said, "they walked over to their grandmother and picked her up. Literally. Just put their hands under her behind, and paraded her around the campus while everyone watched, and she laughed and screamed and begged them to put her down. I just stood back with the parents and smiled, until my parents came back to get me."

"Was that the end with Dmitri?"

"Oh, more or less," Philip said. "I visited him once after that, in the summer, at his parents' place in Southampton. He had a whole locked filing cabinet full of pornography that no one had ever found. And I remember I told him that my great fantasy of domestic happiness would be if we put all our underwear in the same drawer and got them mixed up so we couldn't tell whose was whose."

"What did he say to that?"

"Oh, just what you'd expect. He said, 'That's funny, because my brother Alex and I used to do that when we shared a room, but I always knew which was which.' Apparently Dmitri was secretly turned on by wearing his brother's underwear. It's funny, he had no compunction about admitting things like that, even though he would have murdered someone before anyone in his department found out about him. Anyway, after that the weekend just sort of dragged on, and we spent a lot of time sitting on the porch, and Dmitri and his father would talk about engineering, and Dmitri's mother would say things to me like, 'Well, Philip, I know how you feel—when the men in this family start talking science, I just feel left out at sea. The next time, we'll go into the kitchen and talk about literature.' But we never did. Then I went home."

The blanket pulled away, and Eliot turned onto his side, facing the window. Philip looked up at the stars on the ceiling, which were fading fast. Now bruise-colored streams of sunlight were beginning to pour through the window, keeping the little stars steady and faint. It annoyed Philip that after a night of happy sleeplessness, exhaustion would still punch him awake with the alarm clock in the morning; he would shave, dress, head off to work, while Eliot shifted in bed, turned, gave a small sigh of contentment. He never said goodbye. Once Eliot was asleep he was dead to the world. There was no waking him.

"Eliot?" Philip said.

"Yes?"

"I'm thinking of telling my parents. About us. Which, of course, means telling them about me."

Eliot said nothing.

"I'm thinking of telling them this Sunday," Philip said. "Do you think it's a good idea?"

"I don't know your parents," Eliot said.

"Well I do. And I can tell you now, I don't think this is going to be a big shock for them. They're going to think, 'Of course.' Then they'll understand why I never had a girlfriend and all. I mean, my parents are liberal people. They won't be destroyed by this."

"Probably not," Eliot said.

Philip nodded to himself. "No," he said, "the problem is not going to be my being gay, as much as getting beyond that. Because it's not enough, you know, just telling them and shutting up and never talking about it again. I feel like I should let them know what it's been like for me—what it felt like, growing up, keeping this secret. I feel like I should let them know what it means, having the life I have, having you. They deserve to know."

"That's what Jerene thought," Eliot said. "And look what happened to her."

"My parents are not like Jerene's parents," Philip said; there was a hint of anger in his voice.

"Oh, probably they won't disown you. But don't be sure it's going to be all sweetness and light, Philip. It's hard for you to realize how new this thing is going to be for them because you've lived with it all your life. But they haven't. They probably haven't even thought about it."

"Oh, I'm sure they've thought about it. They're not stupid." . . . Philip glared at Eliot.

"Look," Eliot said, "relax. I'm not saying you shouldn't tell them. I'm just saying that you should think about it very carefully before you do anything rash. And you should be sure you're doing it for them and not for yourself. This is going to be a big deal. Be careful. I know Jerene's case is an extreme, but think about it.

The terrible tragedy of all this is that she still loves her parents. And they love her. And if she hadn't told them—well, they could all still have that."

He yawned, closed his eyes. Philip, wide awake still, stared at the ceiling. What was his motive in telling his parents, he wondered, when for years he had so successfully avoided this confrontation? Was it for them that he wanted to make this revelation, because they deserved to know the truth? Or was it for himself, as Eliot had suggested, to relieve himself at last of the burden of secrecy? It didn't seem to him there was anything wrong with that. Anyway, he had Eliot now. He could show his parents Eliot, scion of Derek Moulthorp, and then how could they say he was throwing his life away? How could they argue he was making a mistake, damning himself to a life of eternal solitude? He wanted to stick Eliot in front of their distracted faces the way he used to stick finger paintings and cookie-dough Santa Clauses—only now they couldn't turn away from him, they couldn't absently say, "How nice." They would have to pay attention.

"Eliot?" he said. "If I tell them, would you come with me to meet them? Would you come to dinner sometime?"

"Sure," Eliot said. He was falling asleep. "Sure." He shuffled a few times, settling. A half an hour later his breath was coming in even rhythmic waves. In only a few minutes the alarm clock would blare. Philip lay in bed, his shoulders rigid, waiting for it.

Family

Coming Out to My Mom

Travis Wise

Travis Wise, a high school junior from San Jose, California, "came out" to his mother at the end of 1992. In the month that followed, Travis wrote extensively in his journal, recording the changes that he observed in his relationship with his parents and exploring his own attitudes toward being openly gay. Selections from his journal appear below.

I'm 17 years old, I live in San Jose, CA (south of San Francisco), and I'm a junior in high school. I am gay. I have told a few trusty friends at school, and met some people who know I am gay on various computer bulletin board services (BBSs) in this area. They have become my underground support network. My parents don't know that I am gay.

I usually go back to my home state of Ohio and visit my Dad (my parents are divorced) for Christmas, but I have decided not to this year, because I have a term paper due soon in AP US History, and I'm working on my school's yearbook, so that takes a lot of my time.

My intent is to write in this journal for a period of one month after I "come out" to my mom, which I hope I can build up the courage to do today. I don't plan on writing every day, but I will tell enough to give a general idea of how coming out to my mom changes my life.

Dec 27—Sun.

Today was a very exciting day for me. It started out normally, I got a lot of schoolwork done, and at 3 pm, I started talking to another gay teen on the phone. His name is "Ryan." We met on a local gay BBS. He told me about how when he came out to his parents, they had basically shut him out of their lives. Well, maybe not shut out . . . he didn't get kicked out of his house, but from what he told me, their relationship went bad. He has a boyfriend, so we're just exchanging our experiences with our parents . . . nothing romantic.

Well, by 6 pm, I was really nervous . . . I just had to tell my mom that I am gay, but I didn't know how. Actually, I didn't know why either . . . I just felt like this was the time. Especially after talking to Ryan. I ate dinner with her, and then called a female friend, the second person who I had told I was gay, the first heterosexual person who I had told. I just needed to hear her voice.

At 7 pm, Mom came into my room and overheard part of my conversation with my female friend. She knew something was wrong, and wanted to know what was the matter. I was really nervous about how to start the conversation . . . once we started talking, it wouldn't be a problem . . . but what would be my opening line? I started talking about how kids my age are dating at school, and I gave specific examples of how "Nick" is going out with "Susan," etc.

She asked if I felt out of place because I didn't have a car to go out on dates in. I said that that wasn't what I was concerned about . . . I said, "Mom, haven't you ever wondered why I've never had an interest in girls?" She started talking about how I had never really played sports (been masculine), but just because of that, that doesn't mean I'm gay.

I told her that that wasn't it . . . that for the last 5 years I have known that WITHOUT QUESTION I am gay. That's hard for her to accept.

By 8 pm, she knew I was gay, and was asking me questions about my lifestyle . . . sex, AIDS, boyfriends, school, PFLAG, DeFrank Center,* the BBSs that I use. She was concerned about

---

*PFLAG (Parents and Friends of Lesbians and Gays) is a nationwide support network for people who have gay family members or friends. The Billy DeFrank Center is a community center for gay men, lesbians, and bisexuals in San Jose.

gay bars . . . I assured her I wasn't interested in that scene, which I'm not.

Everything was going well. She didn't really expect it at all . . . she was starting to go into shock, I could tell. We talked until 10 pm, when we basically had everything ironed out. No yelling, no crying, just talking.

She had many questions . . . I answered most of them. Some were very personal, and we just didn't talk like that . . . stuff like "Does it excite you to think about kissing and making out with guys?" I just don't talk to my mom about stuff like that.

Right now, she is starting to accept it, but still in shock. She is just beginning to understand that this is not something that I suddenly DECIDED on overnight, and that it has been my life for many years.

She also accepts that I have been and will continue to talk to gay teens on the phone, and will probably, at some point, have a boyfriend.

We agreed not to tell my dad, who lives in Ohio, because if we did, he wouldn't pay for my college education, as he is now going to do.

She was very understanding, and left my room saying that she wants to keep the "communication lines open." That's good, I guess.

Anyhow, this was a big day—I came out of the closet a bit more.

Dec. 28—Mon.

Ryan called at 6:30 am . . . Mom picked up the phone and when she realized who it was she said, "This is ridiculous." The new rule is no phone calls before 8:30 am. I can live with that . . . at least she lets my gay friends call.

She came into my room this morning . . . concerned about my friends, and their names (we use aliases on the local BBS). I assured her my friends DO have names. She wants to go to counseling with me. Not to get me to convert, she knows that's impossible, but just to make sure that "it's really the way you feel" . . . she just doesn't get it that for FIVE years its been the UNQUESTIONABLE way I feel.

She tells me that I've never tried dating, so how could I be certain. Oh brother. She said, "You haven't even given heterosexuality a chance!" Oh brother.

Then she had a concern I wasn't prepared for. She said, "People like John Sculley and Steve Wozniak and Steve Jobs* aren't gay." In other words, you can't be gay and successful at the same time. I had no backup for that . . . all I had was a list of famous gays in the early 16th century . . . all I could say was, "Well, how do you know THOSE GUYS aren't gay? Maybe they can't come out because they are so much in the public eye that they would have something bad happen to them if they did come out." She accepted that . . . I have to get some more facts, though.

She was very concerned that if I led an openly gay lifestyle, I would be ostracized so much that I wouldn't be able to advance in whatever career I choose.

Mom and I went out for lunch, and to run some errands. We got to our first stop, and the store wasn't open yet, so we sat in the car. Mom brought up the subject of my homosexuality . . . she was worried that I would be in danger if I went to a college dorm (that I might get beat up or something). She told me that my homosexuality was against nature, and abnormal. I understood where she was coming from, but it didn't change my feelings.

She didn't understand that I liked guys just like most girls do . . . some I find attractive, but not all, and that I might want to have a boyfriend sometime. She didn't seem to really object, but when it hits her she might. She started getting scared that I was going to get in trouble—with AIDS or something. She didn't want me to go around wearing pink triangles, and she didn't want me to change my clothing style, or start acting effeminate. She also

---

*John Sculley is chief executive officer of Apple Computer Corporation. Steve Wozniak and Steve Jobs are computer executives and codesigners of the Apple I Computer.

said she was afraid I would start bringing home a "string of those people" ("those" being gays who are quite effeminate).

I told her I was frequently talking with two other gay teens, and that our conversations were helping me understand what their parents went through. I told Mom I expected her to treat them the same as any of my other friends when they called, and that I had never seen them, so I couldn't tell if they acted really effeminate.

She didn't grasp the concept of me liking other guys, but I think she will eventually.

Well, it's now been 24 hours since I told Mom. Overall, things are going well, but there is definitely a detectable change in our relationship. I volunteered to sweep the whole house (I'm going into "kiss-up mode" so she can't have any complaints against me), but she is almost acting as if I have committed a sin or something . . . she's not avoiding me, I think she's just extremely concerned and CONFUSED.

We went out to a restaurant tonight . . . as I was walking out the door, I heard her call up a psychiatrist friend to make an appointment for her . . . I don't think I have to go . . . she would have told me.

Then, when we were at the restaurant (my homophobic 56-year-old stepdad went with us . . . we don't get along well at all, but he doesn't know I'm gay), Mom suddenly said, "Travis, I want to say something." I knew instantly what it was. I stopped her. I said, "No." She said, "Yes, we need to talk about it." Knowing how my stepdad would have reacted, I said, "If you say anything, I'm walking out of here." My stepdad said, "Well, I'm usually the one who says dumb things, but if it's that bad, DON'T SAY IT!" That ended it.

I don't know why she would be so STUPID to tell MY secret to a person who doesn't drink homogenized milk because it says "homo" on the label!

One of the topics she brought up today was that before I get in a "relationship" with someone, I need to see proof of their negative AIDS test. While I would never get in a risky relationship with someone who was HIV +, I think it is ridiculous for her to think that every 17-year-old, some of whom are NOT away from their parents, have the ability to GET an AIDS test. I think she and I ironed out that rule when I told her that I have enough common sense not to do something to risk my life. I'm sure a large chunk of her shock is the realization that she has to deal with stuff like this now.

Dec. 29–Tues.

Today was interesting . . . we didn't have any major discussion like we had the last few days. I'm tempted to say that Mom is coming out of shock, and she may be, but I suspect it's half acceptance, and half "the same old stuff." She seemed upset, maybe mad . . . I don't know why . . . I've never quite seen the expressions on her face or her mannerisms before. For some reason, I'm reminded of when my parents got a divorce ten years ago.

Tonight my mom called up her best friend in Southern California and told her I was gay. Her friend told my mom to think positively; she was sure I would end up being the same well-paid, successful businessperson I was previously expected to be.

She and her friend talked about me dating other guys, whether I had a boyfriend right now, etc. Mom told her it was mainly limited to talking on the phone, which is true, and which I have been doing a lot of lately. My social life has almost quadrupled in terms of time spent on the phone, which is cutting into my homework schedule, but it's Christmas break . . .

Jan. 6—Wed.

Christmas break is over, I am back in school. I'll give a brief rundown of what has happened in the last week:

Overall, relations are pretty good. Mom has reached out to some friends, made some new acquaintances, and has learned much about the gay community. We are going to a PFLAG meeting in a few weeks, and she is seeing a psychotherapist to help her deal with the news.

Ryan has become my boyfriend. We met once at a roller rink, and have talked endlessly on the phone. He broke up with his old boyfriend, and we've become very close.

Ryan has become a major support system in my coming-out process, and it is very important that parents not hinder their children from talking on the phone to other gay people their age . . . it's safe, and it's probably the only support they get.

My mom doesn't seem to have a problem calling friends up on the phone saying, "Guess what, my son is gay!" . . . as if it was any of their business.

Jan. 18—Mon.

The last few weeks have gone much better. My mom and I are getting along well; my stepdad now knows I'm gay, and we are also getting along much better. Overall, my parents' relationship with me has greatly improved since coming out, and in the last two weeks, we haven't really argued about my homosexuality at all.

My mom went to a PFLAG meeting last week, and she seemed to learn a lot, or at least enjoy it. Ryan and I are celebrating our two-and-a-half-week anniversary (Mom lets me take the bus to meet him at the mall). Yesterday I went to a local gay-youth support group meeting. I'm looking forward to going again next week . . . it was very educational and reassuring.

I've undergone a serious change in mood over the last two weeks, I'm very happy at school and at home, and my life is going very well. Mom is getting literature in the mail from gay groups all the time, and reading everything she can about the subject in order to become more educated. She's really doing well.

Jan. 21—Thurs.

I asked Mom this morning if she could take me to a coffee place tonight where a group of gay guys (college age on up) all get together weekly . . . she said it wasn't a problem. This afternoon, after we had a good time at Burger King, I was on the phone with Ryan for less than five minutes when Mom walked in the door, and blew up . . . there I was, "stupid" (she called me that) me on the phone being used my by "sleazy" boyfriend (she called him that). She told me to sweep the house (which I would have been glad to do if she had asked me).

For the next hour, we yelled and screamed, me mostly trying to justify my 3.0 GPA (3.6 overall) to her, apologizing for "putting her through hell" for the last three weeks, listening to her tell me how hard a child I have been to raise, and how hard it is for her to take me places when she's getting her third master's degree (gee, I can't wait until she gets her PhD . . . even more studying), teaching and tutoring so we can have a nice lifestyle.

I said I'd get a job; she said, "No, your job is to live up to your potential and get better grades."

Well, this evening we sat down, and talked things out . . . she admitted she was wrong in yelling at me, but she wants me to spend more time studying. There's only 24 hours in a day . . .

Jan. 23—Sat.

Well, I'm nearing my one-month anniversary of coming out of the closet, and of having Ryan to help me through everything. Mom and I are getting along well, as well as could be expected. She is still getting used to having a gay son. I've noticed a definite shift in clothing taste . . . I feel like I'm undergoing some sort of a transformation. For some reason, all I want to wear is black . . . I must be in my "black phase."

I wore my pink triangle button today while rollerblading.

My Mother's Worst Fears

Nancy D. Kates

Nancy D. Kates, a writer and filmmaker, grew up outside of Boston in the late 1960s and early 1970s—a time when many adults, including Nancy's mother, still believed that it was not proper for girls to wear pants. In this essay, Nancy recalls her mother's views on "ladylike" dress and behavior, and considers the impact these views on gender have had on her own development as a woman and as a lesbian.

It never occurred to me that I had had a "gay childhood." After all, I didn't know I was a lesbian until my late twenties. Nor did my childhood seem particularly unusual, growing up as I did in an affluent white suburb of Boston. I know that my childhood years were filled with pain and unhappiness, and that I was often lonely. Yet we were never poor, or hungry, or uncomfortable in any physical way, for which I am profoundly thankful, given the misfortunes of so many people. My own experience is all that I know, of course, but I remember as a child how willing I would have been to give up my nice clothes and summers at camp in exchange for what I desperately wanted: the support and understanding of my family. They loved me, of course; they just couldn't accept me. In recent years, it has become clear to me that this lack of acceptance had everything to do with my then nascent sexuality, and almost nothing to do with me as a person. It took me close to three decades to come out to myself, but my mother had me pegged as a dyke by the age of five.

Recently, I heard a middle-aged gay man tell an audience that, growing up, he "knew he was bad but he didn't know why." His words echoed so much of my experience: I was the ideal child and student, never in trouble, generally obedient, but still somehow I was "bad." Simply put, I could not measure up to my mother's expectations. She wanted me to be perfectly feminine, an idealized little girl in pink dresses and patent leathers. I couldn't be that girl, much as I tried, nor would I become her adult counterpart (Laura Ashley dresses and high heels). As a child, I guess I would have been a tomboy, given my druthers. Instead, when I was about five years old, my mother mysteriously transformed herself into a special agent for what I later called the "Gender Police." I was her sole assignment, and she took to the job with a rare sort of vengeance.

This was the start of my mother's ongoing attempt to socialize me in proper female gender roles. It happened some twenty-five years ago, but I still remember the day it all began. She went into my closet and removed my two pairs of dark blue corduroy pants, saying I was a "big girl now," and that, once they reached a certain age, girls didn't wear pants. She was very firm, almost severe, and somehow, even at five, I knew my mother was giving an opinion, but not necessarily telling the truth. I also remember having the sinking feeling that something was about to go terribly wrong. It was 1967, after all. Lots of women were wearing all sorts of clothes, including pants and other unacceptably "male" attire. But from that day forward, until the age of fourteen, I wore pants only to go skiing (at least as far as my mother knew).

My wardrobe soon became an enormous source of friction between us. We would go to the nearby mall, brand new circa 1968, and argue endlessly about what I was to wear. Most of what I selected wasn't "feminine" enough to pass muster with Mom; the clothes she picked for me were far too frilly for my taste, with itchy lace and silly bows that always got in the way. It was a battle of wills, and I was destined to lose most of the time. I was just a little kid, and she was a grown-up. Oftentimes, I would relent and let her buy me something I hated, just to avoid an argument. This strategy always backfired in the end. Six months later, I'd catch hell because I'd never worn the offending garment, on which she'd spent so much money.

Since I grew up in the sixties, my mother's rules often put me in conflict with generational norms, not to mention my own instincts. When I started first grade in the fall of 1967, for example, girls weren't allowed to wear pants in my elementary school. By the winter, some enterprising first-grader had actually organized a protest against the policy, creating a picket line outside the principal's office. The first demand was to be allowed to wear pants to play in the snow; later, the entire policy was questioned. I marched along with my classmates, knowing full well, of course, that a victory at school would have no effect on *me*. Soon after, the school changed its policy. My mother did not.

To be sure, I was somewhat successful in thwarting my mother's watchful gaze. I lived under a litany of rules and restrictions. But there were some facets of life outside her control. Sometimes, I snuck around and did things I knew I wasn't supposed to do. I rarely got caught. I also became an escapist. Whenever possible, I fled into the woods behind our house, finding a solace in nature that was missing in the rest of my life. I read incessantly, sitting in my rocking chair with the red cushions, my feet propped up on a stool. And I developed a very active fantasy life. I remember standing in front of the bathroom mirror, around the age of seven, wearing only my pajama bottoms, pretending I was the man on my Spanish tambourine. There he/I was, in a blaze of red, bare-chested, dancing suggestively with a beautiful, buxom, scantily clad Flamenco woman. I read everything I could, from *Harriet the Spy* to adult books I'd sneak off my parents' bookshelves. Sometimes I identified with the hero, sometimes the heroine. It didn't seem to matter. Perhaps my most grandiose fantasy concerned my mother. One day, I decided she was really a Russian spy sent over to conquer America and win the Cold War, one family at a time. Now, with the clarity of hindsight, I find it hard to imagine I could make up something so awful about the woman who gave birth to me. I loved her dearly, even if I hated her restrictions.

My tangles with the Gender Police got worse as I grew older. In third grade, I was forbidden to play with my best friend, who lived across the street. No explanation was given. I was crushed. A shy, quiet kid with only a couple of friends couldn't afford to give one up. Later, as a teenager, I finally asked my mother what possible harm it could have done for me to play with Dana. She said my friend wasn't an appropriate playmate, because she was exhibiting "tendencies." How my mother arrived at this conclusion, I'll never know. Dana was the straightest girl on the block. She always wanted to play with dolls, which bored me to tears, and only occasionally relented to do what I wanted: go outside and horse around. Of course, my mother wasn't worried about Dana, she was worried about *me*. As I look back upon it now, it seems perfectly incredible that anyone could possibly construe the innocent play of nine-year-olds for proto-lesbian behavior. It doesn't matter. Back then, my mother's word was law. Her irrational fears of homosexuality governed my behavior, my friendships, and my day-to-day world.

By fourth and fifth grade, I was having trouble with my peers. I was a smart kid, too nerdy to be cool, and I was weird. I never wore pants. I also never brought friends over after school—I preferred to visit other people's houses, away from my parents and their rules. I'd also developed an interest in sports, but that didn't last long. As I tearfully explained one day to Mr. Celie, my gym teacher, my mother didn't want me playing after-school basketball, because it wasn't "ladylike." Ugh! I had only one friend, a girl whose mother didn't object to her "tomboy" tendencies. In direct contradiction to my mother's operating theory—that being a tomboy leads to lesbianism—my friend turned out straight. She's still kind of butch, though. At her wedding, one of her sisters joked that in her wedding gown, she seemed to be in drag.

As I got older, I got more and more used to hiding things from my parents, particularly my mother. My father rarely got involved—he thought some of the restrictions were kind of silly, I think, but just wasn't around as much. He had heard my vocal opposition to having to wear skirts all the time, but he refused to get involved, though he often championed my cause on other issues.

Around the age of nine or ten, I discovered the apparent source of all the rules. My mother had consulted a psychiatrist about me, a member of a group practice. These "professionals" instructed my mother to emphasize feminine clothing and behavior as a way of insuring that I would turn out "normal," i.e., heterosexual. Back then, psychologists still classified homosexuality as an illness; I guess my mother perceived me to be developing abnormally, and was trying to "save" me. I didn't even know these people, but they made my life as a child utter hell, just as they tortured thousands of adult lesbians and gay men by promising "cures" for their "abnormal tendencies." Rationally, I know my mother was just trying to do the best thing for her child. Yet sometimes I still wonder what might have happened if she had never bothered.

More than anything, my childhood was filled with confusing mixed messages about being a girl. My mother wanted me to be an ultra-femme; my father seemed to expect that I would excel at seemingly masculine activities like school and business. The message was a common one, I think: girls were supposed to be proud of being female, yet understand their places in a world run by men. My older brother didn't live under the kind of rules governing my life. He seemed to do what he wanted, for the most part. Sometimes I resented it. My parents built him a basketball court in our backyard when I was ten or eleven. He used it for a little while, then moved on to street hockey and other sports. I, who was dying to play basketball, was not even allowed to set foot on the court. Of course, I'd sneak out and use it every chance I got. Eventually, when I was in ninth grade, I summoned up all my courage and tried out for the basketball team. My peers—who had known me only as shy, overweight, and nerdy—were shocked that I actually made the team. I was ecstatic, just to play on the JV. No one knew about my secret life practicing in the backyard.

My mother did eventually give up trying to enforce her dress code. Scrimping and saving my junior high babysitting money, I finally had enough cash to purchase a pair of Levi's. I was immensely proud of these pants; they seemed to represent the personal freedom I'd been craving for years. At first, I would sneak around and wear them behind my mother's back, but I think she got tired of fighting with me. In the end she simply relented.

In adolescence, I started to develop crushes on the girls in school, and sometimes adult women. Was I simply going through a "phase," as I told myself, as if I were a subject in a psychology textbook? I never discussed my feelings with anyone. No doubt I would have denied them vehemently if anyone had dared to ask. It turns out that my school had quite a thriving gay underground, though

I was more or less oblivious to it at the time. There were a couple of fairly overt gay male teachers, and a young lesbian faculty member who was sort of "out," as well as a few highly closeted older teachers. I was intrigued with my lesbian teacher, but also terrified. My conscious awareness of homosexuality was pretty limited back then: I must have thought being gay was contagious, like the mumps or the chicken pox, and that too much contact with this woman would give me her disease. I also admired some of the girls on my various sports teams, unaware that many of them were baby dykes. All I knew is that I didn't want to date the boy who kept asking me out, even though dating was "normal." Frankly, the idea of sex terrified me.

College was difficult socially. All my female friends seemed to have boyfriends; most of my male friends were gay. I guess you could have called me a "fag hag," a term I despised. These young men had furtive affairs, for the most part, not steady boyfriends, but still I felt left out. Everyone seemed to be having so much fun. I had fun, too, but not much in the romantic department. Eventually, I did have a few brief, unsatisfactory relationships with men, although I didn't really understand what all the fuss was about. At nineteen, I met a woman who was "interested" in me. I was quite leery of her, but we became friends somehow, though we went to different schools. Eventually, near the end of our senior year, we had a brief romantic interlude during a weekend visit. We managed to get together in spite of her girlfriend and my vehement protestations that I was straight. If my life was fiction, I suppose we would have become lovers and I would have come out then. Instead, she and her lover moved to California when school got out, and I convinced myself I had simply been satisfying my curiosity.

I didn't date much in my twenties; nothing ever seemed to work out with the men I fell for. Perhaps the most obvious things are the hardest to see. When I took up soccer at the age of twenty-five, I quickly developed infatuations with some of the dykes on my team. It was completely mystifying. It couldn't be a "phase," like in high school—I was too old for that. Denial runs pretty deep, though. It still didn't occur to me that I was a lesbian. Finally, at twenty-seven, I developed an intense crush on Pauline, the "girl next door." We never got past the heavy flirting stage, but she did help me figure out that I really *was* attracted to women. She also started to convince me that maybe it wasn't the end of the world, either. That was my first, painfully tentative, step out of the closet.

I do not know what might have happened if things had been different when I was young. My mother's attempts to socialize me had enormous repercussions. For years, I was unaware of my sexuality, cut off from my own feelings and desires. There is a legacy of shame that I carry with me still, a feeling of failure that runs deep. Sometimes, even now, I wish I could fulfill her wishes for me, even if they wouldn't make me happy. But most of the time, I'm just grateful to have my sexuality. I still get confused once in a while about what it really means to be female. Maybe I never learned. Women aren't idealized packages of femininity, as my mother would have led me to believe (though she herself hardly fits that description). What we are remains an ongoing question.

Recently, when I came out to my mother, I asked her about her all-consuming effort to imprint traditional gender roles on me. She finally admitted she had done it because she was worried about my sexual orientation. "It was always on the basis of professional advice," she added. I paused for a moment, then I asked her, "But don't you think it was kind of cruel?" She didn't respond at first. "Well," she replied, her voice barely audible, "I guess it didn't work, did it?"

Black, Queer, and Out

Karl Bruce Knapper

Karl Knapper grew up in El Paso, Texas. During his sophomore year in college, Karl decided to "come out," to friends at school as well as to members of his family. The responses he got were surprising.

It was spring quarter of my sophomore year at college, and I had finally decided to come out to my friends. I'd known that I was gay since the age of twelve, but so far I'd only told a handful of friends from my AAU swimming team and high school. I hadn't even come out to my family yet, though they knew that whenever I was home on break I would frequent the Old Plantation with my best friend, Sue. The O.P. was El Paso's only gay disco, which they knew because I had told them. I've always been honest with them, and I didn't think that this was something that I needed to lie about. They just assumed that I was being my usual "cutting-edge" self by hanging out with the hip, urban (hardly), underground demimonde of El Paso. After all, they knew from TV and magazines that "trendy" people often hung out at gay bars.

I was suffering from the Mohammed Syndrome (wanting to go tell it on the mountain, shout it from the rooftops, etc.) and felt this burning desire to let my college friends know that I was gay. I had decided that the best way to handle it was to get a few of them together at a time and tell them. It would take less time than telling them individually, yet wouldn't be as potentially intimidating as having to tell them all at once in a large group. Despite the fact that I was determined to tell them, I was still a little nervous (scared is more like it) about coming out. I hoped that because we were supposedly at one of the more liberal institutions of higher learning that my chances of suffering a traumatic rejection were slight, but one could never be sure.

I decided to start with the friends that I felt were most tolerant and work my way through to those I wasn't as sure of. I also decided to space it out over a few days and have my friends come by my room in small groups of two or three people. I was so nervous about my planned revelation that I hadn't been able to eat. Instead, I paced back and forth in my room, listening to music, and preparing myself for what I thought was going to be an earth-shattering disclosure.

After all that build-up, though, the actual coming-out was a bit of a letdown. I sat each group of friends down and went into a spiel about having something really important to share with them, something that I had never told anyone before, but something that I had to tell them if we were to continue to remain close friends. I told them that I hoped that what I was about to tell them wouldn't change the way they felt about me or change our relationship. (At this point, I'm sure they probably thought I was about to tell them that I was an ax-murderer or had violated the Honor Code by cheating on my last midterm.) Then I would blurt out that I was gay.

In every case, my friends would tell me they already knew or had assumed that I was gay. ("We knew that no straight man could possibly be as compulsive about fashion and clothing as you are." "Your dorm room is just too well decorated." "Besides, you're too compassionate and sensitive to be a straight man—they're usually macho, boorish jerks.") In fact, they'd been discussing it since fall quarter, but no one had thought to let me in on the discussion. I felt hurt and betrayed. I'd made my big announcement for nothing. My thunder had been stolen. Instead of being happy that my friends didn't care, I was upset that they'd been discussing my personal life for six months and that no one had bothered to consult or ask me about it!

So I hid out in my room and sulked for a few days. My friends were totally confused by my reaction. They couldn't understand why I was so upset, and I didn't feel like telling them that I just needed to lick my imaginary wounds for a while till I snapped out of my funk. Eventually, they confronted me about my moping around. I explained to them why my feelings had been hurt, and they apologized and explained that the reason that they hadn't approached me about it was that they assumed that I would come out to them when I was ready. They didn't realize that they had taken the wind out of my sails by not allowing me to surprise them, and I realized that I had been a little naïve to assume that they wouldn't be able to figure out my story. In the end, we laughed about the whole thing (and I got over it), but my coming-out experience with my college friends was nothing like I had either imagined or planned it to be.

My coming-out experience with my family, on the other hand, was not as smooth and uneventful. Fresh from my success with my friends at school, I came home for the summer with an undefined plan to come out to most, if not all, of my family. I started with my sister, Alyson, because I knew that she, being the most liberal of my siblings (as well as a noted champion of underdogs), would probably react well. She basically said "so what" and that it didn't matter to her if I was gay. She even told me that she knew several lesbians on her basketball and track and field teams and got along fine with them. I had figured that she wouldn't be upset, but it was still a relief that she had responded so positively.

Next, I told my youngest brother, Aubrey. I had always been closer to him than to my other brother, Erich, so I figured he would handle it better. At first, he seemed to take it well. He said that it didn't matter to him whether I was gay or straight. Within a few weeks, though, our relationship became strained, and I was forced to confront him about the apparent rift that had developed between us. He said that he was having trouble dealing with his feelings about homosexuality and my being gay. He'd always looked up to and admired me, and it was proving difficult for him to reconcile his feelings for me with the negative feelings he had about homosexuality, which he'd presumably absorbed from the dominant, popular culture. We talked for a while, and although we didn't get everything worked out or resolved right then and there, we did manage to salvage our faltering relationship.

I never got a chance to tell my brother Erich that I was gay. He beat me to the punch and told me that he had figured out I was gay on his own. We had a long, heated discussion in which he said that he thought that there had to be something wrong with a person who was gay because it wasn't normal to be that way. He naïvely compared it to having a speech impediment or being disabled. I told him that there was nothing wrong with me and that my being gay did not make me sick, weird, or abnormal, but to no avail. I had to settle for him telling me that it didn't really matter whether I was gay or not because I was still his brother and he would always love me. I wasn't totally comforted or satisfied with that kind of acceptance (or more accurately tolerance), but there also wasn't much I could do at the time to raise his consciousness or change his mind. Over the years, his attitude has improved (though not as much as I would like), and he has turned out to be generally supportive of me.

My mother was the most difficult person to tell because she was also one of my closest friends. I was really afraid of being rejected by her; though knowing how liberal she was, I was hoping that it wouldn't be a big deal. Soon after I got home that summer, the mother of one of my best friends found out that he was gay and kicked him out of the house (but only for a day or two—she later relented and begged him to come home). I was so upset by the ordeal that I asked my mother what she would do if she found out that one of her kids was gay (not thinking that this might cause her to start wondering about me). She answered pretty much the way I had assumed she would and said that even though it wasn't what she would choose for one of her children, because of the probable hardship involved, that we were her children and she would love us no matter what.

Over the course of the summer, though, our relationship really deteriorated. I distanced myself both physically and emotionally from my mother, in an effort to avoid being around or talking to her, or coming out to her about my sexuality. I occasionally didn't come home at night and then lied about where I'd spent the night. I used every excuse possible to avoid either being at home or alone with her. I stopped confiding in her. I stopped talking to her about anything but the most superficial things.

Finally, my mother took the bull by the horns and confronted me. We had been having an argument about my behavior, when out of the blue my mother asked me if I was gay. I was taken aback and paused for a second before shooting back that I was. She asked me if I'd been so difficult all summer because I was struggling with keeping it a secret from her, and I said yes. After that, I relaxed a bit and opened up to her, and we had a long conversation about my being gay.

I asked my mother what had caused her to ask. She said that she'd gone in my room to put something away and seen a gay porno mag next to my bed. (I had called my sister that morning to tell her to keep everyone out of my room because I had forgotten to hide the magazine, but I guess it had been too late.) She said that she had first started to suspect when I had asked her what she would do if she discovered one of her children was gay and that finding the magazine sort of clinched things for her. It had never occurred to me that my question earlier in the summer would have triggered her suspicions. (I obviously hadn't been thinking clearly when I asked her in the first place.)

She told me that she worried about how difficult life might be for me. It was hard enough being black, and to add to that being gay was going to make things tough. I told her that I could handle it; after all, being black in America, I'd come from a long line of survivors. She said that she only wanted me to be happy. I told her I was, especially now that I didn't have to hide things from her, and she said that she couldn't ask or wish for anything more.

Since then, my mother has been an amazing source of strength and support for me. I can talk to her about my life and my loves without having to edit anything. She is still one of my best friends. I also have the benefit of knowing that she understands some of the oppression that I have to face in being twice a minority (and twice-blessed) in a prejudiced world.

Cat

Julie Carter

*This short story by Julie Carter is told from the point of view of Cat
(short for Catherine), a young African-American woman who develops a romantic relationship with a neighbor named Sheila. Cat is
later accused by her father of being a "bulldagger." (The term* bull-
dagger *is a derogatory name for a lesbian, particularly one who has
a "masculine" appearance.) Carter's story appears in* Home Girls:
A Black Feminist Anthology.

It is three days after my twelfth birthday and my mother is sitting beside me on the edge of my bed.
She is holding a box of sanitary napkins and a little booklet that
reads "What Every Young Girl Should Know" and telling me for
the third straight year that I am to read the book and keep the
pads hidden from the sight of Daddy and Leroy. I am hardly
listening. I am sneaking furtive glances out the window and patiently waiting for her to finish so I can meet the boys out on the
lot for our softball game.

My mother is saying, "Look, you've thrown your pretty dress
on the floor." She is bending down to pick it up. It is a white
flared dress with large yellow flowers. Daddy bought it for my
birthday. I am remembering the party, the coconut cake with
the twelve ballerinas holding twelve pink candles. Momma had
straightened my hair but refused to wave it tight to my head so it
would look like a process, the way I usually wear it. Instead she
has fluffed up the curls like she does my sister Dee Dee's hair.
Momma is serving punch in a white apron or just standing around
with her hands in the pockets. When she catches my eye she mo-
tions with her head for me to go over and talk with the other girls

who are standing in a cluster around the record player. I smile nervously back at her, but remain where I am. My friends are all acting strange. Leroy, my brother and very best friend, has been stuck up under Diedra Young all evening and Raymond and Zip-Zip are out on the back steps giggling with Peggy and Sharon. Jeffrey teases me about my knobby black knees under my new dress until I threaten to punch him in the mouth. I wander out to the kitchen to play with Fluffy, our cat, until Momma misses me and comes to drag me back to the party.

Now, sitting on my bed with Momma, she is saying she will have to get me a training bra. I self-consciously reach up and touch my breasts then jerk my hands down again. I hate them. I'm always hurting them when I bump into things and now when I fight I not only have to protect my face and head I have to worry about getting hit in the breast too.

"Momma, can I go now? I gotta pitch today," I say. Momma puts her arm around my shoulder and pulls me close to her. "Sugar, you've got to stop playing with those boys all the time; why don't you go play with Sheila, that nice young girl who's staying with the Jenkins?"

"But I don't know her."

"Well, you can get to know her. She's a nice girl and she doesn't know anybody. You can introduce her to the rest of the girls."

"But Dee Dee knows them better than I do."

"Yeah, sugar, but Sheila doesn't have any girlfriends and you don't either, so you could be friends with each other."

I pull away from her. "I got friends," I say. I'm getting annoyed with the conversation, I want to go out and play. I get up and walk over to the window and stand there with my back to her.

"O.K.," Momma says finally, "but I've invited the Jenkins over for lunch Sunday and if you want to be friends with Sheila fine, if not . . ." She shrugs her shoulders.

"You gonna make Dee Dee be there too?"

"Yup."

"Can we invite Zip-Zip and Jeffrey?"

She hesitates a moment. ". . . Maybe next time."

"O.K., can I go now?" I am inching towards the door.

"All right, scoot." She pats me on the butt as I pass her. I am running down the steps, jumping over the last two. Dee Dee, who has been listening at the door, says, "Can I go with you, Cat?"

"No."

"Why not?"

" 'Cause you can't."

I reach the vacant lot where we play ball. There is no game today. The boys are busy gathering ammunition—dirt clods, rocks, bottles—for the fight with the white boys from across the tracks.

Dee Dee whines to Leroy: "Leroy, I wanna go."

"You can't," Leroy says.

"How come?"

" 'Cause you're too young."

"I'm just as old as Jeffrey!"

"You can't go," Leroy says, ". . . besides you're a girl."

"Cat's a girl," she says indignantly.

We all ignore her. We are gathering sticks and rocks and throwing them into an empty milk crate.

"How come I can't go? Huh? How come?" Nobody answers her. We are all walking across the lot. Raymond and Leroy are carrying the ammunition; Dee Dee is standing where we left her, yelling, "I'm gonna tell Momma what you're up to! I'm gonna tell you going cross the tracks to fight with those white boys." Then, after a moment or two: ". . . And Cat's got Kotex in her dresser drawer!" My neck burns but I keep walking.

I am sixteen years old and sitting in Sheila's dining room. We are playing checkers and I am losing and not minding at all. Her cousin Bob comes in. He is stationed in Georgia and on leave from the army. He says hi to Sheila, ignores me completely and walks through to the back with his green duffel bag in his left hand. His voice drifts in from the kitchen, "Where'd the little bulldagger come from?" Sheila springs back from the table so fast her chair overturns. She yells in the kitchen doorway, "You shut your nasty mouth, Bob Jenkins!" The next day we are supposed to make cookies for her aunt's birthday but she calls to suggest we do it over my house instead. I do not go back over Sheila's again unless Dee Dee is with me, or there is no one home.

. . .

We are in Fairmount Park within some semi-enclosed shrubbery. Sheila and I are lying on our backs on an old army blanket. We look like Siamese twins joined together at the head. The sky is blue above us and I am chewing on the straw that came with my Coke.

"Cat, tell me again how you used to almost be late for school all the time 'cause you used to be waiting for me to come out of my house so we could walk to school together," Sheila says.

"I've told you three thousand times already."

"Well, tell me again, I like to hear it."

"If you hadn't been peeping from behind the curtains yourself and waiting for *me* to come out we'd both have gotten to school on time."

She laughs softly then turns over on her stomach.

"I want a kiss," she says.

I lean up on my elbow, check around to make sure nobody's peeping through the bushes then turn and press my lips to hers. After a few seconds she pulls away. "Man, Cat, I never felt this way about anybody before."

"Me neither." I reach over and touch her hand. We kiss again, briefly, our lips just touching. Then we turn and lie as we were before but continue holding hands.

"Cat?"

"Yeah?"

"I think I'm in love."

"Me too."

She squeezes my hand. I squeeze hers back.

"What would you do if Bob came by and saw us now?" Sheila asks.

"What would you do?"

"I don't know. I'd just say hi, I guess."

"Then I would too," I say.

The sun has moved and is now shining directly over us. I cover my eyes with my arm.

"Bob would say we're both bulldaggers," Sheila says after a while.

"Yeah, I guess he would," I say.

"We aren't bulldaggers, are we, Cat?"

"No, bulldaggers want to be men and we don't want to be men, right?"

"Right, we just love each other and there's nothing wrong with loving someone."

"Yeah and nobody can choose who you fall in love with."

"Right."

Sheila and I are in her bedroom; her uncle is standing over the bed shouting, "What the hell's going on here?" He is home from work early. Sheila and I scramble for the sheet and clutch it across our bodies. I am waiting for her uncle to leave so I can get up and dressed, but he just stands there staring, thunder in his face. Finally I release my end of the sheet and scramble to the foot of the bed. Sheila's stockings are entwined in my blouse. I cram panties into my pocket and pull blue jeans over naked, ashen legs. I am trembling. Her uncle's eyes follow me around the room like harsh spotlights.

Later at my house, Momma, Daddy, and I are in the dining room. Leroy and Dee Dee are in their rooms, the doors are shut tight; they've been ordered not to open them. My mother sits on the couch wringing her hands. I sit stiffly forward on the edge of a straight-backed chair. My head down. My teeth clenched. My father stomps back and forth across the floor, his hands first behind him, holding each other at the butt, then gesturing out in front of him. He is asking, "What's this I hear about you being in bed with the Jenkins girl?" I sit still on the edge of my chair, looking straight ahead.

"I'm talking to you, Catherine!" His voice is booming to the rafters, I'm sure the neighbors hear. It is dark outside and a slight breeze puffs out the window curtains. I am holding a spool of thread that had been on the table. I am squeezing it in my hands, the round edges intrude into my palms. I continue to squeeze.

"You hear me talking to you, girl?" He is standing directly over me now, his voice reverberates in my ear. I squeeze the spool of thread and stare at a spider-shaped crack in the wall above the light switch. There is an itch on my left leg, below my knee. I do not scratch. Dogs bark in the backyards and one of the Williams kids is getting a spanking. I hear the strap fall, a child wailing, and an angry female voice.

My father is saying, "Look, you'd better say something, you brazen heifer!" He jerks my head around to face him. I yank it back to stare at the crack in the wall.

"You're lucky Tom Jenkins didn't have you arrested—forcing yourself on that girl like that . . ."

"What? What? What force? Sheila didn't say I forced her to do anything!"

"If you didn't force her, then what happened?"

"Sheila didn't say that! She didn't say it! Mr. Jenkins must have said it!" I am on my feet and trembling, and screaming at the top of my lungs.

"Then what did happen?" my father screams back at me. I sit back down in the chair and again stare at the crack in the wall over the light switch. Trying to concentrate on it, blot out my father's voice. I cannot. I get up and run to the chair where my mother sits. I am pulling on her arm. "Momma, Sheila didn't say that, did she? She didn't say I forced her?"

Momma sits there biting on her bottom lip and wringing her hands. She does not look at me. She lays her hand on my head and does not speak. My father grabs my arm and yanks me away. I am enveloped in his sour breath as he shouts, "Look, I'm a man of God and don't you dare doubt my word!" I yank my arm from his grip and run towards the steps, toward the safety of my bedroom.

"I haven't dismissed you!" I hear my father's footsteps behind me. He grabs me by my tee-shirt and swings me around. I lose my footing and fall at the bottom of the steps.

"Arthur, Arthur!" My mother is running behind us. My father's knee is in my chest; he is yelling in a hoarse angry voice, "Catherine Johnson, I have one more thing to say to you, then we needn't discuss it anymore, but you listen carefully because I mean every word I say: There will be no bulldaggers in my house, do you understand me? THERE WILL BE NO BULLDAGGERS IN MY HOUSE!"

• • •

I am sitting beside Sheila on a bench in Fairmount Park; we are within walking distance of the spot where we used to meet with our lunch on Daddy's old army blanket. The grass is completely green except for one long crooked brown streak where the boys trampled a short cut to the basketball court. The leaves are green too, save for one or two brown and yellow ones beneath the bench at our feet. Sheila's head is bent.

"I'm sorry," she is saying. She is picking minute pieces of lint from a black skirt. "I'm really sorry but you don't know how my uncle is when he gets mad." I am silent. I am watching three boys play basketball on the court about twenty yards away. A tall white kid leaps up and dunks the ball.

"I just didn't know what else to do," Sheila continues. "I was scared and Uncle Jim kept saying, 'She made you do it, didn't she? She made you do it, didn't she?' And before I knew it, I'd said yes." A short black kid knocks the ball out of bounds and a fat boy in a green sweatshirt darts out to retrieve it.

"Cathy?" Her hand is on my forearm and I turn to look her full in the face. "I'm sorry, Cat, I just didn't know what else to do." I turn again towards the basketball court. The tall white boy is holding the ball under his arm and shaking the hand of a short kid. The fat boy in the green sweatshirt is pulling a navy blue poncho on over his head.

"Cathy, please?" Sheila is saying. I turn to look her full in the face. "It's all right, Sheila, it's all right." It is getting windy. The basketball court empties and Sheila asks if I'll meet her at our spot next Saturday. I lie and say yes. She checks to make sure no one's looking, pecks me on the cheek, then gets up to leave. I sit watching the empty basketball court for a long time, then I get up and take the long way home.

f rom

Becoming a Man

Paul Monette

In addition to six novels and three collections of poetry, Paul Monette is noted for his nonfiction, including Borrowed Time: An AIDS Memoir. *In the passage below from the autobiographical* Becoming a Man: Half a Life Story, *Monette takes us back to his family's home in Andover, Massachusetts, and to the day in the mid-1950s when his mother walked into his room and discovered him having sex with a boyhood friend named Kite.*

I thought one could live on wildness. More and more I couldn't wait to grow up and be rid of childhood, and not so I could start filling cavities. But how could I have overlooked that Kite and I were headed for a showdown with the world? We took no special precautions not to be caught. And if Kite could so casually spread the story of Ruthie's show in the Thompson barn, then what did he say about me? We were hardly playmates otherwise, and he hated school. We'd pass each other in the hallways, barely nodding. There was nowhere else to go. . . .

Kite was over to play at my house, a dank cold day, and just as the winter dusk was falling, the two of us were kneeling by the bedroom window, the one that looked out on the cherry tree. When Kite announced he had a boner, we unzipped our flies and waggled our weenies, snickering. No big deal. I had enough self-control not to break out the *Kama Sutra* with parents in earshot. But I left the light off and the door open.

"What're you boys doing?"

The scald of my mother's querulous voice seared the dwindling day with judgment. In an instant our two flies were zipped, and

I swung around and said, "Nothing." She stood there silent, making me squirm, but neither of us spoke another word.

In the next two days, the squirm became a way of life, as I filled up every silence in the household with bright chatter. My mother and I avoided being alone together, but I could feel the edge of her preoccupation. My nervous happy-talk was a frantic attempt to make an unspoken deal, that we both forget the whole thing. Was she torturing me by letting me swing by my own grinning rope? Did she even remotely understand that her damning silence was turning sex into something strangely private, just between her and me?

On the third day, I came home from school and found her brooding at the kitchen table, smoking a cigarette. Right away I started to talk, changing the unspoken subject, strewing the table before her with A's. She finally looked at me grimly and upped the ante: "What were you doing with Kite?"

No deal. "I told you—nothing," I flung back, skittering away to the living room door. Then tossed it again, with bitter emphasis. "*Nothing.*"

She looked down at the cigarette in her hand, tapping it into the ashtray, and said no more.

I was right, of course—it *had* been nothing. Yet I knew as I walked lead-footed to my bedroom that the high-wire act of passion was over, because it was somehow wrong. Even if I'd had the wherewithal to challenge her confusion, it wasn't worth the fight. There had already been enough damage to our family, more than enough of the pain of being different. The last thing they needed was something weird from me. Thus did the subtext of my growing up get set in stone: *I had to be the normal one.* To compensate for the family curse, my brother, whose laughing demeanor and scrappiness were already at odds with the tragic whispering of neighbors and gawkers.

So I told myself I would give it up, even prayed at night for it to be taken away, not knowing that "it" was love. *Forgive me for what I did with Kite, and don't let it happen again.*

No moment of my first twenty years is more indelible than the kitchen inquisition of my mother. All the ambiguity of sex reduced to a single question, the implication crystal clear that something very bad had happened—unnatural, even. The flinching of my heart from that point on would ensure our brief exchange a central place in therapy, fifteen years later. Eventually I would come to see that it wasn't the crime of homosex so much as sex itself that had so overwhelmed my mother.

Oh, we finally had it out, she and I, combing it over like ancient myth in those dialogues of the dining room table, the oxygen hissing softly from the tank that followed her everywhere now. She swore she'd put the entire incident out of her mind, but that, I think, was wishful thinking. She should have told my father, she said, and let *him* have it out with me. Poor lady—how many mothers hide the first queer evidence from the fathers, compounding the distance all around? And how exactly would it have come out any better if my father had asked the question? My answer would have been just the same—*Nothing*—and I still would've ended up gritting my teeth to be normal.

I think she just felt helpless, out of her depth. When she came upon me and Kite in the winter dusk, it was one more thing she couldn't handle. The last straw of who knows how many disappointments and humiliations she and my father faced, defying the world that thought of us as anything but normal. We were all victims of the peculiarly American obsession that everyone be the same, once the pot has melted down. A sameness decreed by the advertisers, and the white-bread fantasies of the tube. Little did we know that being different was our only hope, my brother's as much as mine.

I've long since forgiven my mother and me. But it used to bother her terribly to hear how unbearable my growing up felt, worse and worse through the minefields of adolescence, on account of the shame of being queer. How fervently she wanted me to remember the happy childhood she swore had taken place. She had all the scalloped pictures to prove it. But I wouldn't budge: the pictures were lies. I had only one small consolation for her, as she battered herself with the very guilt she'd laid on me in the hurricane season on High Street. I told her she and my father must've done it all right in the end, because Bobby and I both managed to find great love. If she'd really fucked up, I'd be all alone.

What My Father Told Me

Paul Phillips

"I thought I was the only one in the world," says Paul Phillips, now in his mid-eighties, as he recalls discovering that he was gay around the year 1919. Paul's father responded to his son's homosexuality in a remarkably enlightened way. Paul's oral history is included in Eric Marcus's Making History: The Struggle for Gay and Lesbian Equal Rights, 1945–1990.

Gradually I began to discover that I was different, besides my color, and I thought I was the only one in the world. I remember when I first discovered that things were not right, sexually, I wanted to kill myself. I'd say this was in 1919. I was about fifteen then. I knew I didn't care anything about girls. Everybody else was chasing after girls, and I couldn't figure out why. Didn't make sense to me and still doesn't. But I just didn't want to go through life this way. I was just completely down and out. I practically gave up.

Finally, my dad came to me one day and told me what he had heard. He told me that I was not natural. Whether he heard it or just looked at me and could tell, I don't know. He never did tell me who told him.

So he said, "We'll go to the Mayo Clinic, get you examined, and see if we can find out what causes this and what to do about it." I was willing to go because I wanted to be changed. So he put Mother and me in the car, and she and I went up to the Mayo Clinic, in Rochester, Minnesota. That was back in the days when you couldn't get a place to stay or a place to eat because we were blacks. We bought crackers and baloney in the store and took them out and ate them. We got one of these ten-by-twelve tents and we stayed in the tent at night.

They had me in and out of the hospital for several days. I was terrified. They asked all kinds of questions. They determined that I was homosexual and that there was nothing they could do about it. They said that because of the final report, according to their state laws they should report me and have me incarcerated. Put me in jail! But they said that since I was a client of theirs, they would not do that, but there was nothing they could do for me. That almost put me under the ground.

So we went back home and reported to Dad. My dad was not really an educated man. He was a lawyer, but he was self-educated and he didn't know anything about gays. I might say this, that I was an adopted child. And I often used to wonder as a kid, "What will he do when he finds it out? Will he put me out? Or will he accept me?"

Dad was very understanding. When I say understanding, I don't think he actually understood, but he was willing to accept. So he finally told me, "Since they don't know what to do about it, find yourself a friend that you can trust. And bring him home. I don't want you playing around on the streets or out on the country roads because you never know who's going to step up behind you. Bring him home. What you do in your room is your business."

My Brother on the Shoulder of the Road

Clifford Chase

In this autobiographical essay, Clifford Chase recalls a series of momentous encounters with his brother, Ken, as both young men were coming to terms with their sexual identities. Chase lives in Brooklyn, New York, and is currently working on a book about his brother and the rest of his family. (That book, On the Shoulder of the Road, *will be published in the fall of 1994 by HarperSanFrancisco.)*

It was the summer before Ken went away to college. My mother, who worked full-time, was paying him to clean house for her, and babysit for me. I had a cruel streak, and I teased Ken mercilessly when he was vacuuming or dusting. Like my parents, he had a terrible temper. It was easy even for me, six years younger, to get his goat. I would stand in the path of the vacuum cleaner and make faces, or I'd follow him around while he was dusting and make farting noises. Sometimes I'd just lean in the doorway of the bathroom and stare at him until he turned from his cleaning and said, "Do you mind?"

I also defied him as much as possible that summer. Perhaps I was angry that he was going away to college in the fall. Perhaps I had simply reached the age to rebel, and Ken was more available than either of my parents.

David Vickers and I had set up the train table in the living room for the summer. In self-defense I had put the Muppets aside and now played with trains every day, a more boyish activity. David and I had built bridges from the train table to the two steps into the sunken living room—and this was the cause of perhaps the worst fight I ever had with Ken.

It was hot, and the sunlight pressed against all the windows of the house. I had no doubt been teasing Ken all day, and now he wanted to vacuum the steps. I remember he came into my room and asked me to move the bridges.

"No," I said, fingering the curtains. "I don't feel like it."

He grabbed my arm, I began to scream, and things went on from there. He managed to drag me out into the entryway above the living room, and he hit me a few times on the shoulder. Still I refused to help him. "Cleaning is your job," I said. By now he had pinned me to the cold tile floor and was kneeling over me, his face and arms red with fury. I struggled, and then came his worst blow:

"Stupid little faggot!"

He had never called me that before. Or if he had, somehow it had never hit me in quite the same way. We stared at each other a moment, and I think my face must have changed its shape. Perhaps I screamed. What I felt, and could not find words for, was this: *Not you, too.*

I tore myself from his grasp and ran down the hall, an incredible and shameful grief pushing up behind my eyes. It was one of the last times until adulthood that I would really cry. Once in my room with the door closed behind me, that privacy did not seem enough either, and, as if to confirm the power of a future metaphor, I ran and shut myself in the closet.

Ken came into my room after me. Somehow I had known he would see the seriousness of the situation and not open the closet as well. He stood outside the sliding door, and I sat fingering the opaque plastic door handle, a cap over a hole in the door and the only light that came in. "Come on," he said. "I hardly touched you."

But I kept still. My head hurt with trying not to cry, and it was hot in there. Ken waited a moment longer. "What's the matter?" he asked.

As much as we fought, and as often as Ken hit me, he was sensitive and he knew when he had really hurt me. I think he was sorry now, but still I didn't speak. I couldn't have explained it anyway, and at that moment I just wanted to be left alone to cry.

"Okay, be that way," he said, and I heard him go out.

. . .

The following spring, it was a chance remark by Ken that made me understand that I was gay.

He came home one weekend from college with his girlfriend, Kathleen. This was Ken's first girlfriend, and I don't remember my oldest brother, Paul, ever bringing anyone home, so this was new to me too. The air seemed charged with sexuality. My mother approached Kathleen gingerly, as if on tiptoe; my father teased her. On Saturday afternoon Kathleen and Ken sunbathed on lawn chairs in the back yard. I followed my mother out with the tray of iced tea, and as Kathleen walked barefoot to the patio in her yellow bikini, her browned hips and breasts flowing out, my mother exclaimed, as she always did during sexy scenes in movies on TV, imitating a huffy matron: "Well!"

I had been lonely since Ken went away to college, and I wanted to sunbathe myself now in his and Kathleen's brief presence. I wanted to know them, their private jokes, their world together. They called each other "Rabbit." They surfed. They smoked pot. They had a communal way of talking, Southern Californian and ironic, with certain phrases that seemed unusual and hip to me: "How odd," they'd say. Or, "Mr. Meat says, 'Make a mess!' " I didn't know where the phrases came from or even what some of them meant.

Saturday night I went to the movies with them. Or maybe we went miniature golfing, I don't remember. By the end of the evening it was like I was drunk on their company. As we drove home, in the darkness of the backseat I grew more and more vivacious, trying to imitate them and their phrases as much as possible. Maybe I was really imitating Kathleen. Anyway, after seven months of junior high constraint, I let go completely.

I like to think of that utterly fluid moment in seventh grade, before I quite knew the names of things, the proper boundaries between masculine and feminine, gay and straight—where my personality was so unformed and changeable that I could, with a little encouragement and excitement, let my guard down and emerge as a flaming queen of a child.

"Oh, how odd!" I cried, giggling. "Make a mess!"

I was scarcely aware of whether Ken and Kathleen were listening or not, so happy was I to be with my brother and his girl-friend, this wonderful alternative to my hate-filled life at school.

"Why are you acting so strangely?" Ken asked as we turned onto our block. All the houses were dark.

I stopped and thought. I was so happy, I wasn't even offended by his question. "I don't know," I said. "I usually don't act this way. How am I acting?"

"Really femmy," was his reply. Maybe he was embarrassed in front of Kathleen. And yet I like to think there was a strangely nonjudgmental quality in his voice, as if he were simply describing a fact.

"Really?" I said.

"Yeah, femmy," agreed Kathleen genially. She didn't seem to care.

"Hmm," I said. I looked for a reason. "I am acting differently. Maybe it's because of being with you two."

Then Ken said something very strange. I'll never forget it, though I don't remember his exact words, and it was only a joke. He said something like, "Maybe you're a *contact homosexual.*"

"What's that?" I asked.

And he explained that it was someone who was homosexual only in contact with certain people, or in certain situations. It was a phrase he and Kathleen had learned in psychology class.

Shame began to ring in my head like a bell. We had pulled up in the drive a few minutes ago, and now we got out of the car. As I followed them up the dark walk to the house, in the California night air, I was beginning to put it together—what homosexual was, what fag was, what I was. Inside, I said goodnight to my parents, who were getting ready for bed. Ken and Kathleen went to their rooms—they had to sleep separately—and I went to my own room quickly, as if holding my discovery close to my breast. I closed the door and looked up the "H" word in the *Encyclopaedia Brittannica* and confirmed that I really was what the other boys at school said I was.

Ken came out to me when I was twenty-one. He had been living with Kathleen nearly six years when he started seeing men. He had moved with her to the East Coast, where she was getting her Ph.D., but he couldn't find work in Vermont and had to move to Boston. Now, a year and a half later, they had broken up and he had just moved back to California. He was staying with my parents while he looked for a job, and so now it was I who came home from college to visit one weekend.

Saturday night we went to a ferny, brightly lit bar in the next town where you could play backgammon. We sat down and had beers.

I didn't know Ken had something to tell me. His initial strategy was to remark on how other men in the bar were cute. I was so far from letting myself look at men that I had no idea what he was talking about. I remember at one point a stocky blond guy came in the door, at the far end of the room. Ken pointed discreetly. "Oh, there's a cute one," he said.

I turned. "Uh-huh," I said vaguely, guardedly.

I must have been frowning.

"Do you think it's strange for me to say that?" Ken asked.

"I don't know. I guess you're scoping out the competition, huh?" I meant his competition for the women in the bar. I genuinely thought this was some sort of "swinging singles" technique.

Ken did one of his joking double takes, a fidgety gesture he had. He was always very nervous, his hands shaky and his eyes darting, in the manner of everyone in the family, to your face and shyly away again. He had ruddy skin and a high forehead that furrowed easily. "Not exactly," he said. Then he just blurted it out: "I'm trying to tell you that I'm gay."

I almost think I had the same feeling of fear as that night when I was thirteen, when Ken made that chance remark—only now the feeling was more like elation. "Really?" I said. I saw him fidgeting with his beer, waiting for my reaction. It was as much to put him at ease as to satisfy any desire to talk about these things that I told him about myself too. "I've had those feelings," I said, faltering. Then I was a little more honest: "Actually, I've had them a lot."

Ken did another one of his false double takes. But he was happy now.

We talked first about our mutual surprise. "I guess I always thought you were basically straight," Ken said.

"No . . . I thought that about you, too." And I have a particular image in my mind of Ken as a straight man, which was perhaps my model for any straight man: Ken washing his red Ford Falcon in the drive. His teenager's manly persona was, in fact, part of my own ideal self-image, nurtured throughout high school—that of the kind of guy who fixes things, who swears, who smartly ruffles the newspaper before he starts to read. I wonder at how we had fooled each other all that time with these personas, or rather with the idea that such a persona could not be gay. We believed in this "basically straight" guy, and we each fooled ourselves with him.

my brother

Pat Parker

Many gay men and lesbians have siblings who are also gay. In her poem "my brother," Pat Parker (1944–1989) described the rituals and the struggles of a sister and brother, both of whom are gay. Born in Houston, Texas, Parker wrote half a dozen books of poetry about being black and lesbian.

for Blackberri

I

It is a simple ritual.
Phone rings
Berri's voice
low, husky
'What's you're doing?'
'Not a thing,
you coming over?'
'Well, I thought I'd
come by.'
A simple ritual.
He comes
we eat
watch television
play cards
play video games
some nights
he sleeps over

others
he goes home
sometimes
he brings a friend
more often
he doesn't.
A simple ritual.

II

It's a pause that alerts me
tells me this time
is hard time
the pain has risen
to the water line
we rarely verbalize
there is no need.

Within this lifestyle
there is much to undo you.

Hey look at the faggot!
When I was a child
our paper boy was Claude
every day
seven days a week
he bared the Texas weather
the rain that never stopped
walked through the Black section
where sidewalks had not
yet been invented
and ditches filled with water.
Walk careful Claude
across the plank
that served as sidewalk
sometime tips into the murky water
or heat
wet heat

that covers your pores
cascades rivulets of
stinging sweat down your body.
Our paper boy Claude
bared the weather well
each day he came
and each Saturday at dusk
he would come to collect.

My parents liked Claude.
Each Saturday Claude polite
would come
always said thank you
whether we had the money
or not.
Each Saturday
my father would say
Claude is a nice boy
works hard
goes to church
gives his money to his mother
and each Sunday
we would go to church
and there would be Claude
in his choir robes
til the Sunday
when he didn't come.

Hey look at the faggot!

Some young men howled at him
ran in a pack
reverted to some ancient form
they took Claude
took his money
yelled faggot
as they cast his body
in front of a car.

III

How many cars have you dodged Berri?
How many ancient young men have you met?
Perhaps your size saved you
but then you were not always this size
perhaps your fleetness
perhaps
there are no more ancient young men.

Ah! Within this lifestyle
we have chosen.
Sing?
What do you mean
you wanna be a singer?
Best get a good government job
maybe sing on the side.
You heard the words:
Be responsible
Be respectable
Be stable
Be secure
Be normal, boy.

How many quarter-filled rooms
have you sang your soul to
then washed away with
blended whiskey?

I told my booking agent one year
book me a tour
Blackberri and I
will travel this land
together
take our Black Queerness
into the face
of this place and say

Hey, here we are
a faggot & a dyke, Black
we make good music
& write good poems
We Be—Something Else.

My agent couldn't book us.
It seemed my lesbian audiences
were not ready for my faggot
brother
and I remembered
a law conference
in San Francisco
where women
women who loved women
threw boos and tomatoes
at a woman who dared
to have a man in her band.

What is this world we have?
Is my house the only safe place
for us?
And I am rage
all the low-paying gigs
all the uncut records
all the dodged cars
all the fear escaping
all the unclaimed love
so I offer my bosom
and food
and shudder
fearful of the time
when it will not be
enough
fearful of the time
when the ritual
ends.

Growing Up Gay in Little Havana

Jesse G. Monteagudo

Jesse Monteagudo grew up in Little Havana, a Cuban neighborhood in Miami. In this essay, Monteagudo explains how it felt to grow up as a gay man in this "family-oriented society that expects its sons and daughters to reside with their parents until they get, heterosexually, a means of escape."

Cuban parents would go to any length to save their sons from a fate they believed was worse than death. Many a Cuban boy of uncertain sexuality was subjected to hormone shots, a practice that led to a crop of hirsute, deep-voiced gay men who walk the streets of Miami today. My parents chose a less drastic (though equally popular) measure. Every afternoon after school I would dutifully walk to the local YMCA—where, naturally, Spanish was spoken—and take judo classes, as if my erotic interest in my own gender could be extinguished through physical contact with other males. When that didn't seem to work, my parents sent me to a psychiatrist, an equally futile gesture but one popular with many concerned Cuban parents at that time.

By the time I graduated from high school in 1972, Little Havana had changed. It had expanded its horizons westward as affluent, now naturalized Cuban-Americans began to move to the suburbs. Calle Ocho itself underwent a transformation as the last of the old Anglo-owned businesses closed down and were replaced by Cuban enterprises. Cuban-Americans were ready to assume leadership of the city of Miami from the retreating Anglos, who were now migrating north into Broward and Palm Beach counties.

I turned twenty in 1973. That year I became both an American citizen and a practicing homosexual, no small feat for a man who is naturally reluctant to take chances. My parents had moved into a house just outside of Little Havana and I had moved along with them, commuting to and from college and a part-time job selling shoes at a Hialeah shoe store owned by a Cuban Danny De Vito. I also worked as a dishwasher for a greasy spoon whose manager was a notorious chicken hawk who invariably invited all his young employees to his apartment for some tea and sympathy. Finding both job and boss unattractive, I quit after a few weeks.

Determined to work my way through college, I got a job in the school library, which helped my coming out process in two ways. First, the library carried all the latest "gay liberation" books, which I, an incorrigible bookworm, did not fail to read. Second, the library had a very cruisy men's room, which I used to good benefit during my student years. From tearooms I "graduated" to adult bookstores and then, in 1974, to gay bars.

Though my parents had long suspected, they did not have to face my sexual orientation outright until one night when I, my inhibitions dulled by alcohol, finally blurted it out to them (so much for my education). I offered to move out then and there but my parents, for whom the family unit is paramount, wouldn't hear of it. Apparently they thought that my reputation (and theirs) would be safer if I remained under parental supervision.

Most twenty-year-olds would have taken this opportunity to leave an increasingly uncomfortable parental nest and set up a place of their own. But Little Havana, like big Havana, is a family-oriented society that expects its sons and daughters to reside with their parents until they get, heterosexually, a means of escape that is unavailable to most lesbian or gay Cubans. *La familia* comes first, which means that "little" Jesse (or everyone else in his predicament) was expected to drop everything in order to assist his parents, straight siblings, aunts, uncles, and cousins.

In the Cuban community a façade of heterosexuality must be maintained while living at home. If one's sexual orientation is known it is treated as, at best, an unfortunate vice that should only be indulged elsewhere. It's no wonder that, once away from their parents, many young gay Cubans went wild. This system of repression and hypocrisy also applied to heterosexual singles, though they have the privilege of eventually getting married, thus adding respectability (and children) to their sexual relations.

An institution that developed in order to deal with the plight of the Cuban single was the *posada*, a drive-in motel which rented by the hour. During the early seventies Calle Ocho was home to several *posadas*, places where Cuban gays and straight singles alike went for sexual release before going home to *Mama y Papa*. A couple would check in, do their business, and check out, after which the motel attendant would come in to change the bed and clean up a bit before renting the same room to another couple. To their credit *posada* managers and attendants were very accepting of sexual diversity, though I once tried their sense of tolerance by bringing in a dirty-looking, *Americano hippiado* ("hippyish" American) I picked up somewhere. In any case, with Cuban libidos (my own included) running high, *posada* owners made a tidy profit. I remember trying to find a room on New Year's Eve 1974 only to find an especially long waiting list and impatient couples lining up around the block.

Not having a car or a place of my own, my sex life depended upon the kindness of strangers. Still, I was able to enjoy Little Havana's lively but furtive gay male social scene, one that centered around bars, beaches, a few private homes (for not all gay Cubans lived with their parents), and the newly opened Club Miami baths. Camp humor combined with Latin high spirits to create a light and lively atmosphere, which, within its limitations, offered Cuban gay men a break from the problems of living in a society that hated them. Some gay Cubans stood machismo on its head by adopting outrageously effeminate behavior, at least within the confines of gay space, while others sought to let off steam through heavy drug or alcohol use and promiscuous sex.

Being a relatively handsome and newly uninhibited young guy in his early twenties, I was able to enjoy many of the pleasures Little Havana's gay demimonde had to offer. From other gay Cubans I learned how to dress (bell-bottom pants and platform shoes were then the rage), to stay up late, to hold my liquor, to cruise and deal with rejection (nonchalantly). I even "learned" to adopt an effeminate pose and to refer to myself and others as "she," though this was something I never cared for. Though I did not have a car, I joined friends who did for joyrides to the gay beach on Virginia Key and north to Fort Lauderdale's hot spots. My sex partners—and I was seldom without one—ranged from my first lover, a Cuban eighteen years older than me who eventually left me to join a Pentecostal church, to a Mexican doctor on vacation and the above-mentioned *Americano hippiado.*

To many Cubans, gay men want to be women. Many gay Cubans took them at their word and got as close to being women as finances and opportunities allowed. Some went into female impersonation, an art form that flourishes in South Florida. Others went the whole route, becoming genital females through hormones and surgery. Many of these were unhappy and confused gay kids who, growing up in an atmosphere of self-hatred, saw a sex change as the only alternative to suicide. They should not be confused with the true transsexuals, people who knew what they wanted and usually got it.

The most memorable of the gender benders who inhabited Little Havana's demimonde was Silvia, who, when I first met her, was a large and imposing *transformista* who lip-synched in straight and gay bars in the neighborhood. (Her impressions of La Lupe, a salsa singer known for throwing her shoes and her wig at the audience, were legendary.) Silvia's goal was to save enough money to have a sex-change operation, a goal that she eventually accomplished. I remember the party Silvia's friends gave her the night before she checked into the hospital, a combination victory party and wake that I, a friend of a friend, was invited to. The operation was a success and Silvia, "the woman who became a legend" (as the title of a never-produced stage rendition of her life proclaimed), settled down as a lesbian, eventually moving in with a tough dyke who managed a Cuban lesbian bar on Miami Beach.

Though gay life in Little Havana was fun while it lasted, this shallow and somewhat neurotic scene became ponderous after a while. I was never happy with the excessive effeminacy, the heavy drug and alcohol use, the backstabbing and catfighting (I was once robbed by a so-called friend), the self-hatred, and the need to pretend. I wanted to break with my surroundings, to finish college and find a place of my own. I also wanted to find a permanent lover and get involved in gay activism, two commodities that were scarce on Calle Ocho. By 1978, a year after Little Havana joined the rest of Dade County in overturning a gay rights ordinance, I accomplished all of these goals and moved out of Little Havana, not because of the vote but to be with my lover. I moved to Broward County and a chapter in my life came to an end. . . .

As an openly gay man, I can never be reconciled with Little Havana, as it is personified by my relatives and by other Cubans and Cuban-Americans with whom I come in contact. I recently made a very reluctant appearance at my sister's second wedding, an event to which my lover was not invited. Many of my relatives were there, accompanied, of course, by their heterosexual spouses and their children. Though my sister and cousins have life styles that are vastly different from those of their parents—most of them are married to non-Cubans and most of them have been divorced—their views on homosexuality remain similar to those of the generation before them.

In spite of it all, I have made my peace with my past and do not regret having liked it. Calle Ocho will always be a street of memories that, with the flight of time, become increasingly better. Growing up in Little Havana has made me what I am today, and that can't be all bad.

from

Oranges Are Not the Only Fruit

Jeanette Winterson

*Born in Manchester, England, in 1959, Jeanette Winterson worked
as an ice cream vendor and as a makeup assistant at a funeral home
before publishing her first novel,* Oranges Are Not the Only Fruit,
in 1985. Oranges *tells the story of an adopted daughter's relationship with her mother, a religious woman who believes that sin is
everywhere. The daughter, a high school senior named Jeanette, discovers that she is a lesbian and falls in love with Melanie, who is a
member of the church that Jeanette and her mother attend. In the
passage below, Jeanette has invited Melanie to sleep over at her house.
Jeanette's mother is suspicious of Melanie and sets out to put an end
to their affair.*

Early in the morning, about two a.m.,
when the World Service closed down, we heard her come slowly
up the stairs to bed. I had learned to move quickly. She stood by
my door for a few moments, then suddenly pushed it open. I
could just see the braid at the bottom of her dressing gown. Nobody moved and then she was gone. She kept her light on all
night. Soon afterwards I decided to tell her how I felt. I explained
how much I wanted to be with Melanie, that I could talk to her,
that I needed that kind of friend. And . . . And . . . but I never
managed to talk about and . . . My mother had been very quiet,
nodding her head from time to time, so that I thought she understood some of it. When I finished I gave her a little kiss, which I
think surprised her a bit; we never usually touched except in anger. "Go to bed now," she said, picking up her Bible.

Since that time we had hardly spoken. She seemed caught up in something, and I had my own worries. Today, for the first time, she was her old self, busy, and obviously wanting company, if Mrs. White was around. I wanted to know what had happened to cheer her up, so I set off down the hill again with our dog circling behind.

"Hello," I shouted, wiping my feet on the mat. The house was quite still. She had been there recently because the coffee table in the parlour now had her Bible and Promise Box on it. She'd taken a promise out too. I looked at the rolled-up bit of paper. "The Lord is your strength and shield." Mrs. White's coat had gone, but she'd left her dishcloth on the chair. I took it into the kitchen. There was a note on the cupboard. "Gone to stay at Mrs. White's. Come to church in the morning."

Now my mother never stayed in other people's houses except when she went to Wigan on her business. It suited me though; I could go and stay with Melanie. So I fed our dog, had a wash and set off. As usual, when I had no money for the bus, I walked the couple of miles through the cemetery and round the back of the power station.

Melanie was doing the gardening.

"What's your mum planning tonight?" I asked her.

"She's going to the club, then staying with Auntie Irene."

"What do you want to do?" I went on, pulling up a few weeds.

She smiled at me with those lovely cat-grey eyes and tugged at her rubber gloves.

"I'll put the kettle on for a hot water bottle."

We talked a lot that night about our plans. Melanie really did want to be a missionary, even though it was my destiny.

"Why don't you like the idea?" she wanted to know.

"I don't like hot places, that's all, I got sunstroke in Paignton last year."

We were quiet, and I traced the outline of her marvellous bones and the triangle of muscle in her stomach. What is it about intimacy that makes it so very disturbing?

• • •

Over breakfast the next morning she told me she intended to go to university to read theology. I didn't think it was a good thing on account of modern heresies. She thought she should understand how other people saw the world.

"But you know they're wrong," I insisted.

"Yes, but it might be interesting, come on, we'll be late for church. You're not preaching are you?"

"No," I said. "I was supposed to, but they changed it."

We bustled through the kitchen and I stood on the stairs to kiss her.

"I love you almost as much as I love the Lord," I laughed.

She looked at me, and her eyes clouded for a moment, "I don't know," she said.

By the time we got to church, the first hymn was under way. My mother glared at me, and I tried to look sorry. We had slid in next to Miss Jewsbury who told me to keep calm.

"What do you mean?" I whispered.

"Come and talk to me afterwards," she hissed, "but not till we're out of sight."

I decided she had gone mad. The church was very full as usual, and every time I caught someone's eye they smiled or nodded. It made me happy. There was nowhere I'd rather be. When the hymn was over I squeezed a bit closer to Melanie and tried to concentrate on the Lord. "Still," I thought, "Melanie is a gift from the Lord, and it would be ungrateful not to appreciate her." I was still deep in these contemplations when I realised that something disturbing was happening. The church had gone very quiet and the pastor was standing on his lower platform, with my mother next to him. She was weeping. I felt a searing pain against my knuckles; it was Melanie's ring. Then Miss Jewsbury was urging me to my feet saying, "Keep calm, keep calm," and I was walking out to the front with Melanie. I shot a glance at her. She was pale.

"These children of God," began the pastor, "have fallen under Satan's spell."

His hand was hot and heavy on my neck. Everyone in the congregation looked like a waxwork.

"These children of God have fallen foul of their lusts."

"Just a minute . . . ," I began, but he took no notice.

"These children are full of demons."

A cry of horror ran through the church.

"I'm not," I shouted, "and neither is she."

"Listen to Satan's voice," said the pastor to the church, pointing at me. "How are the best become the worst."

"What are you talking about?" I asked, desperate.

"Do you deny you love this woman with a love reserved for man and wife?"

"No, yes, I mean of course I love her."

"I will read you the words of St. Paul," announced the pastor, and he did, and many more words besides about unnatural passions and the mark of the demon.

"To the pure all things are pure," I yelled at him. "It's you not us."

He turned to Melanie.

"Do you promise to give up this sin and beg the Lord to forgive you?"

"Yes." She was trembling uncontrollably. I hardly heard what she said.

"Then go into the vestry with Mrs. White and the elders will come and pray for you. It's not too late for those who truly repent."

He turned to me.

"I love her."

"Then you do not love the Lord."

"Yes, I love both of them."

"You cannot."

"I do, I do, let me go." But he caught my arm and held me fast.

"The church will not see you suffer, go home and wait for us to help you."

I ran out on to the street, wild with distress. Miss Jewsbury was waiting for me.

"Come on," she said briskly, "let's go and get some coffee and decide what you're going to do." I went along with her, not thinking of anything but Melanie and her loveliness.

When we reached Miss Jewsbury's house, she banged the kettle on the gas ring, and pushed me by the fire. My teeth were chattering and I couldn't talk.

"I've known you for years and you were always headstrong, why haven't you been a bit more careful?"

I just stared into the fire.

"No one need ever have found out if you hadn't tried to explain to that mother of yours."

"She's all right," I murmured mechanically.

"She's mad," replied Miss Jewsbury very certainly.

"I didn't tell her everything."

"She's a woman of the world, even though she'd never admit it to me. She knows about feelings, especially women's feelings."

This wasn't something I wanted to go into.

"Who told you what was going on?" I asked abruptly.

"Elsie," she said.

"Elsie?" This was too much.

"She tried to protect you, and when she got ill that last time, she told me."

"Why?"

"Because it's my problem too."

At that moment I thought the demon would come and carry me off. I felt dizzy.

What on earth was she talking about? Melanie and I were special.

"Drink this." She gave me a glass. "It's brandy."

"I think I'll have to lie down," I said feebly.

I don't know how long I slept, the curtains were drawn, and my shoulders felt very heavy. At first I couldn't remember why my head hurt, then as the panic in my stomach got clearer I started to go over the morning's events.

Miss Jewsbury came in.

"Feeling better?"

"Not much," I sighed.

"Perhaps this will help." And she began to stroke my head and shoulders. I turned over so that she could reach my back. Her hand crept lower and lower. She bent over me; I could feel her breath on my neck. Quite suddenly I turned and kissed her. We made love and I hated it and hated it, but would not stop.

· · ·

It was morning when I crept home. I had a plan to go straight off to school hoping no one would notice. I expected my mother to be in bed. I was wrong. There was a strong smell of coffee and voices coming from the parlour. As I tiptoed past, I realised they were having a prayer meeting. I got my things ready and was all packed up to leave. On the way out they caught me.

"Jeanette," cried one of the elders, dragging me into the parlour. "Our prayers have been answered."

"Where did you stay last night?" asked my mother sulkily.

"I can't remember."

"That Miss Jewsbury's I'll bet."

"Oh, she's not holy," piped up Mrs. White.

"No," I told them all, "not there."

"What does it matter?" urged the pastor. "She's here now, and it's not too late."

"I've got to go to school."

"Not at all, not at all," the pastor smiled. "Come and sit down."

My mother absently passed me a plate of biscuits. It was 8:30 a.m.

It was 10 p.m. that same night before the elders went home. They had spent the day praying over me, laying hands on me, urging me to repent my sins before the Lord. "Renounce her, renounce her," the pastor kept saying, "it's only the demon."

My mother made cups of tea and forgot to wash the dirty ones. The parlour was full of cups. Mrs. White sat on one and cut herself, someone else spilt theirs, but they didn't stop. I still couldn't think, could only see Melanie's face and Melanie's body, and every so often the outline of Miss Jewsbury bending over me.

At 10 p.m. the pastor heaved a great sigh and offered me one last chance.

"I can't," I said. "I just can't."

"We'll come back the day after tomorrow," he confided to my mother. "Meantime, don't let her out of this room, and don't feed her. She needs to lose her strength before it can be hers again."

My mother nodded, nodded, nodded and locked me in. She did give me a blanket, but she took away the light bulb. Over the thirty-six hours that followed, I thought about the demon and some other things besides.

I knew that demons entered wherever there was a weak point. If I had a demon my weak point was Melanie, but she was beautiful and good and had loved me.

Can love really belong to the demon?

What sort of demon? The brown demon that rattles the ear? The red demon that dances the hornpipe? The watery demon that causes sickness? The orange demon that beguiles? Everyone has a demon like cats have fleas.

"They're looking in the wrong place," I thought. "If they want to get at my demon they'll have to get at me."

I thought about William Blake.

"If I let them take away my demons, I'll have to give up what I've found."

"You can't do that," said a voice at my elbow.

Leaning on the coffee table was the orange demon.

"I've gone mad," I thought.

"That may well be so," agreed the demon evenly. "So make the most of it."

I flopped heavily against the settee. "What do you want?"

"I want to help you decide what you want." And the creature hopped up on to the mantelpiece and sat on Pastor Spratt's brass crocodile.

"Everyone has a demon as you so rightly observed," the thing began, "but not everyone knows this, and not everyone knows how to make use of it."

"Demons are evil, aren't they?" I asked, worried.

"Not quite, they're just different, and difficult. You know what auras are?"

I nodded.

"Well, the demon you get depends on the colour of your aura, yours is orange which is why you've got me. Your mother's is brown, which is why she's so odd, and Mrs. White's is hardly a demon at all. We're here to keep you in one piece, if you ignore us, you're quite likely to end up in two pieces, or lots of pieces, it's all part of the paradox."

"But in the Bible you keep getting driven out."

"Don't believe all you read."

I started to feel ill again, so I took off my socks and pushed my toes into my mouth for comfort. They tasted of digestive biscuits. After that I went to the window and burst a few of the geranium buds to hear the pop. When I sat down the demon was glowing very bright and polishing the crocodile with its handkerchief.

"What sex are you?"

"Doesn't matter does it? After all that's your problem."

"If I keep you, what will happen?"

"You'll have a difficult, different time."

"Is it worth it?"

"That's up to you."

"Will I keep Melanie?"

But the demon had vanished.

When the pastor and the elders came back, I was calm, cheerful, and ready to accept.

"I'll repent," I said, as soon as they came in the parlour. The pastor seemed surprised.

"Are you sure?"

"Sure." I wanted to get it over with as quickly as possible; besides, I hadn't eaten for two days. All the elders knelt down to pray, and I knelt down beside them. One of them began to speak in tongues, and it was then I felt a prickle at the back of my neck.

"Go away," I hissed. "They'll see you." I opened an eye to check.

"Not them," replied the demon, "they talk a lot but they don't see nothing."

"I'm not getting rid of you, this is the best way I can think of."

"Oh that's fine," trilled the demon, "I was just passing."

By this time all the elders were singing "What a Friend We Have in Jesus" so I thought it wise to join in. It was all over very quickly really, and my mother had put a joint* in the oven.

"I hope you'll testify on Sunday," said the pastor, hugging me.

---

a joint: a roast.—Ed.

"Yes," I said, squashed. "What will Melanie do?"

"She's gone away for a while," Mrs. White put in. "To recover. You'll see how much better she is in a few weeks."

"Where's she gone?" I demanded.

"Don't you worry," the pastor soothed. "She'll be safe with the Lord."

Dawn

James Purdy

At what point does a young man or woman become an adult in the eyes of his or her parents? That is the question James Purdy tackles in his short story "Dawn." Born in Ohio in 1923, Purdy has published thirteen novels and several collections of short stories and poetry. He currently lives in Brooklyn, New York.

It wasn't as if Timmy had made his living posing nude and having his picture in the flesh magazines. Tim modeled clothes mostly and was making good money. But he did do one underwear modeling job and that was the one his dad saw in North Carolina. Wouldn't you know it would be! So his dad thought there must be more and worse ones. Nude ones, you know. His dad was a pill.

His dad came in to New York from the place he had lived in all his life. Population about four hundred people, probably counting the dead.

Well, his dad was something. He arrived in the dead of night or rather when the first streaks of morning were reaching the Empire State.

"Where is Timmy?" he said without even saying hello or telling me who he was (I recognized him from one of Tim's snapshots). He pushed right past me into the front room like a house detective with the passkey.

"Well, where is he?" He roared his question this time.

"Mr. Jaqua," I replied. "He just stepped out for a moment."

"I bet," the old man quipped. "Where does he sleep when he is at home?" he went on while looking around the apartment as if for clues.

I showed him the little room down the hall. He took a quick look inside and clicked his tongue in disapproval, and rushed right on back to the front room and helped himself to the big easy chair.

He brought out a raggedy clipping from his breast pocket.

"Have you laid eyes on this?" He beckoned for me to come over and see what he was holding.

It was the magazine ad of Tim all right, posing in very scanty red shorts.

I colored by way of reply and Mr. Jaqua studied me.

"I suppose there are more of these in other places," he accused me.

"Well!" He raised his voice when I did not reply.

"I don't poke my nose into his business," I said lamely. I colored again.

"I can't blame you if you don't." He was a bit conciliatory.

"See here, Freddy . . . You are Freddy, I suppose, unless he's changed roommates. Pay me mind. I wanted Tim to be a lawyer and make good money and settle down, but he was stagestruck from a boy of ten." Mr. Jaqua seemed to be talking to a large assembly of people, and looked out through my small apartment window into the street. "I've sent him enough money to educate four boys," he went on. "I could even have stood it, I think, if he had made good on the stage. But where are the parts he should have found? You tell me!" His eyes moved away from outdoors, and his gaze rested on me.

"He failed," the old man finished and looked at the underwear ad fiercely.

"But Tim had some good parts, Mr. Jaqua. Even on Broadway," I began my defense, but I was so stricken by this man's rudeness and insensitivity that I found myself finally just studying him as a spectacle.

"There's a screw loose somewhere." He ignored my bits of information about Tim's acting career. "I've come to take him home, Freddy."

He looked at me now very sadly, as if by studying me the underwear ad, the acting career, and the loose screw would all at last be explained.

"See here. Everybody saw this ad back home." He tapped the

clipping with his finger. "The damned thing was in the barber-shop, then it turned up in the pool parlor, I'm told, and the dentist's office, and God knows maybe finally in Sunday school and church."

"It paid good money, though, Mr. Jaqua."

"Good money," he repeated and I remembered then he was a trial lawyer.

"I should think it would, Freddy," he sneered as if finally dismissing me as a witness.

"It's very tough being an actor, Mr. Jaqua." I interrupted his silence. "I know because I am one. There's almost no serious theater today, you see."

"Do you have any coffee in the house, Freddy?" he said after another prolonged silence.

"I have fresh breakfast coffee, sir. Would you like a cup?"

"Yes, that would be nice." He folded the advertisement of the red shorts and put it back in his pocket until it would be produced again later on.

"What I'd like better, though," he said after sipping a little of my strong brew, "would you let me lie down on his bed and get some rest pending his arrival?"

Mr. Jaqua never waited for my nod of approval, for he went immediately to the bedroom and closed the door energetically.

"Your dad is here," I told Timmy as he came through the door.

"No," he moaned. He turned deathly pale, almost green. "Jesus," he whimpered.

"He's lying down on your bed," I explained.

"Oh, Freddy," he said. "I was afraid this would happen one day . . . What does he want?"

"Seems he saw you in that underwear ad."

Tim made a grimace with his lips that looked like the smile on a man I once saw lying dead of gunshot wounds on the street. I looked away.

"He expects you to go home with him, Timmy," I warned him.

"Oh, Christ in heaven!" He sat down in the big chair, and picked up the coffee cup his dad had left and sipped some of it. It was my turn to show a queer smile.

Tim just sat on there then for an hour or more while I pretended to do some cleaning up of our apartment, all the while watching him every so often and being scared at what I saw.

Then all at once, as if he had heard his cue, he stood up, squared his shoulders, muttered something, and without a look or word to me, he went to the bedroom door, opened it, and went in.

At first the voices were low, almost whispers, then they rose in a high, dizzy crescendo, and there was cursing and banging and so on as in all domestic quarrels. Then came a silence, and after that silence I could hear Tim weeping hard. I had never heard him or seen him cry in all our three years of living together. I felt terribly disappointed somehow. He was crying like a little boy.

I sat down stunned as if my own father had come back from the dead and pointed out all my shortcomings and my poor record as an actor and a man.

Finally they came out together, and Tim had his two big suitcases in hand.

"I'm going home for a while, Freddy," he told me, and this time he smiled his old familiar smile. "Take this." He extended a big handful of bills.

"I don't want it, Timmy."

His father took the bills from him then—there were several hundred-dollar ones—and pressed them hard into my hand. Somehow I could accept them from Mr. Jaqua.

"Tim will write you when he gets settled back home. Won't you, Tim?" the old man inquired as they went out the door.

After their footsteps died away, I broke down and cried, not like a young boy, but like a baby. I cried for over an hour. And strange to say I felt almost refreshed at shedding so many bitter tears. I realized how badly I had suffered in New York, and how much I loved Timmy, though I knew he did not love me very much in return. And I knew then as I do now I would never see him again.

A Chinese Banquet

Kitty Tsui

Kitty Tsui, the author of the poetry collection The Words of a Woman Who Breathes Fire, *grew up in Hong Kong and England. In "A Chinese Banquet," Tsui evokes the feelings of isolation, frustration, and hope she experiences upon attending a family gathering to which her partner was not invited.*

for the one who was not invited

it was not a very formal affair but
all the women over twelve
wore long gowns and a corsage,
except for me.

it was not a very formal affair, just
the family getting together,
poa poa, kuw fu without *kuw mow**
(her excuse this year is a headache).

aunts and uncles and cousins,
the grandson who is a dentist,
the one who drives a mercedes benz,
sitting down for shark's fin soup.

they talk about buying a house and
taking a two week vacation in beijing.

---

* *Poa poa:* maternal grandmother; *kuw fu:* uncle; *kuw mow:* aunt.

i suck on shrimp and squab,
dreaming of the cloudscape in your eyes.

my mother, her voice beaded with sarcasm:
you're twenty six and not getting younger.
it's about time you got a decent job.
she no longer asks when i'm getting married.

you're twenty six and not getting younger.
what are you doing with your life?
you've got to make a living.
why don't you study computer programming?

she no longer asks when i'm getting married.
one day, wanting desperately to
bridge the boundaries that separate us,
wanting desperately to touch her,

tell her: mother, i'm gay,
mother i'm gay and so happy with her.
but she will not listen,
she shakes her head.

she sits across from me,
emotions invading her face.
her eyes are wet but
she will not let tears fall.

mother, i say,
you love a man.
i love a woman.
it is not what she wants to hear.

aunts and uncles and cousins,
very much a family affair.
but you are not invited,
being neither my husband nor my wife.

aunts and uncles and cousins
eating longevity noodles
fragrant with ham inquire:
sold that old car of yours yet?

i want to tell them: my back is healing,
i dream of dragons and water.
my home is in her arms,
our bedroom ceiling the wide open sky.

Commitments

Essex Hemphill

Essex Hemphill is the author of Ceremonies *and the editor of* Brother to Brother: New Writings by Black Gay Men. *In his poem "Commitments," Hemphill describes himself as "the invisible son," unseen by his family, who do not acknowledge that he is gay. Hemphill lives in Philadelphia.*

I will always be there.
When the silence is exhumed.
When the photographs are examined
I will be pictured smiling
among siblings, parents,
nieces and nephews.

In the background of the photographs
the hazy smoke of barbecue,
a checkered red-and-white tablecloth
laden with blackened chicken,
glistening ribs, paper plates,
bottles of beer, and pop.

In the photos
the smallest children
are held by their parents.
My arms are empty, or around
the shoulders of unsuspecting aunts
expecting to throw rice at me someday.

Or picture tinsel, candles,
ornamented, imitation trees,
or another table, this one
set for Thanksgiving,
a turkey steaming the lens.

My arms are empty
in those photos, too,
so empty they would break
around a lover.

I am always there
for critical emergencies,
graduations,
the middle of the night.

I am the invisible son.
In the family photos
nothing appears out of character.
I smile as I serve my duty.

Gun-Shy

Sean Mills

Born in Iowa, Sean Mills grew up in the Land of Lincoln and attended Knox College. His novel-in-progress, Gun-Shy, *explores the friendship between Sonny and Jack, two college students at a midwestern school. In the excerpt below, Sonny's parents come to visit their son in an apartment he has just moved into with Jack. Sonny's father knows that his son is gay and wonders whether Sonny and Jack are more than "just friends."*

"So . . . is he a, a friend or a . . . *friend?*"

"Dad, he's just a friend."

"A friend," his father tried his luck, "a friend . . . who you've *been* with?"

Sonny overreacted, came back with, "Oh Dad, why don't you just come out with it?! Just say it. Have I lain with him? Do I know him in the biblical sense? The answer is no. Not yet."

His father was a tough nut to crack, thought Sonny, but he was coming along. He remembered the end of his first (and only) therapy session with his father's friend, "a good Catholic psychiatrist," when his father was asked to join them, and talk of "behavior modification," psychotherapy, buzzed in the air. It was one of the original bees, one that stung like a hornet when Sonny was defenseless, allergic. His father didn't want him to "act on his desires"; he wanted to take steps to systematically prevent the possibility of sex with men—or sex, period, for that matter. "And what about the AIDS thing," his father catechized his friend in front of wincing, exasperated Sonny on the slippery leather couch. His father discovered that his friend hadn't done psychotherapy in twenty-

five years, that when he had tried it, he never really had much
success. Sonny wondered about the sort-of success cases, some of
whom married or were "more comfortable" with members of the
opposite sex. They were probably lost souls rattling the chains of
purgatorial marriage; he thought of tearooms, back rooms, the wives,
frustration, beatings, pain . . .

"Jerry, I'll tell you now, it just won't work," said the therapist.
He shifted his cross-legged, pedantic inquisition to Sonny and asked,
"Sonny, do you *want* to be gay?" He couldn't remember his answer, and it didn't matter, because he sensed he was only being
listened to, not heard, then; talked at and over, not with.

They discussed the option of Sonny marrying into some sort of
stable configuration where a wife and possibly children were kept
in outer orbits separate to that of a proposed male lover who could
stay in a free range somewhere close to his sexual nucleus. To
Sonny, who hated chemistry in high school because it was too
abstract, this sounded like juggling, something he never got the
hang of either because if he got two balls going, the introduction
of the third usually fumbled everything.

He also registered, "Now it's my understanding that one man
can just look at another and tell whether or not he's gay, isn't this
true, Sonny?" He answered affirmatively, but was saved from
saying anything else by more compulsive AIDS questions from
his father. Luckily, his ignorance undermined the aimless hour as
he revealed the real clincher: Sonny found out his dad imagined
that AIDS just happened when two men had sex, like sponta-
neous generation. He realized his father really did think then that
if Sonny lusted, or even fell in love, if he gave in to himself just
once, he'd get sick if he touched another man with sex in mind—
he'd be the cause of his own disease. Then the session turned
completely toward his father, ended with a ". . . let me find you
something to read, Jare, or maybe Sonny has a few suggestions
. . ." Sonny excused himself to go to the bathroom, and he never
went back. . . .

One unseasonably hot day in April, a few weeks before his move,
Sonny ventured on a whim to a barber in town, where he had all
his long winter hair buzzed off down to an eighth of an inch.
When he returned, cooled, he walked his bike slowly, habitually

running his hand back and forth over the top of his head, getting used to the velvety bristles of his GI Joe hair. As he locked the bike up outside his suite, he heard "fag" whooping from a shady upper balcony across the quad. He was unmoved, unsure he was even the target for the name, which didn't sink in but beaded up and rolled off him anyway, like rain. But then, "Hey, nice hair! Did you catch AIDS, faggot?!" whipped across the way from a pale beefcake in a Raiders cap and boxer shorts. These words hit him like snot dredged up, gutturally, and spat at him with viscid rancor. Unflinching, he secured the shaky Kryptonite bike lock and retreated slowly through the suite to his room, trying the lock on his door with one, then another misguided key. Sonny sat on his bed, snuffed, shade drawn against the world, still rubbing his hair; he was paralyzed in the dark, a quiescent, festering adult packaged in a nest, a lair, one his parents took comfort in because it was economical, safe.

Sonny's parents stood very close together by the front door, eyeing the furling ceiling tapestries, Aztec wall blankets, incense burners, and a two-foot-long water bong peeking out suspiciously from behind a tie-dyed curtain. His father finally made an attempt at bolstering the perfunctory introductions: "So, Jack, I hear you're a painter," he said, as his mother tensed visibly, having already taken in Jack's Delta Ninety-Eight censoriously when Sonny received his parents in the driveway. It had been finger-painted with handprints, footprints, and animal effigies. "Sonny, whose is that?" she gasped, knowing, but fearing, the answer.

Things limped along, like beginning tennis players trying to establish a volley. "Well, I paint, too," his father tried to identify with Jack, "but not like anything you do. I paint houses, just in the summer when I'm out of school. I'm not artistically inclined—I've never done paintings or . . . cars."

Sonny, of course, tried to stay as far away from Jack as possible, moving to opposite corners of the room. He couldn't get any closer. They repelled like two tiny dog magnets pushed against one another the wrong way. He viewed Jack distantly, sizing him up as his parents did, but from another oblique angle. Jack had dressed in tight jeans and a moth-eaten brown turtleneck; his hair was wet, slicked back so the scraggly blond ends disappeared. He looked good. He'd have been perfectly acceptable if he offered a handshake or removed his hands from his pockets in some sort of accommodating gesture, or even said, "Come on in and have a seat." Sonny wished he'd doff his tattered, olive-drab army coat, but restrained himself and didn't dare ask him to do this, let alone suggest it. Jack drew it around his slumping figure like broken wings, one of the protective layers he required and often wore indoors. There was also the corona of haze framing Jack's un-shaven face, the ghost of a nervous cigarette lying curled and dead in the ashtray, its life cut short by their footsteps on the stairs outside their rooms. The smoke softened his sunken features, air-brushed tiny lines and occasional pimples out like an Olan Mills portrait, a senior picture.

Sonny tuned back in, hearing his father inviting Jack to come along with them to mass and breakfast later at The Family Table. Sonny'd forewarned Jack of the requisite Sunday mass when his parents stopped through town on weekends, so Jack declined more or less politely when he was invited along. Jack chuckled warmly, to Sonny's disbelief, about the restaurant, replying, "Oh, The Stable." He smiled more sheepishly now, and looked at his feet. His parents were befuddled, intrigued by Jack's sudden anima-tion. "Sorry, I mean . . . that's what we like to call it. Great place, you get tons of food for cheap." He said no more.

"Yes," his father agreed, reciprocating the chuckle stiffly, his eyes roving first to his wife, then to his son. Sonny volunteered an alibi for Jack, and Jack piped up again, agreeing, said he had to keep working. At least the tension had broken, there was ner-vous moving about. "Mom, Dad, come see my room before we head out." Sonny led his parents to his cleaned-up room and showed them around. His father fixated immediately on safety things: the overloaded wall socket, an extension cord run under a rug, a lamp placed too close to a curtain. Sonny's father sniffed the air, smell-ing smoke, cleared his throat and spoke up. "Sonnyboy, I know your roommate smokes, right? But you don't, do you?" Sonny shook his head, shushed him.

"Well even if you do occasionally, just don't smoke in bed, okay?"

"Dad, that's just incense you smell in here, I don't smoke," he lied. "Also the oil lamp, and candles."

"Well, you just be careful," he went on, "stay by these things at all times when you're using them." He pulled back the tattered throw rug to inspect the cord, businesslike as a fire chief. "And this," he clucked, "I don't like the looks of this either."

As he began again to lecture on more fire safety tips, Sonny changed the subject, turning to his mother, and began discussing the upcoming presidential election.

"Who're ya voting for, Mom? Not for Bush again, are you?" They moved out of his room, back through the living room now, his father eventually following.

She was defensive, matter-of-fact. "Well, honey, you know my stance. Bush is the only choice as far as I'm concerned. How can you think of voting for someone who's *for* abortion?" They were all on their way out, except Jack, who was still pacing in the living room. Sonny's exiting parents were tacitly sweet, his mother's White Shoulders lingering behind her like room freshener.

"Well, Jack, it was sure nice to have met you," Sonny's father said at the door. "Hope you and Sonny make out all right." Sonny remembered thinking, Dad, do you really mean what you're saying? If he only knew; Sonny could only hope. He continued the discussion through the front door and down the stairwell, which he was sure Jack was overhearing. "But Mom, Bush used to be for abortion, over a decade ago, before Reagan. He's a hypocrite, a Trojan horse, he'll say anything to get reelected." He was reacting assertively, like Jack. His mother was wounded; her face read something like, "So is this how you think now. Who's taught you to be like this?" She responded, "Sonny, how can you say that?"

Sonny escorted his parents to church now; Jack, the atheist, stayed behind. Outside, as they approached the curb, Sonny stopped in his tracks at seeing a new red, white, and blue bumper sticker on the back of their gleaming Mercury. He dropped behind them. It read: "I (heart) BABIES, BORN AND UNBORN (fetus)." He hoped Jack wasn't watching out the window. As Sonny plopped into the back seat and slammed his door, he found his mom and dad already belted in securely, the eyes of father stray-

ing on son in the rear-view mirror until Sonny caught them, caus-
ing a reflexive wrist flick of the ignition key. The engine turned
over immediately and idled high for its prescribed couple of minutes as they all just sat there, settling in, not wanting to take off
prematurely. Sonny's parents looked ahead beneath their visors
with glazed reticence; his father pulled a garish Reebok off the
accelerator and absentmindedly massaged his khaki thigh, his pulled
hamstring, Sonny speculated, the chronic ailment of an amateur
runner who didn't like to race, the jogger who rarely ran. He
awaited commentary from the front seat, some sort of validation
of his new life with Jack, about which he sensed they'd just as
soon not react to as remain in a state of dumbfounded piety (or
pity). Cluelessness is next to godliness, he thought.

"So what'd you think?" Sonny ventured. Their silence, their
timidity, vexed him. He would take anything at this point, a re-
affirming grunt, nod, or sigh somehow bringing closure to the
encounter. His mother, finally, unable to turn her face to the back
seat, sniffled. Having come to some sort of conclusion, she pulled
a limp wad of lipsticky Kleenex out from her purse and pushed it
up against her nostrils; they flared as fingertips dabbed luxu-
riantly, pugging her nose. She braced herself and spoke: "You live
like flower children," she blurted, cushioning it with a laugh as
she began to cry.

Night Kites

M. E. Kerr

In M. E. Kerr's novel Night Kites, *Erick Rudd, a straight high school student, discovers that his older brother, Pete, has contracted the virus that causes AIDS. "How could Pete get* that?*" asks Erick. As the story progresses, Erick learns that HIV, the virus that causes AIDS, cannot be transmitted through casual contact but only through an exchange of bodily fluids, such as blood or semen. The novel also charts the bond that develops between the two brothers as Pete opens up about being gay and having AIDS. In the scene below, Erick is visiting Pete in his New York City apartment the day after Pete informed the family of his illness.*

"How's Dad taking this?" Pete asked me. "I couldn't really tell."

"He's worried about your health. I am, too."

"I don't mean my health."

"I think he's hurt."

"Because I told Mom I'm gay but not him, hmmm?"

"Yeah."

"And you, pal? I was planning to tell you."

"When I grew up, or what?"

"I don't blame you for being pissed off, Ricky. I was waiting for the right time."

"You act like you had a crime to confess or something. I'm not Dad, Pete. I told Dad last night: It's just another way of being. It's not a crime. It's not anything to be ashamed about."

Pete got up to play the other side of the tape. "I thought you sort of knew anyway."

"How would I sort of know?" I said. "You sort of know about someone like Charlie Gilhooley, but how would I sort of know about you?"

Pete went back and sat down. "I never brought any women home. I never talked about any women. I'm twenty-seven years old."

"You talked about going out to discos, dancing all night."

"Yeah, I guess I did. I didn't say they were gay discos."

"What about Belle Michelle?"

"That was ten or eleven years ago," Pete said. "Michelle always knew about me. I never tried to fool *her*. I didn't want her to think the reason I didn't make any passes had anything to do with her."

"We always thought she was your big love. Dad thought she threw you over and you never got over it."

"Michelle and I were just great pals, at a time when we both needed pals. She was in her wheelchair, and I was in my closet." Pete smiled. "Michelle said as long as I stayed in my closet, she'd understand perfectly if I parked my car in a handicapped space, too."

"So when did you tell Mom?"

"Right before I went to Europe last summer."

"Dad made it sound like she'd always known."

"Maybe she did, deep down—I don't know. . . . Getting up the courage to tell Mom was the hardest thing I ever had to do," Pete said. "How many times have you heard Mom say we were the perfect family? She and Dad never played around on each other, never even had a fight that lasted overnight . . . and while all their friends' kids were raising every kind of hell, we were the good boys. We didn't do drugs, or drink, or cheat in school, or wrap the family car around trees."

"You came close," I said.

"I got a few speeding tickets."

"I know what you mean, though," I said. "Mom always thought we were the Waltons, or the Lawrences on 'Family.' "

"My God, the Lawrences!" Pete winced. "I forgot how Mom loved to watch the Lawrences: Buddy and Willy and Kate and Jim, et cetera, happy ever after in that big blue house, wrapping up every problem from adultery to abortion in sixty minutes flat, with time out for commercials."

"She still watches the reruns," I said. "Yeah, I always thought *I* was going to be the one to blot the family record."

Pete chuckled. "Not your big brother, hmmm?"

"I didn't mean that you're blotting the family record, Pete."

"I know you didn't," Pete said, "but I'm not exactly enhancing it. . . . So I kept thinking, why do Mom and Dad have to know? I managed to grow up without opening that boil. Why start all the guilt/blame machinery going now? I was never crazy about self-revelation, either. I always hated people who got on the tube and confessed they were alcoholics or anorexics or Jesus freaks or some other damn thing!"

I said, "When I'd watch gays on talk shows, I'd wonder why they'd announce it. Dad said they were exhibitionists."

"I thought they were, too," Pete said. "I used to sit watching those things hoping to God they'd look as straight as possible. I used to hate seeing any Charlie Gilhooleys coming out of the closet."

"Poor Charlie just got beat up at the Kingdom By The Sea bar," I said.

"I'm sorry, but I'm not surprised," Pete said. "I used to stay as far away from Charlie Gilhooley as possible. Sometimes, when I was a kid, *I* felt like beating him up. I'd tell myself I might be gay, but I'm not a Charlie Gilhooley fairy!"

"Well, you're not," I said.

"So what?" said Pete. "Do I get extra points for not looking it? . . . I used to think I did."

"Then what changed you?" I said. "What made you tell Mom?"

Pete took a fast gulp of coffee, and it sloshed down the side of his mug to the tabletop. "Jim Stanley went to work on me," he said.

He started to get up, for something to wipe up the coffee.

"I'll get it," I said.

I went into the kitchen for a sponge. I was trying to remember Jim Stanley. I'd met him only once. He wrote science-fiction stories and screenplays as J. J. Stanley, and called himself "bicoastal" because he traveled back and forth from New York to Beverly Hills. Pete had gone to Europe with him last summer.

When they came back, we'd all had dinner together, at a restaurant in SoHo, in lower New York. Pete and Jim had just come from having drinks at Stan and Tina Horton's loft down there. Jim was Pete's age, tall, sandy-haired. I remembered he'd talked a lot about Rachter, this program that rigged a computer to write novels. He was working on an idea for a TV series about a Rachterlike character in an office, who told stories about the employees. . . . I couldn't remember anything else about him.

While I wiped up the coffee, Pete said, "Jim's a political gay. I used to hate gay activists! I used to think they were a bunch of self-pitying sissies who blamed everything on the fact they were homosexuals. I used to tell Jim that what I did in bed was my own private business. Jim said that was right: What I did in bed *was*, but what about life out of bed? What about lying to everyone, trying to pass for straight, never letting family or friends know what was going on in my life? . . . He convinced me the only way to get past that kind of self-hatred was to come out of hiding. He said anyone who loved me wouldn't love me any less if I came out, and I'd like myself a lot more. So I started with Mom. You were next on my list."

I tossed the sponge at the sink, missed, left it on the kitchen floor. "What'd Mom say when you told her?"

"She said she wasn't surprised. She said she was glad I told her. And she said she used to worry that I was too much of a loner."

"That's what I always thought you were, too," I said.

"A loner." I sat down.

"I was. A busy loner."

"What's a busy loner?"

"Active, but not really attached," Pete said. "Too busy. . . . That's why I never did anything about finishing *The Skids*—or finishing my Ph.D."

"Oh, *that*," I said a little contemptuously, as though Dad was in the room with us.

"Dad was right about that," Pete said. "I should have gone to Columbia, or N.Y.U., and finished it. I should have worked on my book, too," Pete said. "But when I landed here right out of Princeton, I couldn't believe the gay scene. It was still the seventies. There'll never be another time like it. I thought I'd died and gone to heaven. I wasn't out at Princeton, naturally. When I saw all the gay bars and discos here, I just wanted to dance and drink and play."

I couldn't imagine Pete dancing with another guy.

I said, "When I get out of college, if I ever get into college, I'll probably want to dance and drink and play, too."

Pete shook his head. "No. You're having your party right now. My adolescence was on hold. . . . I could hardly take Tim Lathrop to the Seaville High Prom, or Marty to the P-Party. We sneaked around like guilty thieves. Tim spent half his time at confession, and Marty was seeing if a shrink could make him straight. . . . That's when I became the world's foremost authority on gay books." Pete laughed. "Migod! I don't think there's a book that even remotely touched on the subject that I didn't read. I spent hours in the library looking under H in the card catalog!"

I was remembering Tim Lathrop as Pete talked. Tim had been a lifeguard on Main Beach when Pete was. He was this blond hunk who was at our house a lot when Pete was in his teens, one of the star tennis players at Holy Family High. . . . Marty Olivetti was still one of Pete's closest friends. He was from Tulsa, Oklahoma. He'd come from Princeton with Pete for weekends years ago, and they'd spent most of their time out on the boat. When Dad first met him, I remembered Dad'd imitate Marty's thick Oklahoma accent, and tease, "What kind of an Italian says 'far' for 'fire' and 'pank' for 'pink'?"

Pete got up to get himself another cup of coffee. A minute later he zapped me with the soggy sponge I'd left on the kitchen floor, calling me *"Cochon!"*

I threw it back at him, and for a while we were feinting punches at each other, and ducking, horsing around in the old familiar way.

But Pete looked beat. When I said I ought to be leaving soon, Pete didn't protest. He said he probably shouldn't have any more coffee—it'd only give him the trots.

Pete said he needed a nap, too, that Stan and Tina were coming by later, and Jim was flying in from the coast that night. He said he'd try to bring Jim out to Seaville for dinner one night next week.

"Does Jim know you have this thing?" I asked him.

"Say AIDS, Ricky," Pete said. "Mom and Dad are calling it a thing, a bug, everything but AIDS. . . . Yes, Jim knows. We were both sick all through Europe. I kept telling myself I had what he had, some kind of dysentery. But my lymph nodes were swollen, and I had these little red spots on my ankles. I had all these explanations to myself for what they were. But I couldn't ever get my strength back, and there were more spots. I began to really panic by the time I came out to Seaville last time. Mom wanted me to go see Doctor Rapp there. By then I had this big purple bruise under my arm. When I saw that, I began to face the fact I could have AIDS. I figured old Rapp would broadcast it all over the Hadefield Club. Dad would like that a lot!"

"Stop worrying about Dad," I said, as Pete helped me get on my blazer.

"I worry about him the most," Pete said. "I think this is going to be hardest on Dad. Most of the time he spent here last night, he was on the phone to Phil Kerin. Do you remember Doctor Kerin? One of Dad's old golf cronies?"

"Dad told me he called him."

"Dad must have said 'This is confidential' a dozen times during the conversation. . . . I could have gone from the hospital to Dad's place last night, but Dad was afraid to let you kids stay here. He said if it ever got out that I have AIDS, and he'd known you kids were here, he'd be responsible for putting you at risk."

"I don't get that," I said. "Dad told me there was no way you could catch it casually."

"He's worried that other people don't know that."

"Dad makes everything hard!"

"No, Ricky. This time it's just hard. It's not Dad."

We stood there facing each other a minute.

I said, "I just want you to get well."

"You've made me feel better, pal. Thanks," Pete said. He slung his arm around my shoulder. "The last thing Dad said to me last night was 'Whoever got the bright idea to come up with the name "gay"?' " Pete was doing a good imitation of Dad at his darkest. " 'It doesn't sound like a very *gay* life to me!' "

A Whisper in the Veins

Terry Wolverton

When does a person stop growing up? In her short story "A Whisper in the Veins," Terry Wolverton suggests that growing up and coming to terms with one's parents is a lifelong process. Gregory, the central character in Wolverton's story, thinks back on a variety of childhood memories as he searches for the right moment to tell his now elderly mother, whom he has not seen in several years, about the results of his HIV test. Wolverton, a writer of fiction, poetry, essays, and drama, is currently writer-in-residence at the Gay and Lesbian Community Services Center in Los Angeles.

The apartment is small and ugly modern, and I stand tracking mud and melted snow onto the nondescript linoleum of its tiny kitchen. My mother rises from her rocking chair where she's been reading the paper, padding into the kitchen in her stockinged feet.

I stare at her feet as I remember a story she used to tell me when I was a child. "I always wanted to have fat feet," the story begins. "Mine are skinny and narrow and I thought it would be just wonderful to have fat feet." She never explained where this standard of beauty originated—she takes it for granted that anyone would understand the desire. "So one day I was walking outdoors and I stepped on a bee. I did it on purpose because I knew it would make my foot swell. What I didn't know is that it would be so painful!"

Her arms close around me and I lean down to kiss her cheek. She takes my coat and spreads a newspaper where I can leave my wet shoes. The darkened leather warns me that these Cole-Haan loafers will never be the same. It wasn't snowing in D.C., where I started from this morning. I tell her I have only the afternoon, a more or less impulsive stopover on my way home from a business trip.

I follow her in my damp socks into the living room. I recognize a few of the pieces of furniture that I grew up with—an old desk, a large oak bureau, my father's stuffed green chair—but they seem unfamiliar in this square room. Against one wall a television is flickering, though the sound is turned down. It's not the same one that I last saw in my parents' house. Most of the furniture is new, bought from Sears or Montgomery Ward on time payments.

I sit in my father's chair. She is anxious and shy with me, bustling around making coffee, tidying up the scattered pieces of the paper, wanting to get me a sweater, though the room isn't cold. She asks if I need to go to the bathroom. I don't. I pick up the front page of the paper and retreat into reading it, sinking into news of a plane crash, a treaty negotiated, the predictions of a dire year for agriculture.

My mother brings me a cup of pale brown coffee. She's always made her coffee weak. "Looks like rain, but it smells like coffee," my father used to joke. She interrupts my reading to ask if I'd like some toast or a cinnamon roll. Monosyllabic, I indicate my preference for the former and begin studying Ann Landers's advice to a woman whose relatives criticize her housekeeping.

After I've scanned the comics, my mother pulls the card table over in front of my chair. The table is draped with a lacy crocheted tablecloth, which covers a cotton cloth printed with red cherries. I remember the cherries from the kitchen table in my childhood. She sets a plate of toast on top and moves my coffee cup beside it. I lay the paper aside, pick up a heavily buttered slice of toast and dunk it in my coffee cup. This is something I do only when I'm with my mother. It is her custom, and in her house I observe it.

Little crumbs bob in the cup and a puddle of melted butter creates a rainbow slick on the surface of the coffee. The soaking bread dissolves easily in my mouth.

"How are you? Have you been healthy?" my mother asks, still shyly. This is an innocent question, standard in my mother's repertoire.

I nod, noncommittally. I'm caught off guard, and glance at her suspiciously. I've come here to tell her something, but I can't just blurt it out to her, not in this small ugly room with the television flickering.

My mother doesn't wait for an answer. Her attention has wandered to the screen, where characters in a soap opera act out their dramas. When I was a child I used to watch these with my mother when I'd stay home from school. I have friends who are too sick to work anymore and they stay home every day and watch the soaps. When they're not talking about their symptoms or a new doctor or the latest experimental treatment, they talk about the stories on the soaps.

"Erica's going to get what's coming to her now," my mother remarks, referring to the woman on the screen whose evil good looks invite fascination and loathing. I don't know what Erica's got coming to her, but I can tell by looking at her she has karmic debts to pay. I've heard Jerry and Stuart talk about Erica, but since I don't follow the soaps, I've never paid much attention.

"How've you been feeling, Mom?" I change the subject.

She starts a little, shifts her attention back to me, and blinks behind her glasses. My mother's never worn glasses before, I realize, and she's picked out a really stupid pair, ones which are not flattering to her face or coloring. They're also at least ten years out of fashion.

It makes me crazy when my mother's cheap. I know that my father left her a comfortable sum of money, but here she is in a drab apartment, shopping at Sears and buying tacky polyester pantsuits and stupid glasses. I really ought to take her shopping.

I used to do that when I was younger. My father was appalled, but as a fifteen-year-old boy I liked nothing better than to take my mother shopping. We'd drive over to one of the better department stores—I always insisted on that—and spend the afternoon amid the racks of women's Sportswear, Better Dresses, Town and Country. My mother was amazed that I had such a sense of women's clothing; I knew fabrics, lines, designer labels. She always swore I had better taste than she did. My mother was still an attractive woman then, and I loved to make her look gorgeous.

Now she has terrible glasses and a bad perm. This makes me sad. It's been a couple of years since I've seen her—the last time was at my father's funeral.

"Oh, I'm all right, I guess. I have such a hard time sleeping," she complains softly in answer to my question. "And I still have these stomach pains when I eat."

"Didn't the doctor tell you to stop drinking coffee?" She has told me this about her stomach in several of our phone conversations. I've tried to call her more regularly since my father died.

"Well, yes, but I don't drink it very much." She is distracted; she really wants to find out what's going to happen to Erica.

My mother and I were very close, up until I was about nineteen. That's when I told her I was gay. She took it hard, a lot harder than my father. I suppose he had always known. It disgusted him, but it wasn't a surprise. I think my mother blamed herself. Maybe she heard my father's hundreds of admonishments—"You're spoiling him, Mae"—and took them to heart for the first time.

Anyway, we'd said some terrible things to each other then, and I upped and moved to L.A. My parents became a distant memory, a photograph. I'd send presents at Christmas and cards on birthdays, but they had no part in my daily life.

The soap ends and my mother moves across the room and presses the button that turns the TV off. The picture disappears from the screen, collapsing in on itself, and the room is suddenly darker. She shuffles to the other corner of the room and turns on a lamp. I recognize the lamp from my father's den in the old house, but as with the other familiar objects in the room it is unfamiliar here.

"Do you want some more coffee," she asks awkwardly, standing by the window with its cheap lace curtains, "or some more toast? Can I make you a tuna sandwich?" She's happy to see me, but doesn't know exactly what to do with me.

"Let's play some cards," I suggest, and she smiles in relief. She indicates for me to lift my plate and saucer, then she peels the crocheted cloth off the table, revealing more fully the faded splendor of the printed cherries below. She goes to the bureau and slides open a drawer, easily finding the deck in its proper place. She pulls a folding chair to the opposite side of the card table, and sits.

The cards are well worn—I recognize the deck with its illustration of hunting dogs on the back. The game is gin rummy, the continuation of a ritual begun in my early childhood. Whenever I'd be home sick, or on nights when my father didn't get home on time, or on holidays when there was no place to go, even on the night of my father's funeral after the guests had gone home—my mother and I would compete for the Gin Rummy Championship of the World.

She liked to devise an elaborate score sheet, with three games at once. If you won a hand, your score was entered in the first game. When you won another hand, that was added to your earlier total while at the same time got you entered into the second game.

Gin rummy brings out a competitive streak that is seldom seen otherwise in either of our personalities. My mother is a cutthroat card player, and she'll watch with cunning which cards I pick up, which I discard, and plan her strategy accordingly.

I spread my hand open in front of my face and sort through: a pair of dark kings and the jack of spades—I can play that either way, hoping for a third king or the queen of spades. I have the four, five, six of clubs. Nothing else to speak of, but I can build from there.

"You," I announce, waving my cards at her, "have dealt me a supreme hand!" We bluff to torment one another. "You really ought to shuffle better."

"One card," she teases back. "Just give me one card."

I once taught this game to Stuart, during one of the bad periods when he was bedridden. It had been hard for him to concentrate and he was easy to beat. I'd felt guilty about winning, but didn't know how not to.

My mother's brow is furrowed as she tries to decide whether to pick up the jack of spades I just discarded or take her chances from the deck. She chooses a new card and her face lights up.

"I'm going to knock with four points!" she crows triumphantly, spreading her cards on top of the cherries.

I lay down my three kings, my four, five, six of clubs. I have two deuces which I toss to the side to offset her four points. I'm still holding the eight of hearts and the ace of diamonds.

"Nine points," I say glumly, and she gleefully records this on her score sheet.

As she deals again I watch her hands. I've always loved my mother's hands. They are strong still, and heavily veined, spotted now with age, but agile as she flips the cards into a pile in front of me.

As has been our custom now for many years, she asks me nothing about my life. "How's your job?" she'll say, expecting and gratified to hear, "Oh, about the same." She'll ask about my house—I've sent her pictures of the Spanish-style home in the Hollywood Hills where Robert and I used to live together—but not about what it's like to live there alone now, or if in fact I am living there alone.

I win the next hand—all the right cards just come to me, as they always seem to do when I don't care about winning—with an extra twenty-five points for ginning. I don't know how I'm going to say what I've come all this way to tell her.

She wants to know if I've seen any movies and we talk about the latest releases. Some of my favorites are independents that won't make it to this part of the country. Outside the window I can see it starting to snow more heavily, and the afternoon is growing dark.

She tells me that my cousin Lenore, her sister's daughter, has had a baby, a boy. She named it Gregory, which is my name, but also my grandfather's. I tell her something cute that my dog Jackson did recently. She smiles vaguely—she doesn't know a lot about dogs.

When Robert got sick, he had to call his parents in Waco, Texas, and tell them for the first time that he was gay. I remember lying in bed that morning, watching his neck flush and the muscles of his back tense as he listened to first his mother, then his father tell him that his illness was God's punishment. That they would pray for him. They never came to visit during those weeks when Robert was in the hospital, and I couldn't decide who he needed me to be most—his lover or his parent.

I want to tell my mother this story, as she quickly grasps the queen of diamonds and positions it in her hand. She discards the five of spades and I pick it up, although I have no use for it at all.

I'm playing recklessly now, totally without strategy, picking up and discarding with no thought for the consequences. When my mother wins, I'm holding seventy-three points in my hand.

She looks at me over the top of those unflattering frames and complains, "You're not concentrating! It's not fun if you make it so easy for me!" She dutifully records that she's won the first game and is perilously close to taking the second as well.

I deal, shuffling the cards automatically. I'm thinking about my test, just a couple of weeks ago, about the earnest counselor who gave me my results. She was wearing green eye shadow that was a bad color for her skin tone, and made more prominent the deep circles under her eyes.

My mother takes this hand easily and throws down her cards in disgust. "You're worse than your father!" she snorts.

My father was a terrible card player. He was a cabinetmaker, as his father had been, as so many men had once been in this lumber-rich part of the country. He trusted the grain of wood, the burls and knots, what he could see and shape with his own hands. The abstract patterns of clubs and diamonds and their possibilities were never real to him.

"I'm sorry." I smile, conciliatory. I glance at my watch. "I've got a couple more hours. Can I take you out for an early dinner somewhere?"

She looks out the window, where the blizzard is raging. "Do you think your plane will really take off?" She sounds both hopeful and fearful. "It's a real Michigan night." Her tone turns apologetic, as if she is afraid she's disappointing me. "I don't really feel like going out in all that. Why don't I just heat up a couple of Lean Cuisines in the microwave?"

I nod my assent, uncomfortably aware of the time passing. She gets up, gathers the cards into their pack before she asks, "You're done with these, aren't you?" I nod again. She returns them to their place in the bureau drawer on her way to the kitchen. I hear her opening the freezer.

"Where's the phone?" I want to know.

"It's in the bedroom. You'll see it. Don't you want to call De-rek?" Derek was a friend of mine in high school, someone I haven't seen since I moved away. My mother's run into him with his family a couple of times at the mall. "Or Elsa? She'll never forgive me if she hears you were in town and didn't call her." Elsa is my aunt, her sister.

"I'm just going to call the airlines and see if my plane is still taking off tonight." I wish I could keep the testiness out of my voice.

I step into her bedroom and am struck by the familiar scent of White Shoulders, the perfume my mother has always worn. Most of the furniture is the same as it was in the house I grew up in—the bed frame, the dresser, the dressing table. Missing is the large armoire that my father built, that housed his things.

I sit on the new rose-colored comforter. It's stuffed with fiber-fill, not down—my mother's cheapness again. The phone by the bed is a new thing; my father would never have put up with that. He had an inherent distrust of telephones—to him they were a vehicle for public, not private, communication. On the rare times he called me in California, probably not more than three times in the fifteen years I've lived there, he always delivered his message quickly, in a self-conscious truncated voice. And he always re-fused to leave a message if he got an answering machine.

An airline attendant with a flat Michigan accent informs me that the planes are flying, and on schedule. Looking outside at the blizzard I find this hard to believe, but I will it to be true. I glance at my watch—I should phone for a cab in about an hour.

I raise the window blind and press my nose to the cold glass. A circle of steam clouds the place where my nose has been. I trace a pattern into it, then watch it disappear as the steam evaporates.

Before leaving the bedroom, I stop to stare at a framed photo on the dressing table. It's a picture of my mother and father when they were in their early thirties, before I was born. She is sitting on his lap, her arms clasped around his neck. His head is thrown back. They are both laughing with abandon, in adoration, per-haps with lust. I never knew my parents like this but I love the photograph. I love knowing that for at least one moment in their lives they felt like this with each other.

Reluctantly, I go back to the living room. On the card table my mother has set out plates of bread; plastic containers of bean salad, coleslaw, cottage cheese; dishes of canned fruit in heavy syrup. The table is set and I stand there, not knowing what to do.

"Is your plane leaving?" she calls from the kitchen.

"Hard to believe, but they swear it's even on time. I should call a cab after we eat."

She sticks her head out of the kitchen. I'm struck by the mixture of regret and relief in her voice as she says, "It's too bad you're here such a short time. Are you sure you can't spend the night?"

I explain again about the clients I have to meet in L.A. in the morning. She bobs her head; she doesn't understand the laws of commerce, but she knows better than to think she can interrupt them.

"Go and wash your hands now. We're ready to eat." She shoos me toward the bathroom as the microwave begins to beep.

The liquid soap won't lather in my hands as I rub them together under a trickle of warm water. I stare at my face in the bathroom mirror. The blond profile, the tanned skin, the good haircut, all serve to hide the shadow that whispers in my veins.

Tell her, I say to the face in the mirror. Do what you've come to do. I nod in agreement, then turn to wipe my hands on the ridiculous tiny pink guest towels my mother has carefully displayed on the rack.

Ever the hostess, my mother has spooned everything from the Lean Cuisine trays onto plates, arranged it like a meal she has really cooked. The television is on again, this time with the sound.

"I hope you don't mind," she apologizes, indicating the screen. "I like to watch the news."

A man in a checkered suit so bad it's comic is drawing in chalk on a map—the local station here can't afford the fancy computer graphics that are routinely used to foretell the weather in L.A. He's chattering on about high-pressure systems, storms from the north, windchill factors.

I chew the bland food, better than airline food, I have to admit, but only by degrees. My mother laughs at some joke made by the weatherman.

When the sports report comes on I think I have a chance to get her attention. "Mom?" I venture.

She turns to me, already anticipating what she thinks I'm going to say. She's out of her seat, saying, "You want more milk? Can I get you anything else? Are you ready for some coffee? I have a nice pumpkin pie and a Dutch apple from the store—I can heat them up for us?"

"Mom, please just sit down!" My voice is harsher than I mean it to be. "I have something to say to you."

An edge creeps over her face, but she sits as I've asked her to.

The national news report has just begun, and I can feel her need to turn her attention there.

I once had to tell my mother about having broken the pocket watch that had belonged to her grandfather. I was about eight. It was real gold. She hadn't given me the watch yet; she told me she was keeping it for me until I was older and could appreciate its value. I kept taking it out to look at it and play with it until finally, somehow, I broke the crystal. I was sure it was irreparable and I was torn with guilt over destroying something that was precious to my mother. I didn't sleep the whole night before and when I finally told her, I cried. She was extremely kind. She said the watch could be fixed and that as soon as it was she would give it to me, since I had obviously learned to appreciate its worth.

When I was nineteen I was madly in love with Michael, a boy I'd met at college, and I expected her to share my elation. She instead responded that she was sickened, she hadn't raised me to be "that way," she was ashamed to call me her son.

After Robert died last year I called to tell her. "I don't know what to say," she said. "I don't understand, but I'm sorry if you hurt."

She sits before me now, her brown eyes cloudy behind her glasses. Her cheeks are soft and lined and tinged with rouge; her permed hair frizzes gently over her forehead. She still goes every two weeks to the beauty parlor, has it tinted a light brown.

She is my mother. She is seventy-one. Her husband is dead and she has one child, who lives in California. I think of all the ways we are known to each other, all the ways in which we are unknown.

Bravely, she speaks first. "What is it, Greg? What is it you want to tell me?" I see in her face a determination to hear whatever it is, and I love her fiercely for this.

I open my mouth, but the words that follow take me by surprise. "I want you to come to California. I want you to come and stay with me. I'll send you a ticket."

This is not what she expected either, whatever that might have been. She relaxes a little while she demurs. She's afraid to fly, especially with all the things that have been happening lately, the plane crashes, the hijackings. She sees them on the news. And she can't get away. She has her doctors' appointments. She helps Lenore out by watching the baby a few times a week. And what would she do in California anyway? She'd just be in the way.

"No," I contradict her, growing more insistent. "You should come right away. Get out of this winter! Come see my house! We'll go shopping! I'll send you a ticket this week!" I am seized with urgency.

She's overwhelmed. It's been years since I demanded anything of her. For this reason, more than any other, she agrees.

"I guess I could take a couple of weeks. But not next week—I get my hair done next week. I'll come the week after that." Her head is already full of plans: cancel the newspaper; get Mrs. Fletcher across the hall to bring in the mail; use up the food in the refrigerator so it doesn't go bad.

I sit back in my father's chair, full of surprise and accomplishment, though this is not what I had intended to accomplish. My news seems less important, somehow, than this plan.

I see it is time for me to start out for the airport. I go into the next room and call for a cab. Peering out the window I see that the snow has stopped, and the night beyond is cold and blue. Perhaps they'll have the runways cleared after all.

As I wait for the cab I help her wash the supper dishes. She washes, I dry and put away, just like when I was a kid. In what seems a very short time I hear the beep of a horn and see from the window a pair of headlights in the driveway below.

My coat is toasty from the heating vent where it's been drying all afternoon. My shoes are mottled, stiff and uncomfortable as I slip them on.

"Remember," I say as I give her a quick embrace, "I'm taking you shopping at Neiman Marcus." She giggles like a girl, and I shut the door behind me.

Mother and Child

Jeanne Manford and Morty Manford

A remarkable sight confronted spectators at New York City's second annual Christopher Street Liberation Day parade in June 1972. A simply dressed, middle-aged woman was carrying a sign that said, "Parents of Gays: Unite in Support for Our Children." No one watching the parade had ever seen anything like it before. For most gay people, who had yet even to tell their parents they were gay, such open support was almost beyond belief.

Jeanne Manford, an elementary school teacher and mother of gay rights activist Morty Manford, didn't think she was doing anything remarkable. She loved her son and believed he deserved her full support. But the experience of the march and the constant telephone calls from gay men and women and their parents in search of help made it clear to Jeanne and her son that there was more to be done than simply show support. They decided there was also a pressing need for an organization for parents of gay children.

Jeanne: When Morty was around fifteen, he asked if he could go to a psychologist. I couldn't believe he had problems, because he was always a leader. He always had a lot of friends. He had parties here. He was president of his student organization in his junior high. One of his teachers told me, "Send him to the best colleges. He's going to be a senator someday." When he said he needed help, both my husband and I said, "You think so? Sure, why not?" But we didn't know why. We later found out when the psychologist told us that Morty was gay. My initial reaction was to tell Morty that I wanted him to be happy and that whatever made him happy was fine with me. Morty was no different from the way he'd been the day before. I didn't look at him in a different light. I was very naïve; I didn't understand society's condemnation.

Morty: My father's initial reaction was to be quiet. He had a lot of thinking to do. He didn't say anything critical, but he just decided he had to think about it. I think he harbored a hope that things would change.

Within a year and a half, I became very involved in the gay liberation movement and was bringing friends home from the Gay Activists Alliance. We would sit down and talk with my parents about our civil rights demonstrations. These friends from the organization would speak with my parents, which was particularly helpful to my father. My father later commented that it was difficult for him to examine his attitudes by talking to me alone because there was a lot of emotional involvement. But as he started to speak to some of my friends, who had this heightened sense of gay consciousness, he felt he could consider the issues and the societal biases from a more detached and dispassionate view. That helped him reexamine his old attitudes.

Jeanne: I remember one night I got a phone call from the police at 1:00 A.M. "Your son is arrested."

Morty: I was in the police station, and the officer made the phone call. I remember that he went out of his way to say, "Your son has been arrested. And you know, he's homosexual."

Jeanne: I think my reply was something like, "Yes, I know. Why are you bothering him? Why don't you go after criminals and stop harassing the gays?"

Morty: I couldn't hear what my mother said, but the officer was scratching his head after he put down the phone. He had just been zapped.

Jeanne: I worried about Morty. I knew he could be hurt physically. That was always in the back of my mind, although I tried not to think about these things. I believed Morty had a right to do what he was doing. I didn't think he did anything unlawful. I believed he was being harassed. But I worried—there was one time when Morty did get hurt. That was in April 1972. He had been at the Hilton Hotel, giving out leaflets to the Inner Circle.

Morty: The Inner Circle was, and still is, an annual get-together of politicians and the political press in New York City. It's organized by the City Hall reporters. They do skits and have a big dinner and give speeches to each other.

I was handing out leaflets to protest media oppression, including an editorial that had run in the *Daily News* about a week before this dinner. The editorial commented on the refusal by the U.S. Supreme Court to consider an appeal by Mike McConnell, who was denied a job at the University of Minnesota because he was gay. McConnell had already been promised a librarian's job, but after the Board of Regents found out that he and his lover had applied for a marriage license, the job disappeared. The *Daily News* editorial was entitled, "Any Old Jobs for Homos?" The lead sentence was, "Fairies, nances, swishes, fags, lezzes, call 'em what you please." And then it went on to say some obnoxious things about gays. It was outrageous.

We went to the dinner to distribute leaflets to people in attendance, many of whom were good people who were supportive of gay rights and had welcomed our arrival. However, there were thugs in attendance who were guests at the dinner, and they proceeded to physically attack six of us. A number of us, including me, ended up hospitalized.

I was beaten up by Michael May, the president of the firemen's union. The guy was a Golden Gloves boxing champion. He punched and kicked me. I didn't have any broken bones or internal injuries, but it was a bad beating. I was on painkillers for a week. At the trial that followed, although everybody identified him as my assailant, he wasn't convicted.

Jeanne: I had a call from the hospital. I was furious. I remember thinking, *What right have they got to assault my son and the others? Why didn't the police protect them? What kind of a police force do we have in New York?* Then I sat down and wrote a letter to the *New York Post*. This was long before Rupert Murdoch owned it. I mentioned that my son was gay and that the police stood by and watched these young gays being beaten up and did nothing. And it was printed. Then Morty called me up and said, "You can't believe how everybody's talking about your letter!" I didn't think anything of it, but I guess it was the first time a mother ever sat down and publicly said, "Yes, I have a homosexual child." I was never quiet about having a gay son. I'd tell strangers; I didn't care. I figured this was one way to educate people.

At one point, my name was in the *New York Times*. The principal of my school told me that parents were complaining because my name was on the front page of the *Times*. She asked if I would be more discreet. I said, "Look, my professional life is one thing. And my private life is another, and I'll do as I please." She never bothered me again.

Morty: I thought my mom was terrific! On one level, her reaction and concern and involvement seemed very natural for a parent. What I thought was extraordinary was that other people weren't doing the same thing at that time. She's a unique person. [. . .]

Jeanne: Not long after Morty was beaten up, he came to me and said, "Will you march in the Gay Pride Parade with me?" I said, "I'll march if you let me carry a sign. What good does it do to have another person marching unless they know why you're marching?"

Morty: The sign said, "Parents of Gays: Unite in Support for Our Children."

Jeanne: My husband was a ham-radio buff at the time. The day of the march, he had his field day, so he didn't go. So Morty and I went without him. As we walked along, people on the sidewalks screamed! They yelled! They ran over and kissed me, and asked, "Will you talk to my mother?" We had so much of that. "Wow, if my mother saw me here . . ." They just couldn't believe that a parent would do this. There were, of course, other parents there, but they weren't visible.

Morty: When people started cheering as we were coming by, did you think it was for you at first?

Jeanne: No, because Dr. Spock was walking in back of us. I thought they were cheering him. After all, he was well known. But more and more people crowded around me and spoke to me.

Morty: We marched shoulder to shoulder. It was a great experience. The outpouring of emotion from our own community was overwhelming. No one else got the loud emotional cheers that she did.

Jeanne: We learned that they were fearful of telling their parents. And many had been rejected because their parents knew. I guess they didn't feel that any parent could be supportive of a gay child.

Morty: We are the only minority whose parents do not share our minority status. In other words, a black child who is fighting for civil rights is going to have his parents share that issue with him. Because of the importance of family to all of us, being estranged from your parents is a very traumatic thing. Being forced to closet your life from them is very devastating. The symbolic presence that my mother provided was a sign of great hope that parents could be supportive, that the people we're closest to, whom we love the most, need not be our enemies. I think the desire on the part of gays to share their totality as people, as gays and lesbians, was very much the reason why the parents have always gotten such an overwhelming response.

Jeanne: As Morty and I walked along during that first march, we were talking about starting some kind of organization. So many people said, "Talk to my parents." Then later there were the phone calls—all day long my phone was ringing. So that's really where it began. We decided during the march that a parents' group might be a good idea.

Each parent thinks, *I'm the only one who has a child who is homosexual,* and nobody was willing to let anyone else know about it. An organization was needed so parents could talk to each other and know that they were not the only ones. So they could get together and say, "Look, there's nothing wrong with them. It's just a different way of life." [. . .]

Jeanne: We had the first meeting at the church. I think there must have been eighteen or twenty people.

Morty: I handled the nuts and bolts of publicizing it. I placed an advertisement in the *Village Voice*. I also coordinated everything with Barbara Love, a respected lesbian writer at that time. You may recall, she and her lover Sidney Abbott wrote a book, *Sappho Was a Right-On Woman.* In those days we were very sensitive to the need for men and women to be working together, that nothing we did should be done solely from a gay male point of view. It was very important that Barbara was one of the organizers of this effort. She was able to reach out to the lesbian community as I reached out to the gay male community in an effort to publicize this meeting. We asked everybody to let their parents know we had a place for them to come.

Jeanne: It was a nice turnout of parents for the first meeting. Gay people also came without parents. There was a young man from Ames, Iowa, who came from a big family. His father and brothers would go hunting, but he was never interested. He had a hard time until a teacher told him to get away from there and go to the big city.

I guess I did most of the talking, with the help of my husband, who was an articulate person. He was a much better speaker than I. He was right along with me on everything.

Morty: Let me just bring things full circle with my father. By the time of this meeting, in March 1973, my father had been fairly well educated about gay issues. He had made the comment to me, "I understand intellectually that this is a civil rights issue, that we've been imbued with prejudices. I still have a lot of those prejudices deep in my gut because after so many years it's hard to get rid of them." I, of course, realized that he was facing his own upbringing and was making a conscious effort to change. So at these meetings he understood the processes that the parents were going through in coming out of their closets, facing the values that they'd been taught by society and grappling with the emotional impact they had. Thereafter he marched in parades regularly and spoke openly and became a great supporter of the gay rights movement.

Jeanne: During this time, I got so many calls and letters—so many. Many people who called were crying. They were upset because they had a child who was homosexual. I told them to come to a meeting and talk. At the meetings they would tell me how much I had helped them on the phone.

You know, some of the meetings made me feel pretty good. A couple would come over to me after a meeting and say, "We were on the verge of divorce, blaming each other. We feel differently now." There was one man, who was a prison warden upstate in a small town, and he started to cry because he had abused gay people and then discovered that his son was gay. He was quite upset when he realized what he had done.

Morty: It was not so much what my mother said, but that she said it. I remember her saying many times, "There's nothing wrong with your son being gay or your daughter being lesbian. We've been taught by society that there's something wrong, but society has been wrong." People had never heard this before. To hear it from another parent, a peer, had an especially compelling effect. They expected to spend the phone conversation in tears with someone at the other end saying, "Now, now, dearie," but that's not what they got.

Jeanne: You don't just believe everything you're told by society. Society could be wrong. I guess that was a revolutionary thing to say because they put me in the revolutionary calendar the following June.

Morty: There was a calendar that somebody published, which I picked up over on St. Mark's Place that next year. For each month it had a picture marking some occasion. For example, for the month of Mao Zedong's birthday, there was a picture of Mao. There was a picture of Martin Luther King, Jr., during his birthday month. And for June, guess who the calendar girl was?

Jeanne: Before Morty turned to June, I said, "This is not a true revolutionary calendar unless there is something about the gay march—about gays—for the month of June." And when I turned the page, there was my picture.

The irony, of course, is that I considered myself such a traditional person. I didn't even cross the street against the light.

IV

Facing the World

A Lesbian in Class!

Beth Harrison

Although one of every ten students in the United States is gay or lesbian, many educators assume that all young people are heterosexual. This situation is changing, as an increasing number of high schools offer counseling and support groups to address the needs of lesbian, gay, and bisexual youth, and many colleges now have well-established social and support groups for gay and lesbian students. In the essay below, from Young, Gay, and Proud!, *Beth Harrison writes about her decision to "come out" in high school, and how it felt to be the only openly gay student in the school.*

This spring I came out in high school. It was one of the hardest things I've done in my life, and it caused a lot of problems, but in the long run I've gained more than I lost.

The way it happened is that my sociology teacher, who is very liberal, was having a special unit on minorities—and one of them was homosexuals. One day he had in a lesbian and two gay men to talk to the class. Everyone had a lot of questions: "Do you want to adopt children?" "Are you attracted to every woman you meet?" (This was asked by a girl in the class to the lesbian, who said, "No, are you?") "How can you say you're discriminated against when you can look and act like everybody else if you want to?" "When did you first know you were gay?"

Most kids were very curious, and they didn't seem to really dislike the speakers; they just didn't know what to make of them.

At one point, one of the men said, "There's twenty-two students in this room. It's pretty likely that two of you are gay." Everybody looked around at everybody else. I don't think anybody really believed that any of *us* were gay. By then I was feeling good about my lesbianism, though, and I had seen that no one else in the class was really hostile toward the gay speakers. I had been thinking for a long time about coming out to people in school and I decided, well, it's now or never! So I raised my hand. "That's right," I said. "I'm one of them." (I just couldn't quite get myself to say, "I'm a lesbian.")

Everybody was silent. Even the gay speakers didn't know what to say for a minute. Some people were obviously bothered, and I clearly remember one girl, who I didn't really know, who scooted her chair back away from me and looked distinctly disgusted. But in a few minutes people were asking me questions. The next day, everybody in school knew.

What's happened now? Well, the lesbian speaker (her name is Madge) was very helpful. She talked to me after school for a long time, and we talked about the problems I was going to face, and how good it felt to be honest with everybody for once, and about dozens of other things. Without her, my life would have been much harder.

In school, most of my friends didn't change how they acted with me. Some of them would talk to me about it, though, and some wouldn't. One girl that I knew (thought I knew) very well wouldn't have anything to do with me, and some of the boys thought it was pretty cool to put me down, as if they couldn't have anything to do with a girl who didn't want to go out with them. I found "DYKE" scrawled on my locker once. I just left it there and tried to pretend I didn't care, though I did sometimes.

So there were good and bad results. But I know I've been honest with myself and with everybody else, and my true friends are still my friends. I thought a few other lesbians might turn up in school. So far they haven't, but I know I've made it easier for any that want to come out later. And I've met Madge, who is now my very best friend. Coming out was a monumental event for me, but it was worth it all.

A Letter to Aunt Shelley and Uncle Don

Tom Shepard

In November of 1992, Colorado voters approved an anti-gay amendment to their state constitution. The initiative, known as Amendment Two, forbids enactment of laws to protect lesbians and gay men from discrimination. Shortly after Amendment Two passed, Tom Shepard, a Colorado native and recent graduate of Stanford University, wrote to his relatives back home to explain how the amendment would affect him.

December 19, 1992

Dear Aunt Shelley and Uncle Don,

As I prepare to come home this Christmas, I have been thinking a lot about community. What is it that makes a community safe enough to reveal one's deepest secrets and then feel absolutely supported? Part of it, I know, is the politics of that community. More importantly, I think, is family.

The reason, then, that I write this letter is because for the first time ever, I am afraid to come home. I am afraid to be in a place where "my hometown community" has basically made a statement which dismisses an important part of who I am. Obviously what I'm talking about is Amendment Two.

For several years, I have been involved in a process of "coming out"—a process which has been both intellectual and interpersonal, both spiritual and political. For a while now, I have identified myself as gay. I have been involved in the Gay, Lesbian, Bisexual community at Stanford doing advocacy and education. Many of my friends, both men and women, are gay and bisexual. I have discovered the larger gay and bisexual community in the Bay Area and particularly in San Francisco, where I am moving in January.

For me, this has been an amazing process which would be impossible to represent in one letter. It hit me, however, after the recent election how important it is for me to share this process more openly with people at home.

I grew up not knowing any gay person, let alone a teacher or a role model. Except for the man who worked at the Lotus Eater Boutique, I thought no gay people lived in the state of Colorado. I am beginning to understand why I felt this way now. I look around and see the influence that right-wing Christians have in Colorado Springs. More importantly, I see within my own family reluctance to discuss gay issues candidly, and misinformation around every corner.

I realize that I cannot influence what ideas and values are taught in Will Perkins's family* or Pat Robertson's family or any other family for that matter. But I can influence those in my own family. I am affected by this law and the ignorance and bigotry that has inspired it. If I wanted to return to Colorado Springs to work, I feel as though I could not do so while being openly gay. I have decided not to apply for jobs even in Denver for this reason.

It seems to me that this legislation will continue to perpetuate ignorance. Gay people will be more afraid to

---

*Will Perkins, head of Colorado for Family Values, was instrumental in writing and campaigning for the passage of Amendment Two. When I was younger, I played tennis with Perkins at the Colorado Springs Racquet Club. I would like him to know that his actions and words have hurt me and many other members of the Colorado Springs community.—Tom Shepard

come out in the workplace and there will be fewer role models in our community. We need role models to dispel myths and stereotypes. If even one of my teachers had been openly gay *and proud*, maybe some of the trauma I experienced in my teenage years could have been avoided. If even one chapter in my history book had covered the gay rights movement or the assassination of Harvey Milk,* maybe I would have felt less shameful and more accepting of myself.

I think by trusting young people with honest information, as opposed to protecting them from what is taboo and controversial, we empower them to make educated and non-bigoted choices in their lives. This has happened frequently in discussions with my sister and has been extremely liberating.

I often find myself feeling angry at how invisible gay people are in our world. I rationalize to myself that people are just misinformed; they are frightened of what they do not know. But I still do not understand why people who have affection and love for other people of the same sex cannot display them? Why can't gay men and lesbians legally get married? Why can't a gay man teach elementary school without accusations of being a child molester? Why do competent men and women get "dishonorably" discharged from the military solely because of their sexual orientation? Why do people call men who are nurses "faggots" and women who are cops "dykes"? Why are gay, lesbian, and bisexual people bashed on the streets because of who they date? *What is*

---

*Harvey Milk (1930–1978) was a crusader for gay rights and the first openly gay official of any big city in the country. Elected in 1977 to the post of San Francisco city supervisor, Milk was murdered in 1978, along with San Francisco Mayor George Moscone; the light sentence given their killer sparked major protests. The story of Milk's life is told in the book *The Mayor of Castro Street* by Randy Shilts and in the Academy Award–winning documentary film *The Times of Harvey Milk*.

it that is so threatening about men loving men and women loving women? As teachers, I would be interested in your feedback to these questions which seem to gnaw at my conscience every day of my life.

I can't say all I want to you in a letter. There is so much more. I just wanted you to know me a little better. It has been hard to stay in touch these past years. I feel as if I know little about what your lives are like right now. And often our family gatherings don't lend themselves to these kinds of discussions. At any rate, I hope that this might be a springboard for future conversations. I certainly feel fine talking openly about *anything*. And whatever you feel is appropriate to discuss with the kids is okay with me. In fact, I encourage it.

I hope that this letter has not been overwhelming in any way. And if it has, I hope that you will let me know how I can help you clarify any misunderstandings. Letters are very formal.

I love all of you.

Love,
Tom

We All Nourish Truth with Our Tongues

Dorothy Allison

Dorothy Allison is a poet and novelist whose books include Bastard
out of Carolina *and* The Women Who Hate Me. *She grew up
in South Carolina and writes about the particular challenges of facing the world as a lesbian in the South. The following is an excerpt
from a longer poem.*

In the dirt country where I was born
the words that named me were so terrible
no one would speak them
so always just over my head
a silent language damned me.

I learned then that what no one would say
was the thing about which nothing could be done.
If they would not say   *Lesbian*
I could not say pride.
If they would not say   *Queer*
I could not say courage.
If they would not name me
Bastard, worthless, stupid, whore
I could not grab onto my own spoken language,
my love for my kind, myself.

I learned there is only one language
and it either speaks truly or lies.
But sometimes it must go on a long time

before the whole truth comes out
and until that moment all the words
are lies.   Still I tell you
there is only one language.

What I am saying is the words
are growing in my mouth.
All the names of god will be spoken,
all the hidden secret things made known.
We will root in dirt our mothers watered
sing songs, tell stories echoed in their mouths.

Then with no walls around us, you and I
will speak of truth to each other,
the soil that grows the vegetable
as deeply as the flower that never
touches the soil.

Honor Bound

Joseph Steffan

Open lesbians and gay men are officially banned from all branches of the U.S. military, on the grounds that their presence compromises discipline and creates morale problems. Despite the ban, hundreds of thousands of gay people have served in the military. Increasingly, these gay men and lesbians have chosen to "come out" in protest of a policy that they say is the last form of government-approved discrimination in American society. In this selection from his 1992 memoir, Joseph Steffan, a midshipman at the Naval Academy (the navy's college for future officers), describes a meeting he had with his commanding officer. Rumors had begun to circulate at the academy that Steffan was gay, and he decided to come out to his commanding officer just weeks before graduation—even though he knew that to acknowledge he was gay might put an end to his dream of a career in the navy.

I tried to keep calm, but it was difficult to ignore the obvious importance of this meeting. What would happen in the next few moments would likely determine, to a very large extent, the rest of my life. My feelings were a strange mixture of fear, anger, and pride, and I was determined that, no matter what, I was going to maintain my sense of dignity.

Finally, the EA signaled that the commandant was ready and led me into his office. The commandant of midshipmen, Captain Howard Habermeyer, was waiting just inside the door as we entered. He greeted me, shaking my hand, and motioned for me to sit as he returned to his desk. The office was relatively opulent by military standards, with dark wood paneling and blue carpeting.

Behind the commandant's large wooden desk stood the United States flag and the blue-and-gold flag of the Brigade of Midshipmen. The walls were covered with pictures and plaques, memorabilia from his service as an officer in the submarine service.

Captain Habermeyer was tall, bespectacled, and quite thin, almost to the point of frailty. He and the superintendent had taken over during the previous summer, replacing Captain Chadwich and Admiral Larson, both of whom I had come to know quite well during my previous years. I regretted that they were not here now, and that my fate rested in the hands of two officers who barely knew me. I sometimes wonder if they had been there instead whether it would have changed the outcome at all. Perhaps it would at least have been more difficult for them.

I had first met Captain Habermeyer at a small leadership retreat held for the top incoming stripers of my class. The retreat was relatively informal and was held at an Annapolis hotel. At the time, he impressed me as an intelligent and articulate officer, and we had shared a conversation about his admiration of Japanese culture. It was an interest that had grown through several tours of duty he had in Japan.

I had heard since then that Captain Habermeyer was a stickler for regulations. He played everything exactly by the book. My suspicion was confirmed when the EA remained standing in the doorway as the commandant began to question me about my request. He had apparently been ordered to remain as a witness to the conversation. Despite an outward sense of cordiality, I was beginning to feel like a criminal under interrogation.

As with the previous officers, I refused to discuss the purpose of my request with the commandant, but he continued to question me. He finally stated that no one in the military has an inherent right to meet with anyone above his own commanding officer, which for midshipmen is technically the commandant. If I refused to disclose the purpose of the meeting, he would deny my request. When he again questioned me, I finally answered, "The meeting concerns a situation of which you are already aware."

"You're referring to the NIS investigation presently under way?" he asked.

"Yes, sir."

He responded: "Are you willing to state at this time that you are a homosexual?"

The moment of truth had arrived. In a way, I was surprised that he was even asking the question. Captain Holderby had already basically told him the answer. Was he offering me an out, a chance to deny it, to say that it was all a big misunderstanding? Was he offering me a chance to lie?

I looked him straight in the eye and answered, "Yes sir, I am."

It was a moment I will never forget, one of agony and intense pride. In that one statement, I had given up my dreams, the goals I had spent the last four years of my life laboring to attain. But in exchange, I retained something far more valuable—my honor and my self-esteem.

In many ways, the commandant's words were more than a simple question—they were a challenge to everything I believed in, and to the identity I had struggled to accept. In giving me the opportunity to deny my sexuality, the commandant was challenging that identity. He could just as well have asked, "Are you ashamed enough to deny your true identity in order to graduate?" More than anything I have ever wanted in my entire life, I wanted to be an outstanding midshipman and to graduate from the Naval Academy. And I firmly believe that if I had been willing to lie about my sexuality, to deny my true identity, I would have been allowed to graduate.

I had come to the academy to achieve my potential as an individual. These four years had been filled with trials and lessons from which I learned a great deal about life and about myself. But none of these lessons was more difficult, important, or meaningful than coming to understand and accept my sexuality—in essence, to accept my true identity. By coming out to myself, I gained the strength that can come only from self-acceptance, and it was with that added strength that I had been able to persevere through the many trials and difficulties of life at Annapolis.

The commandant's question was also a challenge to my honor as a midshipman. The Honor Concept at Annapolis is based on the tenet that personal honor is an absolute—you either have honor or you do not. No one can take it from you; it can only be surrendered willingly. And once it is surrendered, once it is compromised, it can never again be fully regained.

I knew that my graduation would mean absolutely nothing if I had to lie to achieve it, especially if that lie was designed to hide the very fact of my own identity. I would have given up my honor, destroying everything it means to be a midshipman. And I would have given up my identity and pride—everything it means to be a person.

The only way to retain my honor and identity, both as a midshipman and a person, was to tell the truth. I was honor bound not simply by the Honor Concept, but by its foundation: the respect for fundamental human dignity. The academy had the power to take away everything tangible that I had attained, but only I had the power to destroy my honor. Even if the academy discharged me for being gay, I could live with the knowledge that I had passed the ultimate test. I was willing to give up everything tangible to retain something intangible but far more meaningful: my honor and my identity. Even the military could not take them away from me now.

Captain Habermeyer said that he could not grant my request to speak with the superintendent because he would eventually sit in judgment over me. A performance board would be scheduled the next day, the first step toward discharge from Annapolis. Although I explained that I still desired to graduate, the commandant assured me that he did not believe the superintendent would allow it.

Before leaving, I looked at the commandant and said, "I'm sorry it had to end this way." He answered, "So am I." I truly believed him, which didn't make the imminent destruction of my life much easier to deal with. It would have been so much easier to have someone to hate, a person to blame for everything that was happening. But there was no one to blame. I couldn't blame myself because I had done what I believed right. There was only a military policy, a rule like countless others that define life in the military, rules that we learn to instinctively enforce and obey.

Speaking Up

Erna Pahe

Erna Pahe is a Navajo who was raised on the Apache Indian reservation in Window Rock, Arizona. She later moved to San Francisco, where she became president of Gay American Indians (GAI). In this interview, she discusses the special challenges facing gay and lesbian native Americans.

Q: Where did you grow up?

A: I was born on the Apache reservation and lived there until I was about six, because my mom and dad worked at the boarding school. Then we moved to Phoenix and lived there a couple of years. I graduated from high school in Flagstaff, Arizona. After a couple years in college, I moved back to the reservation (Window Rock, Arizona) until I was about twenty-three—365 days a year on the reservation. I left when my son was just a baby and came to California and have lived here for fourteen years now. . . .

Q: How old were you when you came out?

A: I was about twenty-three or twenty-four.
  Back home on the reservation, I knew the feeling that I was having. But being that close and being the youngest one of the family, I didn't have much of a chance to be an individualist, I guess.
  It's not anything that's ever talked about. It's not dealt with. You're a member of the family, that's the priority. The chain of command in our family is real sturdy in

that the oldest boy is more or less the father. So we all work real hard to make sure we don't do anything or say anything that is going to upset him.

In our tradition, we don't talk back to our elders, whether they're a few years older or ten or twelve years older. It's a respect that we're taught. They say, "I don't want to talk about it," you don't talk about it.

When I came out here I finally got that feeling that I had control over my own life and didn't have anybody else to answer to. So it was good for me, because when I did go back to the reservation I was ready to deal with "Hey, I'm just me. I'm the baby sister of the family, but I'm independent and I do have my life to live, whichever way I choose to live it."

Q: Do you think that gay Navajo people have to leave the reservation to be able to come out?

A: I think they can be gay and still live there. A lot of it depends on the area that you're in. If you're way secluded, like in Snake Flats or Chinle, it isn't going to make any difference to anybody. If you get into Window Rock, which is the capital with a big population, and you have a lot more of the educated Indians who have lived in Flagstaff and heard the criticisms, there's quite a bit of discrimination. Not that I've necessarily felt it. It seems that way.

Q: What are your positive memories of the reservation?

A: Well, what I think about the most is the openness. When you wanted to get away there was a place to do it. There's accessibility where you can just go out and find an old shed to stay in—and you know you're not going to be bothered. And then, I miss the closeness of my family. Being able to call them up and say, "Let's have a picnic this afternoon."

I do like the city in the sense that you have a lot of things you can do. You have access to all kinds of things without having to travel miles. When you need to go out and talk to people, you can always find someone that doesn't know you or doesn't know your family. Out home, everybody knows you.

Q: Why do many Indians have a hard time accepting gay people?

A: In the past, there was very little talk about your personal life or personal feelings. The basic thing was our traditions—and not so much feelings. It took me until I got out of college and moved to this area before I started speaking up—"Well, yeah, I am gay"—after I had heard the word and realized its interpretations.

Even when I go back home now, and even though my family knows, we never talk about it. The spiritual way is always put as a priority . . . your personal side of life is a little different.

For the elders, that's the way it was in their home. So it's like a new idea. All of a sudden Indians are starting to speak up—and it's not all around politics. Now they see a new generation of kids coming up that are actually saying, "This is the way I am, that's it"—where they were always real quiet and never were taught to speak with their heartfelt feelings unless it dealt with the whole tribe—what *our* people want.

But, you know, it's kind of like they've led us into it, too, saying, "Speak up, speak up—say your piece." You can just see how excited they get as older people. It's a trip. . . .

Q: What advice would you give to a young woman who is Indian and discovers she'd rather go on softball trips than to the prom?

A: The advice I most hope that young Indian women would have is to be patient. It's hard coming out—coming out to your family, being able to sit down and talk with them. It's something I've yet to do with my family. Yet I know they understand; we understand each other. But it's being patient.

I see a lot of young Indian girls and they come out and they're just gung-ho about it. Then the first time they go home, especially after being in an urban area where it's so free, you get discouraged real easy because of the simple fact that at home we don't talk like that. It's just kind of understood. So they get all gung-ho, and they expect a lot of changes in a short period of time, and you can't expect that, especially of your family. Patience is probably the most important thing.

Then as you go through these different types of relationships—I imagine I'll go through a few more in my life—but that's part of life, meeting people. The first time I fell in love with the first woman and it didn't work out, it about tore my heart out. I thought, "Why am I doing this to myself?" It takes being patient and searching and not expecting too much out of the gay life, because it's just as hard as straight life, if not a little bit harder.

There's women that have children that are coming out now. With them you have to be very patient. Bringing them up with the idea that there isn't anything wrong with it. As my son goes out now with his teenage girlfriends, I can imagine the things he goes through to explain the lifestyle in our home. He's had the neighbor kids tease him and talk to him about dykes, and come home saying, "What does 'dykes' mean, Mom?" Bringing him up to not be bitter about it. That all falls into that patience. You have to be very, very patient.

And especially the personalities of gay people. It seems to me that gay people are a lot more intense about life in general. They're a lot more keen on feelings, other peoples' feelings. I don't know why that is but it just seems that way to me.

There's a lot of caring in gay people that is toward all lifestyles, from children all the way up to grandparents. Society is getting used to it now because of this sensitivity. I think it might wear off after a while—we'll get everybody thinking like us. Even dealing in politics, we're a lot more aware of everything—how it is to go through parenthood, how it is to have babies—more so than anybody else. Yeah, we are special, because we're able to deal with all of life in general. It's very special.

In My Own Space

Calvin Glenn

Calvin Glenn grew up in Dallas and studied creative writing at Dartmouth College, where he served as secretary of the lesbian and gay student organization on campus. He wrote this piece of short fiction when he was eighteen.

It was with extreme precaution that I came to know myself. I had concluded, as a young boy, that there was a part of me that I did not want to be; but there was nothing I could do. Almost all of my life I had felt like a drone, following some set path toward my future, not living, but operating according to some preprogrammed specifications. I am older now, and understand who I am. I am thankful I didn't listen to all those people who told me I could only be what the rest of the world would let me be.

Going away to school was a shock for me. I had attended a small college-prep school that was very conservative. I wasn't quite liberal, but I surely wasn't conservative. During my life at the prep school, I had several run-ins with people who thought I was outrageous. I wore the same types of clothes they wore. I spoke the same language that they spoke, and I certainly used the same type of money they used. I was "outrageous" simply because I didn't think their thoughts. When I graduated I moved to the Northeast, to a small private college in the country.

When I arrived on campus, I was sure I had not done a great job of selecting a college. The college was just as conservative as the school back home. I had looked for a small campus where I hoped to explore my identity without inhibition. The day I graduated from high school, I made a pact with myself to "come out" on campus before returning home for winter break. I had no fears. I had come this far and didn't care what anyone else might think of me. My parents knew I was gay, which I considered a plus, but being typical black parents, they first berated me, then alienated me, then sent me to a psychologist to be cured. The local Baptist minister was called in to scare the sickness out of me. (If there had been any sickness there, believe me, he would have scared it out.) My parents have simmered down since then, but I am not sure they accept my sexuality; we simply don't discuss it.

I got off the bus in early September, feeling very good about being at college, away from the stifling silence that engulfed my home. I looked around a bit, and finally mustered the courage to ask someone for directions to my dorm.

"It's straight down the road," a fellow student instructed me. "You'll know it when you get there," he continued. "It's the only building that doesn't look old." I thanked him and proceeded on my way.

When I found the new-looking dorm, I walked in and went up to the second floor to search for room 204. I found it and entered. I was assigned to a triple—three rooms, to be occupied by three very different roommates. One was Jim, a quiet fellow from the Midwest. My other roommate, Sam, was a pseudo-jock from the South. And, of course, there was me. When I moved into my room, I had no idea Jim and Sam would never become my friends.

A couple of weeks into the school year, I decided my room was just a little too drab. Everyone else had vivid posters and cut-outs from magazines plastered all over their walls. I thought I should do that, too. It took two weeks to complete the job. I started out, innocently enough, with a poster of a lion that I hung directly over my bed (with that image, anyone would think twice about upsetting me). And I progressed from there; being a typical teenager, I put up posters of my favorite rock bands. And then it dawned on me; there was something I really wanted but didn't have on my walls: a picture of a perfect man. I looked through my various catalogs and ordered the most innocently seductive poster I could find. When it arrived, I closed the door to my room and tacked up the poster. "There," I said with satisfaction, "now the walls all have a spirit that is purely me."

Later that week, Jim came in to talk with me. "Great posters you've got," he said, walking in. "Kinda picks the place up." We sat on my bed talking about our classes and complaining about our social lives. And then it happened. He turned and spotted the poster on my door. He asked hesitantly, "What—who is that?"

"Some model. It's just a poster I ordered. But he is gorgeous." When those words came from my mouth, Jim gasped and jumped up from the bed. I became wide-eyed, and somewhat offended. I asked, "What's wrong?"

The fear in his eyes was apparent. What was he afraid of? I'm sure I hadn't touched him at all since he walked in commenting on the new scenery.

"Are you," he started, then hesitated. He sighed and continued slowly, "Are you gay?"

Equally slowly, I replied, "Yes, I am gay." Jim looked as though his heart had stopped. I had prepared, somewhat, for this confrontation, but I didn't know how to handle his fear. "Calm down," I said, but he just stared at me, his eyes bulging out of his head and his mouth agape. He turned quickly and left. I sat looking at myself in the mirror. What could he have seen to make him so afraid?

It was not long before Sam knocked on my door and entered. I was still sitting on my bed facing the mirror when he walked in.

"Jim told me about the poster you have up on your wall. Where is it?"

"Turn around; it's behind you," I said wearily.

He looked at the picture and gave it a few nervous taps. Pointing at the poster, he said, "You *can't* have this picture up." His plea was in vain. He looked at me with desperate eyes as though I had physically abused him.

"Why can't I have it up?"

Sam paused to search his fears for coherent reasons. "Look, Chris, when people see this up here they'll think you're a homosexual."

"But I am gay."

Sam's nose began to twitch. "Why the fuck didn't you tell us?"

"What the fuck does it matter?"

"I can't believe this," he screamed, putting his hands on his head. "I'm living with a black faggot." He slammed the door behind him as he left. That was the end of our short friendship.

The next day my roommates confronted me. They said they had been conferring and had come to a conclusion. They put it simply: I had to move out.

"No."

"Come on, Chris," Jim urged. "Wouldn't you be happier in a single?"

"I'm comfortable where I am," I replied.

"But you'd be more comfortable in a single," Sam added.

"You guys are out of your minds. I'm not moving out." I got up and went into my room. "Fucking idiots!" I yelled, as I slammed the door. What the hell was their problem? I hadn't made any advances at them; I didn't even think either was attractive. I hadn't even had any overnight visitors. "How the hell am I bothering them?" I asked myself.

I woke up the next morning feeling lousy, and when I left my room I became angry. Someone had written the letters *F* and *G* around the *A* sticker on my door. I had never been so angry. I went back to my room and pulled out a sheet of paper and began to write. But I stopped. "I'm not going to let myself stoop to their level." I crumpled the paper and went on with my life.

There was a small gay and lesbian organization on campus, and I attended the weekly meetings. I told some of the members about the situation with my roommates. They couldn't believe it. Nothing like it had ever happened before. But then, they told me, none of them had ever had the courage to "come out" to their roommates. "Why?" I asked. "Am I the only one who isn't afraid? Am I the only one who is tired of hiding?"

The next week I received a letter from the director of student life. I was told that my roommates had brought complaints against me to her attention. I had to report to her office the next morning for a conference.

The director called us in separately to get an overview of the circumstances. Then we all sat down: Jim and Sam on one side of the table, me on the other, and the director at the head.

"Now what seems to be the problem?"

"Well, a couple of weeks ago we found out that Chris . . . he's a homosexual," Jim began.

"He put up this big poster of a guy on his door," Sam added. "Everybody can see it."

"We think he would feel more comfortable in a single," Jim concluded.

The director looked at me. "Is this so?"

"Yes, I am gay," I replied, "but I'm comfortable where I am. There's no reason for me to move out."

"But think about us, Chris," said Jim.

"I'm not hurting you," I paused, and then added, "You mean to tell me I can't put up a poster of a man in my own space?" There was silence. "I don't even bother you. Unlike Sam, I don't even have people staying overnight," I sneered.

Sam yelled, "If the guys find out I'm living with a fag—"

"That's enough!" the director interrupted. "It seems to me that this is a very simple case. Chris is gay, and according to this school's policies, there is nothing wrong with that. He's done nothing wrong, as opposed to you two. You will both share the expenses to have his door repainted, and you both may possibly appear for disciplinary action if Chris plans to pursue harassment charges. Finally, I cannot, and will not, force Chris to move out of his room."

"But what can we do? He makes us feel uncomfortable."

"Gentlemen, you will have to learn to handle your own insecurities. But, if you feel so uncomfortable, I suggest that *you* move out."

Teamwork

Lucy Jane Bledsoe

In "Teamwork," a short story by Lucy Bledsoe, a spectator forces the members of a college basketball team to confront homophobia, both within the team and within the individual players' lives. Led by Coach Montgomery, the women succeed in tackling the homophobia head-on.

On the night of our third home game, as I jogged out onto the court with my team, I was so happy I thought I could die right then and be satisfied with my life. Jackie and I had finally started up our love affair. A sweetness coursed through my limbs, making me feel like an Olympic hurdler flying over life's obstacles with perfect elegance. On top of that, our team was winning. Our record was a tremendous 7–0. Thalia's family donated brand-new uniforms to the team (she had been complaining all season about how ghastly ugly the old ones were), so we were looking pretty good, too. When we lined up for lay-ups the school band blasted into action. Even the cheerleading squad pranced onto center court and whipped their pom-poms around. Understand that the band and cheerleaders did not attend women's games until we were on a winning streak, until there was glory to be reaped. I wasn't bitter, though. I loved it. I even loved the hordes of fraternity boys that packed the gym. The night was fine.

We were playing North Carolina State, and we held a decent lead during most of the first half. I sat back on the bench and watched Jackie speed up and down the court. The movement of each muscle was a precious sight to me.

Shortly before halftime, Montgomery benched Thalia to give

her a breather and put in Carson. Suddenly, the game turned around. North Carolina State broke our lead and then, in a quick ten minutes, proceeded to fast-break themselves to an eight-point lead. Seconds before halftime, North Carolina State got the ball again, and went for the fast break. The guard tipped the ball in for a lay-up just as the halftime buzzer sounded. The official called the basket good. Montgomery lunged onto the court toward the ref, screaming that the basket sunk *after* the buzzer.

The ref slapped his hand to the back of his head, pointed at Montgomery, and called a tech on her. The crowd went crazy, because Montgomery was right. That girl wasn't anywhere near the basket when the buzzer sounded. But someone pulled Montgomery back on the bench, and we lined up at half court while the player toed the line for her free throw. Carson was kicking the floor like a mad bull, because she knew everyone would interpret our sudden slide as a result of Montgomery putting her in and taking Thalia out. The North Carolina State player made her shot.

After a good talking-to at halftime, we trotted back out onto the court and warmed up. Then Montgomery did something that surprised us all. She started Carson instead of Thalia. I figured she thought Carson was losing her confidence and so put her in there to let her know she wasn't to blame for the score. Montgomery always emphasized that we were a *team*, that one woman couldn't make or break anything.

A nervous silence fell on the gym as the ten players took positions for the tip-off. A cold sweat saturated the air. I could see Carson's mouth working and would have thought that she was praying if I didn't know better. Jackie wiped her hands on her hips and glanced at me. I felt instant warmth again. The ref held the ball up and glanced around the circle. He hesitated as two players suddenly traded places. Then, just as he bent his knees to make the toss, a male voice in the bleachers erupted like a geyser out of the perfect silence: "Bench the dyke! Play Thalia Peterson."

For a split second, everyone in the gym was stunned. The air felt yellow and still, like in the eye of a storm. Even the ref, who stood between the two centers with the ball balanced on his fingertips, stepped back and squinted up in the stands for a moment.

Then a gurgling of fraternity laughter eased some people's discomfort, and the ref tossed the ball.

Something turned sour for me in that moment at halftime against North Carolina State. Everyone knew the fraternity boy meant Carson, but I also knew that he meant Stella and Montgomery, Jackie and myself. The raw hatred in that boy's voice felt like a boot stomping on a tender green shoot.

We lost that game and the next one, too. Every time I stepped into the big, silent gym for practice, I would hear an echo of that boy's voice. Sometimes, for a flashing second, I could even see the group of fraternity boys in the stands, jeering, *knowing*. Montgomery and Stella were no help anymore; they were as indicted as I. Jackie and I had our first fight that week.

Looking back, I think it's a miracle we ever won any games. So many of us were in some stage of coming out, no one really comfortable, none of us able to say "lesbian" without cringing. We were scared, we were in love, we were all little bundles of explosive passion. Sometimes this energy fairly drove us to victory on the court; other times we crumbled under it.

By midseason Jackie and I were solid. We were crazy for each other. But love isn't everything. We fought constantly. She didn't know what she was doing messing with a white girl, and I didn't know what I was doing messing with any girl at all. Our common ground lay in the realm of ideals and primal loves and fears. But our earthbound experiences were different enough to drive us both crazy. We loved each other and we drove one another to fierce anger. But we carried on, just the same.

After the North Carolina State game, Montgomery began switching around the starting lineup. It's not like she substituted one starter for another (say, Carson for Thalia), but out of the top six players she tried different combinations and often Carson was in there. Sometimes Thalia was not.

Mixing up the starting lineup too much might not be smart basketball (though in this case it might have been), but it sure made me like Montgomery. I don't really know why she did it, but I suspect she saw it as a morale issue. She probably noticed how that boy's remark registered on some of our young faces. Maybe she knew she had some power to erase the imprint of that boot. With me, she was right. I secretly drew from her strength like an invisible leech. But the morale of the rest of the team sagged.

When Thalia didn't start, she lounged on the bench as if it were a settee, as if she was entertaining in a drawing room and hadn't the faintest interest in the game. And when Montgomery put her in, she gave only seventy-five percent. If Montgomery started her, however, Thalia gave her all. The insult to Montgomery, even the *idea* that she could be manipulated by Thalia's insolence, infuriated me. I was glad when Montgomery started her less and less often. A rumor circulated that Thalia's parents offered a large donation to the women's intercollegiate fund on the behind-closed-doors stipulation that Thalia be reinstated as a permanent first stringer. I don't really know if this was true, but people swore it was. Someone knew someone who knew someone who worked in Dean Roper's office. She'd *heard* the offer. I believed the story more than I disbelieved it.

Carson saw the changing lineup as an opportunity to reestablish her position on the team. Her attitude improved. She kept her mouth shut and played ball like it was a matter of life and death. At the same time, Carson became more and more out about her lesbianism. And she thought everyone else should come out as well. "A bunch of fucking closet dykes," she semi-joked at me and Jackie one night in the library. She took that boy's word like it was a piece of clay and fashioned her own meaning out of it. Still, I cringed and quickly looked over my shoulder to see if anyone was within earshot. Jackie just shrugged. "With Montgomery and Stella, we're talking about a job," she said. Yeah, I thought. And for me, we're talking about fear. Jackie didn't want to come out, and I happily hid behind her wishes. So, for lesbians on the team, that just left the jealousy *à trois*, as we called them, three women who had not yet managed to come out even to themselves but were involved in a triangle of jealousy complicated, in my opinion, by a lack of sex. And, of course, there were the four definitely straight women on the team, Susan Thurmond, Amanda Severson, Kathy Jones, and Thalia Peterson. Somehow we were all more and more aware of who was who. Somehow that individual clarity seemed to dissolve our team clarity.

Language of Violence

The Disposable Heroes of Hiphoprisy

The Disposable Heroes of Hiphoprisy use rap music to confront homo-phobia, racism, and brainwashing by the mass media. "Language of Violence," a rap song from the group's 1992 album, Hypocrisy Is the Greatest Luxury, *recounts the beating of a fifteen-year-old student on the first day of a new school year.*

The first day of school was always the hardest
the first day of school the hallways the darkest

Like a gauntlet
the voices haunted
walking in with his thin skin
lowered chin
he knew the names that they would taunt him with
faggot, sissy, punk, queen, queer
although he'd never had sex in his fifteen years

And when they harassed him
it was for a reason
And when they provoked him
it became open season
for the fox and hunter
the sparks and the thunder
that pushed the boy under
then pillage and plunder
it kind of makes me wonder
how one can hurt another

But dehumanizing the victim makes things simpler
it's like breathing with a respirator
it eases the conscience of even the most conscious
and calculating violator
words can reduce a person to an object
something more easy to hate
an inanimate entity
completely disposable
no problem to obliterate

But death is the silence
in this language of violence
Death is the silence
But death is the silence
in this cycle of violence
death is the silence

It's tough to be young
the young long to be tougher
when we pick on someone else
it might make us feel rougher
abused by their fathers
but that was at home though
So to prove to each other
that they were not "homos"
the exclamation of the phobic fury
executioner, judge and jury
the mob mentality
individuality was nowhere
dignity forgotten
at the bottom of a dumb old dare
and a numb cold stare
On the way home it was back to name calling
ten against one
they had his back up against the wall
and they reveled in their laughter
as they surrounded him
But it wasn't a game

when they jumped and grounded him
they picked up their bats
with their muscles strainin'
and they decided they were gonna
beat this fella's brain in
with an awful powerful
showerful an hour full of violence
inflict the strictest
brutality and dominance
they didn't hear him screaming
They didn't hear him pleading
they ran like cowards
and left the boy bleeding
in a pool of red
'til all tears were shed
and his eyes quietly slid
into the back of his head
DEAD. . . .

But death is the silence
in this language of violence
Death is the silence
But death is the silence
in this cycle of violence
death is the silence

You won't see the face 'til the eyelids drop
You won't hear the screaming until it stops

The boy's parents were gone
and his grandmother had raised him
she was mad she had no form
of retaliation
the pack didn't have to worry about
being on a hitlist
but the thing they never thought about
was that there was a witness
to this senseless crime

right place wrong time
tried as an adult
one of them was gonna do hard time

The first day of prison was always the hardest
the first day of prison the hallways the darkest
like a gauntlet
the voices haunted
faggot, sissy, punk, queen, queer
words he used before had a new meaning in here
as a group of men in front of him laughing came
near for the first time in his life
the young bully felt fear
He'd never been on this side of the name calling
Five against one
they had his back up against the wall and
he had never questioned his own sexuality
but this group of men didn't hesitate their reality
with an awful powerful
showerful an hour full of violence
inflict the strictest
brutality and dominance
they didn't hear him screaming
they didn't hear him pleading
they took what they wanted
and then just left him bleeding in the corner
the giant reduced to jack horner

But dehumanizing the victim makes things simpler
it's like breathing with a respirator
it eases the conscience of even the most conscious
and calculating violator
the power of words
don't take it for granted
when you hear a man ranting
don't just read the lips
be more sublime than this
put everything in context

is this a tale of rough justice
in a land where there's no justice at all
Who is really the victim?
Or are we all the cause, and victim of it all

But death is the silence
in this language of violence
Death is the silence
But death is the silence
in this cycle of violence
death is the silence.

Abominations

Lev Raphael

"My Jewish and gay stories," author Lev Raphael has said, "focus on coming out and finding a lover, coping with the impact of the Holocaust, how gay and straight Jews feel about traditional Judaism, and the place of gay Jews in the Jewish community." In "Abominations," a short story from his collection Dancing on Tisha B'av, *Raphael addresses each of these themes and shows the love and understanding that a straight sister has for her gay brother. Nat, the brother, has returned to his college dorm only to discover that a fire has gutted his room, most likely as retribution for Nat's outspoken activism on behalf of gay men and lesbians.*

She was pulled from sleep by her insistent doorbell and she glared at her alarm clock as if it should have protected her from this intrusion. She shoved it off the night table, found her robe on the floor, and hurried out to the door, rubbing at her eyes.

It was Nat, sickly pale, eyes down, hands cold when she grabbed them to pull him inside. He smelled strange to her.

"It's gone," he said, drifting to her kitchen, mechanically filling the fat black teakettle with water, setting it on a burner.

His car's been stolen, she thought—or vandalized. She saw white letters of hate—and then wondered if it wouldn't happen to *her* car, too. . . .

"It's all gone. My dorm room."

She sank into a chair at the table as if his words were heavy hands weighing down her shoulders.

"I went back to get some stuff for my eight o'clock class. And from the parking lot across the street, I could see this big black hole on the first floor of the dorm. Fire, I thought, and then I saw all these puddles of sooty water and you could smell plastic, burned plastic. It was my room. Everything's gone, my clothes, the books, even the phone . . . it's melted. I found the RA, Dave, he said it happened at night—it looks like someone broke in and torched the place—and they were lucky it wasn't worse. Lucky? Someone called the fire department before the smoke alarm even went off. The marshal said it looked like arson to him, but he wasn't sure."

She realized that Nat smelled of smoke, as if he'd been in a bar all night. "Everything's gone?" She was suddenly flooded by all the terrible films she'd seen of Germany in the thirties, with JU-DEN RAUS ("Out with the Jews") whitewashed across Jewish-owned storefronts, synagogues collapsing in flame, religious Jews beaten, bloody, dead.

He looked at her, eyes heavy, grim. "Except this." Nat reached into his jeans pocket and tossed a two-inch black button onto the table. It had one of those Gay Liberation pink triangles she had argued with Mark about. "But you're Jewish, too!" she had said. "Don't you hate that they use something from the camps? You never see Jews wearing yellow stars in a parade!" Mark had tried to convince her that the triangle's origin was precisely the point: shocking people, reminding everyone of the worst that could happen, that *did* happen.

Now the pink and black button glared up at her like a baleful witch in a fairy tale, gloating over the princess's crucial mistake, which was about to plunge her into darkness and slavery. Nat was telling her about the campus police, how aloof and matter-of-fact they were, even wanting to know where he had been all night, how much insurance he had, if any—and how everyone on his floor said they had no idea what had happened, hadn't heard or seen anything. Nobody would look at Nat—as if it was *his* fault, as if *he* had humiliated everyone in the dorm by not only being gay but also the victim of an attack.

"I called Mark . . . I asked him to meet me here. Okay? Is that okay?"

The teakettle—*tchynick* in Yiddish—started whistling and Brenda said in her father's Yiddish, *"Hock mir nisht kein tchynick"*—don't make such a fuss. It was stupid, not at all funny, but Nat smiled a little as he made some instant Folger's, stirred in three teaspoons of sugar, which she knew he'd given up years ago. It was as if he were retreating to the year he had begun drinking coffee—when he was fifteen, a year safe from all this.

"Nat, what can I do?"

"Just sit," he said, sipping his coffee. "Listen." And then he went through a terrible inventory of everything he'd checked and looked for in his room. She couldn't stop thinking of all the Jewish homes and apartments throughout Europe that had been looted, burned, destroyed, trainloads of plundered bloody goods snaking back to the Fatherland: mattresses, pianos, candelabras, coats.

Mark rang sharply, and pushed past her, flushed, rumpled, smelling of sleep and sweat. At first, Mark and Nat held each other's arms without hugging, peering at each other like relations meeting at an airport after forty years, not quite sure they had the right person. Then Mark embraced him, looking fierce and defiant, like a king sending off his armies to avenge his honor.

"I've been making lists of phone numbers. We're calling all the papers, the ACLU, the FBI, because it's arson. You need a lawyer."

Nat moved to the couch, sat. "I need a room."

"Couldn't we leave?" Brenda asked, arms out like an opera singer imploring the tyrant for her lover's release. "Just today—go home and get out of this place? I'll cancel my office hours. I want to go home."

Mark shook his head. "I'm staying. We've got lots to do."

"No." Nat stood up. "Brenda's right. Not today. I want you to come down to Southfield with us, so we can *all* tell them what happened before they hear about it on the news, in the paper—"

"Or in the supermarket," Brenda put in. "From a neighbor."

Mark and Nat grimaced. They decided to go back to Mark's, shower and change, and Brenda would meet them there in an hour.

Washing her hair, she thought of Scarlett O'Hara, dirty, desperate, fleeing the flames of Atlanta for her beloved Tara. For the first time she understood the longing to be released from fear by simply being someplace you loved.

She fondly pictured their enormous backyard, a full acre,

blooming now thanks to the unusually warm spring. Putting on the blue silk dress that her mother said made her look like an actress, Brenda saw them all sitting out in the lacy high-peaked gazebo Nat had always dreamed about and finally gotten this last year with money he earned as a waiter. They would sit in the deep cool shade, admiring the crocuses and tulips springing up at the back of the house, and breathe in the rich sweet smell of the thirty white lilac bushes her parents had planted themselves on their thirtieth wedding anniversary. The stench of burnt clothes would be banished.

Her parents would *have* to be on Nat's side—the fire would be too familiar and threatening, like synagogue bombings, cemetery desecrations.

She slipped Nat's triangle button into her purse before she left. She would have to ask Nat the date of Gay Pride Day, and where people would be marching and what time.

In her car, before putting her key in the ignition, she remembered how the king of Denmark had worn a yellow star when the occupying Nazis started persecuting Danish Jews.

She took out Nat's button and used the rearview mirror to help pin it to her dress.

Rubyfruit Jungle

Rita Mae Brown

Rite Mae Brown's novel Rubyfruit Jungle, *originally published in 1973, was a major event in gay and lesbian liberation. The novel charts the coming of age of Molly Bolt, a bold southern lesbian who follows her heart and her own set of values, refusing to bow to traditional rules or pressures. In the passage below, Molly confronts the homophobic women in her college dormitory by explaining to them, quite calmly, that she and her roommate, Faye, are lesbians. Even the dean of students is no match for Molly.*

The rest of that semester we spent in bed, emerging only to go to class and to eat. Faye made her grades because it was the only way we could be together, and she stopped drinking because she found something that was more fun. Chi Omega began to think Faye had died and gone to heaven. Tri-Delta resorted to sending me urgent notices in the mail. We were eighteen, in love, and didn't know the world existed—but it knew we existed.

Not until February did I notice that people on our hall weren't speaking to us anymore. Conversations stopped when one or both of us would amble down the brown halls. Faye concluded they all had chronic laryngitis and decided she'd cure it. She hooked up a Mickey Mouse Club record to the ugly brick bell tower that rang class changes. Then she announced to our dorm neighbors that at three-thirty the true nature of the university would be revealed via the bell tower. As soon as the record blared across the campus Dot and Karen ran in from next door to giggle at Faye's success. Just as quickly they turned on their heels to walk out when Faye bluntly asked, "How come you two don't talk to us anymore?"

Terror crossed Dot's face and she told a half truth. "Because you stay in your room all the time."

"Bullshit," Faye countered.

"There's got to be another reason," I added.

Karen, angered at our bad manners in being so direct, spat at us gracefully. "You two are together so much it looks like you're lesbians."

I thought Faye was going to heave her chemistry book at Karen, her white face was so red. I looked Karen right in the face and said calmly, "We are."

Karen reeled back as though she were slapped with a soggy dishrag. "You're sick and you don't belong in a place like this with all these girls around."

Faye was now on her feet moving toward Karen, and Dot, the picture of courage, was at the door fumbling with the knob. Faye shifted into overdrive and roared her engine, "Why, Karen, are you afraid I might sleep with you? Are you afraid I might sneak over in the middle of the night and attack you?" Faye was laughing by this time and Karen was petrified. "Karen, if you were the last woman on earth, I'd go back to men—you're a simpering, pimply-faced cretin." Karen ran out of the room and Faye howled, "Did you see her face? What an insipid asswipe that creature is!"

"Faye, we're in for it now. She's gonna run right to the resident counselor and we are gonna be in real fucking trouble. They'll probably throw us out."

"Let them. Who the hell wants to rot in this institution of mis-education?"

"I do. It's my one chance to get out of the boondocks. I've got to get my degree."

"We'll go to a private school."

"You can go to a private school. I can't even pay for my own food, Goddammit."

"Look, my old man will pay my way and we can work part-time to pay your way. Shit, I wish he'd give you the money. I don't give a rat's ass about my degree. But that's out of the question. Anyway, he wants me to stay in school, so he'll send bonuses to encourage me and we can get along with that plus a little work."

"I think it's going to be harder than that, Faye, but I hope you're right."

One half-hour after Faye insulted Karen's nonexistent sexuality, she was called to the resident counselor's office while I was sent to the dean of women, Miss Marne. This creature was a heifer-like, red-haired woman who had been a major in the Army Corps back in World War II. She liked to quote her military experiences as proof that women could make it. I walked into her *House & Garden* office with all the painted plaques on the wall. She probably had one up there as proof of her femininity too. She smiled broadly and shook my hand vigorously.

"Sit down, won't you, Miss Bolt? Have a cigarette?"

"No thank you, I don't smoke."

"Wise of you. Now, let's get down to business. I called you here because of the unfortunate incident in your dormitory. Would you care to explain that to me?"

"No."

"Miss Bolt, this is a very serious matter and I want to help you. It will be much easier if you cooperate." She ran her hand over the glass cover on her maplewood desk and smiled reassuringly. "Molly, may I call you that?" I nodded. What the hell do I care what she calls me? "I've been going over your record and you're one of our most outstanding students—an honors scholar, tennis team, freshman representative, Tri-Delta—you're a go-getter, as we say. Ha, ha. I think you're the kind of young woman who will want to work out this problem that you have, and I want to help you work it out. A person like you could go far in this world." She lowered her voice confidentially. "I know it's been hard for you, your birth and, well, you simply didn't have the advantages of other girls. That's why I admire the way you've risen above your circumstances. Now tell me about this difficulty you have in relating to girls and your roommate."

"Dean Marne, I don't have any problem relating to girls and I'm in love with my roommate. She makes me happy."

Her scraggly red eyebrows with the brown pencil glaring through shot up. "Is this relationship with Faye Raider of an, uh—intimate nature?"

"We fuck, if that's what you're after."

I think her womb collapsed on that one. Sputtering, she pressed forward. "Don't you find that somewhat of an aberration? Doesn't this disturb you, my dear? After all, it's not normal."

"I know it's not normal for people in this world to be happy, and I'm happy."

"H-m-m. Perhaps there are things hidden in your past, secrets in your unconscious that keep you from having a healthy relationship with members of the opposite sex. I think with some hard work on your part and professional assistance, you can uncover these blocks and find the way to a deeper, more meaningful relationship with a man." She took a breath and smiled that administrative smile. "Haven't you ever thought about children, Molly?"

"No."

This time she couldn't hide her shock. "I see. Well, dear, I have arranged for you to see one of our psychiatrists here three times a week and, of course, you'll see me once a week. I want you to know I'm in there rooting for you to get through this phase you're in. I want you to know I'm your friend."

If I had had a blowtorch, I'd have turned it on her smiling face until it was as red as her hair. I didn't have one in my purse, so I did the next best thing. "Dean Marne, why are you pushing me so hard to be a mother and all that rot when you aren't even married?"

She squirmed in her seat and avoided my gaze. I had broken the code and put her on the spot. "We're here to discuss you, not me. I had plenty of opportunities. I decided a career was more important to me than being a homemaker. Many ambitious women were forced into that choice in my day."

"You know what I think? I think you're as much a lesbian as I am. You're a goddamn fucking closet fairy, that's what you are. I know you've been living with Miss Stiles of the English Department for the last fifteen years. You're running this whole number on me to make yourself look good. Hell, at least I'm honest about what I am."

Yes, her face was red, inflamed. She slammed her fist so hard on the desk that the glass covering with all the papers pushed under it broke and she cut her meaty hand. "Young lady, you are going directly to the psychiatrist. You are obviously a hostile, destructive personality and need supervision. What a way to talk to me when I'm trying to help you. You're farther gone than I thought."

The noise attracted her secretaries and Dean Marne dialed the university hospital. I was escorted to the looney ward by two campus policemen. The nurse took my fingerprints. I suppose they run them under a microscope to see if there are any diseased bacteria on them. Then I was led to a bare room with a cot in it and stripped of all my clothing. I was put in a nifty gown that would have made even Marilyn Monroe look whipped. The door was shut and they turned the key. The fluorescent lights hurt my eyes and their humming was driving me as nuts as the treatment I had received. Hours later Dr. Demiral, a Turkish psychiatrist, came in to talk to me. He asked me if I was disturbed. I told him that I sure was disturbed now and I wanted out of this place. He told me to calm myself, and within a few days I'd be out. Until that time I was being observed for my own good. It was a matter of procedure, nothing personal. Those next days I beat out Bette Davis for acting awards. I was calm and cheerful. I pretended I was delighted to see Dr. Demiral's greasy, bearded face. We talked about my childhood, about Dean Marne, and about my simmering hatreds that I had repressed. It was very simple. Whatever they say, you look serious, attentive, and say "yes" or, "I hadn't thought of that." I invented horrendous stories to ground my fury in the past. It's also very important to make up dreams. They love dreams. I used to lie awake nights thinking up dreams. It was exhausting. Within the week, I was released to return to the relative tranquillity of Broward Hall.

I stopped at my mailbox, which had two letters in it. One was written in Faye's handwriting and one had a silver, blue, and gold edging around it which meant it was from my beloved sisters at Tri-Delta. I opened that one first. It was official and had the crescent seal on the paper. I was dropped from the sorority and they were sure I'd understand. Everyone hoped I'd get better. I ran up the stairs, opened the door, and found all Faye's things gone. I sat down on the lonesome bed and read Faye's letter.

Dear Sweet Lover Molly,

The resident counselor told me my father is coming to pick me up and I'm to pack everything. Daddy is apparently close to a heart attack over this whole thing because as soon as I got out of my disgusting discussion with the R.C. I called home and Mums answered the phone. She sounded as though she had swallowed a razor blade. She said I'd better have an explanation for all this because Dad's ready to put me in the funny farm to "straighten me out." God, Molly, they're all *crazy*. My own parents want to lock me up. Mother was crying and said she'd get the best doctors there were for her little girl and what did she do wrong. Vomit! I think we won't see each other. They'll keep me away and you're locked up in the hospital. I feel like I'm underwater. I'd run away by myself but I can't seem to move and sounds roll in and out of my head like waves. I think I won't surface until I see you. It looks like I won't see you soon. If they put me away maybe I'll never see you. Molly, get out of here. Get out and don't try to find me. There's no time for us now. Everything is stacked against us. Listen to me. I may be underwater but I can see some things. Get out of here. Run. You're the stronger of the two of us. Go to a big city. It ought to be a little better there. Be free. I love you.

                                                    Faye

P.S. $20 is all I had left in my account. It's in your top drawer with all the underpants. I left an old bottle of Jack Daniels there too. Drink a toast to me and then fly away.

Between a white pair of underpants and a red pair was the twenty dollars. Underneath the whole pile was the Jack Daniels. I drank Faye her toast, then walked down the hall with all the doors closing like clockwork and poured the rest of the bottle down the drain.

The next day in my mailbox was a letter from the scholarship committee informing me that my scholarships could not be renewed for "moral reasons" although my academic record was "superb."

Nesting in the back of my closet with the palmetto bugs was my Girls' State suitcase. I pulled it out and filled it, sat on it to close it. I left my books in my room except for my English book, left my term papers and football programs and my last scrap of innocence. I closed the door forever on idealism and the essential goodness of human nature, and I walked to the Greyhound bus station by the same path that I had taken on my arrival.

Reflections of a Rock Lobster

Aaron Fricke

Aaron Fricke grew up in Cumberland, Rhode Island. In 1980, he made national headlines when a federal district court allowed him to bring a male date to his high school prom. In this passage from Reflections of a Rock Lobster: A Story about Growing Up Gay, *Aaron explains why he decided to fight for the right to attend the prom with the date of his choice.*

In April, Mr. Lynch held the traditional pep talk to jolt the graduating class out of senioritis. Just as he had done the previous autumn, he referred to the "problem" that had existed at the 1979 prom. Naturally, the students exploded in enthusiasm. I wanted to stand up and scream, "I am gay and proud and will not be oppressed!" I was determined that Mr. Lynch would not go on forever stirring up this prejudice in the hearts of my fellow students. But for the time, discretion prevailed. Besides, I valued the use of my two legs.

Everyone buzzed about the prom after Mr. Lynch's speech. The girls planned to make or buy their gowns. Some guys reminisced about last year's prom. But like always, I was left out of these discussions. Through all of my high school years I had been left out and I was tired of it. I wanted to be part of the group like all the other students.

The simple, obvious thing would have been to go to the senior prom with a girl. But that would have been a lie—a lie to myself, to the girl, and to all the other students. What I *wanted* to do was to take a male date. But as Paul had shown the year before, such honesty is not always easy.

There was an important difference between Paul's case and mine, though. Paul had not been able to fight for his rights because he was seventeen at the time. I was now eighteen and legally able to make my own decisions. If I wanted to go to the prom with a male escort and the school tried to stop me, I could take the case to court.

But should I do that? This would require much thought if I was to make a decision without being selfish, uncaring or irrational.

If I went to the prom with another guy, what would be the benefits? For myself, it would mean participating in an important social event and doing so with a clear conscience and a sense of wholeness. But how would it affect the rest of the people involved?

I believed that those who had themselves faced discrimination or prejudice would immediately understand what I was doing and its implications for human rights. There would be others who may never have had direct experiences with prejudice but who would recognize my right to the date of my choice. These people may have been misled to believe that homosexuality is wrong, but they could still understand that my rights were being denied.

At the opposite end of the spectrum were the homophobics who might react violently. But the example I set would be perfect for everyone. We would be just one more happy couple. Our happiness together would be something kids could relate to. I would be showing that my dignity and value as a human being were not affected by my sexual preference.

I concluded that taking a guy to the prom would be a strong positive statement about the existence of gay people. Any opposition to my case (and I anticipated a good bit) would show the negative side of society—not of homosexuality.

To attend the prom with a girl would not be unenjoyable but it would be dishonest to my true feelings. Besides, most kids now knew I was gay. If I went with a female, I would probably have received more taunts than from going with a male. By going with a male I would win some respect from the more mature students, and I would keep my self-esteem.

I tried not to worry about the possibility of violence. Certainly

I would face opposition. It was inevitable given the rampant prejudice against homosexuals today. But the threat of violence was not enough to change my mind, since I encountered that every day to some degree. Perhaps such threats would diminish in the future as people saw more homosexuals participating openly in everyday life.

My biggest concern was for my parents. Although the entire student body and administration of Cumberland High School knew or assumed I was gay, my family had remained blissfully blind to this reality. The news could be heartbreaking to them. Plus, it might get them ostracized by the neighbors, banned from town social gatherings . . . from church . . . from Tupperware parties! Was I willing to take this risk? No! As much as I believed in my rights, I valued my relationship with my parents too much to have it abruptly severed. After all, for years I had hidden my sexuality for fear of losing my parents' love. As a child it had been *the* most important thing to me. Now, as a man, it was just as important as before. I wanted to go to my prom, but it was not as important as eighteen years of love.

I decided to tell my parents of my homosexuality first, then ask them how they would feel about my going to the prom. If it seemed like too much for them to accept, I would forget the prom and just be happy that I no longer had to be secretive with my parents. But if they rejected me merely because I was gay, then I would still pursue my rights, even at the prom, realizing that my parents were good people but were horribly misled.

Until now, I had never spoken to them about my homosexuality. Like many adolescents I had drifted away from my parents lately. Now I had an impetus to improve my communication with them. I decided to approach my parents separately; a thousand times I rehearsed what I would say.

It began, "Ever since I was a kid . . ." and ended, "I hope you love me enough not to reject me." But when the moment of truth came I felt more self-confident and said, "I don't know if you've had any suspicions, but I'm gay."

Long pause. My mother replied, "I'm so glad you were finally able to be honest with me." She had long suspected. My father had not; when I told him he broke down and cried. Yet they both loved me unconditionally. When I explained why I wanted to go to the prom they were supportive. I was my own man, they each said, and I would have to make my own decisions.

It felt great to be able to talk to my parents about this. Their reaction was encouraging and I decided to go ahead. I would invite Paul Guilbert to the prom.

Anne Guillet wrote me a note in environmental science class when I asked for her advice about the prom. She wrote:

Dear Aaron,

Last year, Paul's attempt to bring a guy to the prom was seen by most people, in fact I think by all, as a grab at publicity. That was because no one knew Paul, he just showed up out of a clear blue sky (and raised a ruckus). Since you've been in Cumberland much longer and have more close friends, people won't suspect you of such ill motives so easily, but this is what they will think.

1. Paul made you do it.

2. You're crazy.

3. You believe in gay rights.

In that order. Now *I* know you did it for reason 3 but you should think about how other people are going to react and I think you should make an effort to explain what you believe. I respect any decision you make, as long as you really think about it carefully.

Love,
Anne

I took her advice and painstakingly wrote a letter to the school newspaper, explaining why I decided to go to the prom with a male date. The letter said that I hoped no one would be hurt by what I was doing, that a victory in court would be a victory for every Cumberland High student because it would be a blow against prejudice. The next issue of the school paper had space for all sorts of trivia, but my letter never appeared.

Later in April, the school theater group took its annual bus trip to New York City. Our teacher, Miss Frappier, was an exceptionally warm and friendly person and we were a tight-knit bunch—one of those rare groups of thespians whose members had no pent-up distrust or jealousy toward each other. On the bus Miss Frappier gave out the spring awards; I received one of them, for an outstanding performance in *A Thurber Carnival.*

In New York we went to the Guggenheim Museum and to a Broadway production of *They're Playing Our Song;* then when the group returned to Rhode Island, I stayed in New York to spend time with Paul.

Paul seemed to be getting happier in the city. Our friendship had not faded although Paul and I had not seen each other for months. We took a long walk through the Village, bringing each other up to date on what we'd been doing, and enjoying the feeling of the trees in bloom and spring in the air.

By evening I had settled any doubts I still had about who I wanted to invite to the prom. And so, with sweaty palms and butterflies in my stomach, I finally asked Paul: "I was wondering, um, do you have a date for the Cumberland High prom this year?"

Paul began laughing. "I'd love to attend the senior prom with you," he finally said. My feeling of happiness lasted all the way back to Rhode Island. [. . .]

When we arrived at the prom site, we were greeted with a glare of television lights. Flash bulbs were popping and everybody was talking and trying to ask questions as we walked toward the building. The reporters broke down the velvet ropes that were supposed to hold them back. I was too full of anticipation and excitement to think of anything to say. So a second before walking in the door, in a grand gesture of looniness, camp and high drama, I turned to the reporters, waved, and stuck out my tongue.

Once inside, Mr. Lynch quickly ushered Paul and me away from the door, so the reporters would be unable to see us. We were shown to an empty table, which neither of us enjoyed because there were no kids to talk to. My ninth-grade Spanish teacher, Mrs. Noelte, eventually sat with us.

Dinner was soon served. It was chicken cordon something or other, and consisted of mushed chicken encased in oil. My piece looked like a monster from the film *Alien*. The salad looked better, but when I bit into the cherry tomato, it splattered right onto my pants. I did my best to ignore the stain, but it kept showing up in the pictures people took.

After dinner was cleared away, many students began coming by to offer us a few good words. There was more good feeling than I would ever have anticipated. One after another, students came by and expresed their happiness that we could share the prom with each other. Billy Marlen came up and said he was glad to see us both. Even Dave Beamer approached and softly said, "I'm glad you're here."

Across the room, I noticed my old friend Bob Cote, accompanied by Bea Duvwalge. When Bob saw me he started to walk over, but Bea grabbed his arm and he went back to her.

I wandered over to a big picture window and stared out. Several reporters were talking outside on the lawn. For a moment I thought of all the people who would have enjoyed going to their proms with the date of their choice, but were denied that right; of all the people in the past who wanted to live respectably with the person they loved but could not; of all the men and women who had been hurt or killed because they were gay; and of the rich history of lesbians and homosexual men that had so long been ignored. Gradually we were triumphing over ignorance. One day we would be free.

The dance music came on. Kelleen Driskell came over and asked me to dance the first song with her. I was happy to accept. I'd known Kelleen in elementary school but I had drifted away from her, as from so many other people, during my fat years. We fast danced for that song and just through our physical movements together, without exchanging words, it felt as if we were re-establishing a communication.

After the dance I had to use the bathroom. Throughout the evening, Paul and I would see all kinds of defense mechanisms from the other guys whenever we went to the bathroom. Some of them made a beeline for the door as soon as we walked in. Others stayed, their desire to escape temporarily overcome by their curiosity about how gay people go to the bathroom.

When I got back to the dance floor, Paul asked me if I wanted to slow dance. I did. The next song was Bob Seger's "We've Got the Night," and we stepped out onto the dance floor.

The crowd receded. As I laid my head on Paul's shoulder, I saw a few students start to stare at us. I closed my eyes and listened to the music, my thoughts wandering over the events of that evening. When the song ended, I opened my eyes. A large crowd of students had formed a ring around us. Probably most of them had never before seen two happy men embracing in a slow dance. For a moment I was uncomfortable. Then I heard the sound that I knew so well as a B-52's fan. One of my favorite songs was coming up: "Rock Lobster."

Paul and I began dancing freestyle. Everyone else was still staring at us, but by the end of the first stanza, several couples had also begun dancing. The song has a contagious enthusiasm to it, and with each bar, more dancers came onto the floor.

I glanced over at the tables. Bob Cote was sitting with Bea Duvwalge, who was finishing off her chicken cordon-whatever. Bob was eyeing the dancing students and bouncing his leg with an obvious urge to join. He stood up and tugged at Bea's arm to come with him; she pulled him back and he sat down again with a look of disappointment.

More students were coming onto the floor to dance. I doubt that any two people were dancing with the same movements: the dancing was an expression of our individuality, and no one felt bad about being different. Everyone was free to be themselves.

A quarter of the way into the song, thirty people were on the dance floor. I looked at Bob and Bea again. Bea seemed to be wondering what a rock lobster was.

"Down, Down, Down," commanded the lyrics. Everyone on the dance floor sank to their knees and crouched on the ground. I lifted my head slightly to look around. Dozens of intertwining bodies crouched on their knees as if praying. We were all one; we shared a unity of pure love. And those who did not want to share it, such as Bea Duvwalge, sat on the sidelines. Bea was now arguing with Bob.

> *Red snappers snappin'*
> *Clamshells clappin'*

Everyone jumped to their feet again and resumed dancing. Many more kids had joined us and there must have been sixty or eighty people on the dance floor now.

As Paul and I danced, we had gradually drifted from our original space on the floor. We were now near the table where Bob and Bea sat. Out of the corner of my eye, I saw Bea suddenly stand up and grab a napkin. It looked like a glass of water had spilled on her. She dabbed at her gown.

"Down, Down, Down," cried the B-52's again, and we all went down. The feeling of unity among us permeated the air again. When we came up I heard Bea yelling at Bob, then she stormed off toward the bathroom. Now there were at least a hundred people on the dance floor. The tempo became more frenetic and everyone danced faster.

"Let's Rock!!!" bellowed from the speakers, and to my surprise, when I looked up I saw that Paul had disappeared. In his place was Bob Cote. I looked around; several other guys were dancing with each other, and girls were dancing with girls. Everybody was rockin', everybody was fruggin'. Who cared why? Maybe they were doing it to mock me and Paul, maybe they were doing it because they wanted to, maybe one was an excuse for the other . . . I didn't know and I didn't care. It was fun. Everyone was together. Eventually Bob and I drifted away. I danced with girls, I danced with guys, I danced with the entire group.

Then the music stopped. "Rock Lobster" has an abrupt ending, and no one was quite ready for it to stop. I had been having so much fun that I lost track of time; I had also lost track of Paul, and had to look around the room for him.

I could see that everyone felt a sense of disorientation. For six minutes and forty-nine seconds, the students on the dance floor had forgotten about their defenses, forgotten about their shells. We just had fun.

Does It Matter?

This poem was written by an anonymous high school student.

My father asked if I am gay
I asked Does it matter?
He said No not really
I said Yes.
He said get out of my life
I guess it mattered.

My boss asked if I am gay
I asked Does it matter?
He said No not really
I told him Yes.
He said You're fired, faggot
I guess it mattered.

My friend asked if I am gay
I said Does it matter?
He said Not really
I told him Yes.
He said Don't call me your friend
I guess it mattered.

My lover asked Do you love me?
I asked Does it matter?
He said Yes.
I told him I love you
He said Let me hold you in my arms
For the first time in my life something matters.

My God asked me Do you love yourself?
I said Does it matter?
He said Yes.
I said How can I love myself? I am Gay
He said That is the way I made you
Nothing again will ever matter.

Appendix 1: For Further Exploration

This is not a comprehensive bibliography but rather a selective list of books, magazines, and videos that may be of special interest to young adults. Most of the titles below are in print and available at bookstores and libraries. (If you have difficulty locating a given title, inquire about interlibrary loan services through your school or public library, or contact one of the bookstores listed below to order material by mail.) An asterisk before an entry indicates that a portion of the book is reprinted in this anthology.

BOOKS

Coming Out

*Alyson, Sasha, editor. *Young, Gay, and Proud!* Boston: Alyson Publications, 1985. A practical handbook for young women and men, with sections on coming out to parents and friends, health concerns, and sexuality.

Borhek, Mary V. *Coming Out to Parents: A Two-Way Survival Guide for Lesbians and Gay Men and Their Parents.* New York: The Pilgrim Press, 1983. The mother of a gay son, Borhek draws on personal experience and case histories to provide practical advice to gay young people and their parents.

Curtis, Wayne, editor. *Revelations: A Collection of Gay Male Coming Out Stories.* Boston: Alyson Publications, 1988. Well-known and first-time gay writers share their reflections on the coming out process.

Eichberg, Rob. *Coming Out: An Act of Love.* New York: Dutton, 1990. Contains extensive examples of coming-out letters from young people to their parents, as well as letters from parents and a chapter on "coming out powerfully."

*Holmes, Sarah, editor. *Testimonies: A Collection of Lesbian Coming Out Stories.* Boston: Alyson Publications, 1988.

Life Stories / Autobiography / Biography

*Adair, Nancy, and Casey Adair. *Word Is Out: Stories of Some of Our Lives*. San Francisco: New Glide Publications/Dell Publishing, 1978.

Barrett, Martha. *Invisible Lives: The Truth about Millions of Women-Loving Women*. New York: William Morrow, 1989; Harper and Row, 1990. Draws from more than 120 interviews to present rich and insightful portraits of lesbians in contemporary America.

*Boyd, Malcolm. *Take Off the Masks*. Garden City, New York: Doubleday, 1978.

*Crisp, Quentin. *The Naked Civil Servant*. New York: Holt, Rinehart, Winston, 1968; New American Library, 1983.

*Fricke, Aaron. *Reflections of a Rock Lobster: A Story about Growing Up Gay*. Boston: Alyson Publications, 1981.

Heron, Ann, editor. *One Teenager in Ten: Testimony by Gay and Lesbian Youth*. Boston: Alyson Publications, 1983. Though somewhat dated, this collection is effective in describing the struggles that gay and lesbian young people often face in the process of discovering themselves.

Hutchins, Loraine, and Lani Kaahumanu, editors. *Bi Any Other Name: Bisexual People Speak Out*. Boston: Alyson Publications, 1991. A wide-ranging collection of personal reflections on bisexuality.

*Kopay, David, and Perry Deane Young. *The David Kopay Story: An Extraordinary Self-Revelation*. New York: Arbor House, 1977; Donald Fine, 1988.

*Lorde, Audre. *Zami: A New Spelling of My Name*. Freedom, California: The Crossing Press, 1983.

*Monette, Paul. *Becoming a Man: Half a Life Story*. New York: Harcourt Brace Jovanovich, 1992.

*Navratilova, Martina, and George Vecsey. *Martina*. New York: Alfred A. Knopf, 1985; Fawcett Books, 1986.

*Preston, John, editor. *A Member of the Family: Gay Men Write about Their Closest Relations.* New York: New American Library, 1992.

*————. *Hometowns: Gay Men Write about Where They Belong.* New York: New American Library, 1991.

*Reid, John. *The Best Little Boy in the World.* New York: Putnam, 1973; Ballantine, 1986.

Shilts, Randy. *The Mayor of Castro Street: The Life and Times of Harvey Milk.* New York: St. Martin's, 1982, 1988. A captivating biography of Harvey Milk, the first openly gay elected official in California, who was assassinated in 1978.

*Steffan, Joseph. *Honor Bound: A Gay American Fights for the Right to Serve His Country.* New York: Villard Books, 1992.

Gay and Lesbian History

Cowan, Thomas. *Gay Men and Women Who Enriched the World.* New Canaan, Connecticut: Mulvey Books, 1988. Witty and brief biographical sketches of forty famous gay people, including Leonardo da Vinci, Sappho, Gertrude Stein, and Michael Bennett.

Cruikshank, Margaret. *The Gay and Lesbian Liberation Movement.* New York: Routledge, 1992. A lively and balanced account of the roots of the contemporary movement for gay and lesbian liberation.

Duberman, Martin. *Stonewall.* New York: Dutton, 1993. A history of the momentous 1969 Stonewall uprising, told through testimony of people who participated.

Faderman, Lillian. *Odd Girls and Twilight Lovers: A History of Lesbian Life in Twentieth-Century America.* New York: Columbia University Press, 1991; New York: Viking Penguin, 1992. Uses journals, songs, novels, and interviews to show how "lesbian identity" emerged. Scholarly.

Heger, Heinz. *The Men with the Pink Triangle.* Boston: Alyson Publications, 1980. An account of the Nazi persecution and extermination of gay men during World War II.

Katz, Jonathan N. *Gay American History: Lesbians and Gay Men in the U.S.A.* New York: New American Library, 1992 (revised edition). A fascinating collection of historical documents.

————.*Gay / Lesbian Almanac.* New York: Harper and Row, 1983. Another collection of historical documents, including newspaper articles, book reviews, legal writings, and excerpts from literary works and medical journals; this volume covers gay history from 1607 to 1950.

*Marcus, Eric. *Making History: The Struggle for Gay and Lesbian Equal Rights.* New York: HarperCollins, 1992.

Collections by and about Lesbians and Gay Men of Color

Beam, Joseph, editor. *In the Life: A Black Gay Anthology.* Boston: Alyson Publications, 1986. A powerful collection that contains essays, fiction, and poetry about being black and gay.

*Hemphill, Essex, editor. *Brother to Brother: New Writings by Black Gay Men.* Boston: Alyson Publications, 1991. The sequel to *In the Life.*

*Roscoe, Will, editor. *Living the Spirit: A Gay American Indian Anthology.* New York: St. Martin's, 1989.

Silvera, Makeda, editor. *Piece of My Heart: A Lesbian of Colour Anthology.* Toronto: Sister Vision, 1991.

*Smith, Barbara, editor. *Home Girls: A Black Feminist Anthology.* Latham, New York: Kitchen Table Press, 1983.

Novels

*Baldwin, James. *Giovanni's Room.* New York: Dial Press, 1956; Dell, 1985.

*Brown, Rita Mae. *Rubyfruit Jungle.* New York: Daughters, Inc., 1973; Bantam, 1988.

*Garden, Nancy. *Annie on My Mind.* New York: Farrar, Straus and Giroux, 1982.

Homes, A. M. *Jack*. New York: Macmillan, 1989; Random House, 1990. A fifteen-year-old learns that his father is gay.

*Leavitt, David. *The Lost Language of Cranes*. New York: Alfred A. Knopf, 1986; Bantam, 1987.

White, Edmund. *A Boy's Own Story*. New York: Dutton, 1982; New American Library, 1983. A bittersweet novel about coming of age as a gay man.

*Winterson, Jeanette. *Oranges Are Not the Only Fruit*. London: Pandora Press, 1985; New York: Atlantic Monthly Press, 1987.

Short Stories / Short Fiction

*Birtha, Becky. *Lovers' Choice*. Seattle: Seal Press, 1987.

Leavitt, David. *Family Dancing*. New York: Alfred A. Knopf, 1984; Warner Books, 1991.

*Portillo, Tina, editor. *Dykescapes: Short Fiction by Lesbians*. Boston: Alyson Publications, 1991.

*Raphael, Lev. *Dancing on Tisha B'Av*. New York: St. Martin's, 1990.

Stambolian, George, editor. *Men on Men 4: Best New Gay Fiction*. New York: Dutton, 1992. An anthology of short stories by contemporary gay men. See also the three earlier volumes in the *Men on Men* series.

Poetry

*Allison, Dorothy. *The Women Who Hate Me: Poetry, 1980–1990*. Ithaca: Firebrand, 1991.

Coote, Stephen, editor. *The Penguin Book of Homosexual Verse*. New York: Viking Penguin, 1987. This anthology contains contemporary poetry as well as verse written before the twentieth century; the emphasis is on British authors.

Hughes, Langston. *Selected Poems of Langston Hughes*. New York: Alfred A. Knopf, 1959; Random House, 1990.

Lorde, Audre. *Undersong: Chosen Poems Old and New*. New York: Norton, 1992 (revised edition).

*Morse, Carl, and Joan Larkin, editors. *Gay and Lesbian Poetry in Our Time*. New York: St. Martin's, 1988, 1989.

Health / Sexuality

The Boston Women's Health Book Collective. *The New Our Bodies, Ourselves*. New York: Simon and Schuster, 1985, 1992 (revised edition). A comprehensive guide to women's health, with extensive coverage of lesbian issues.

Bell, Ruth. *Changing Bodies, Changing Lives: A Book for Teens on Sex and Relationships*. New York: Random House, 1980. Clear and matter-of-fact treatment of sexuality, with strong material on gay and lesbian issues.

AIDS

Dietz, Steven D. and M. Jane Parker Hicks, M.D. *Take These Broken Wings and Learn To Fly: The AIDS Support Book for Patients, Family and Friends*. Tucson: Harbinger House, 1989. A clear, factual discussion of HIV and how it causes disease. Offers a positive approach to living with AIDS.

*Kerr, M. E. *Night Kites*. New York: HarperCollins, 1986.

Martelli, Leonard, with Fran D. Peltz and William Messina. *When Someone You Know Has AIDS: A Practical Guide*. A guide for helping relatives and friends to cope with AIDS. Contains practical information on day-to-day issues facing people with AIDS.

Shilts, Randy. *And the Band Played On: People, Politics, & the AIDS Epidemic*. New York: St. Martin's, 1987; Penguin, 1988. An exposé of the federal government's responses to and attitudes about the AIDS crisis, and an investigation of the role that politics has played in funding research on and treatment for the disease.

Reference Books

The Alyson Almanac. Boston: Alyson Publications, 1989. An entertaining and comprehensive reference book with brief entries on gay and lesbian history, literature, publications, and organizations.

Blumenfeld, Warren J., and Diane Raymond. *Looking at Gay and Lesbian Life*. New York: Philosophical Library, 1988. A highly readable reference book that covers history, the causes of sexuality, AIDS, and gay and lesbian culture.

Marcus, Eric. *Is It a Choice? Answers to Three Hundred of the Most Frequently Asked Questions about Gay Men and Lesbians*. San Francisco: HarperSanFrancisco, 1993. A handy reference source for gay and non-gay readers.

Preston, John. *The Big Gay Book: A Man's Survival Guide for the '90s*. New York: Plume, 1991. An excellent resource to contemporary gay culture, with information on political organizations, religious groups, media, and living with AIDS.

MAGAZINES / NEWSLETTERS

The Advocate. Biweekly newsmagazine for gay men and lesbians, featuring national and regional news, arts reviews, and interviews. Subscriptions: $54 for 26 issues. Published by Liberation Publications, Inc., 6922 Hollywood Blvd. (tenth floor), Los Angeles, CA 90028. Tel. (213) 871-1225.

Christopher Street. Monthly magazine for gay men, noted for strong fiction department. Subscriptions: $27 for 12 issues. Published monthly by That New Magazine, Inc., 28 West 25th Street (fourth floor), New York, NY 10010. Tel. (212) 627-2120.

Deneuve: The Lesbian Magazine. Bimonthly magazine for lesbians, featuring news, arts reviews, and interviews. Subscriptions: $24 per year. Published by FRS Enterprises, 2336 Market Street (Suite 15), San Francisco, CA 94114. Tel (415) 863-6538.

Inside / Out Newsletter. Quarterly newsletter by and for sexual minority youth. Published by Bay Area Sexual Minority Youth Network (BASMYN), P.O. Box 460268, San Francisco, CA 94146-0268. No fee.

Out. Bimonthly magazine for lesbians and gay men, featuring news, arts reviews, and interviews; trendy. Subscriptions: $19.95 per year. Published by OUT, P.O. Box 15307, North Hollywood, CA 91615-5307. Tel. (800) 876-1199.

VIDEOS

Another Country (1984; 90 minutes; directed by Marek Kanievska; stars Rupert Everett, Colin Firth). Adaptation of Julian Mitchell's hit play, in which Guy Bennett, a British citizen who became a Russian spy, looks back on his awakening as a gay man at a private British school in the 1930s.

Common Threads: Stories from the Quilt (1989; 75 minutes; directed by Robert Epstein and Jeffrey Friedman). An Oscar-winning documentary about the personal stories of five people with AIDS and the memorial quilt made to commemorate people who have died of the disease.

Desert Hearts (1985; 93 minutes; directed by Donna Deitch; stars Helen Shaver, Patricia Charbonneau). Adaptation of Jane Rule's novel, in which an unhappy college professor goes to Reno to get a divorce in the 1950s and falls in love with an adventurous lesbian.

Gay Youth (1992; 40 minutes; directed by Pam Walton). A powerful documentary about the lives of gay and lesbian youth, featuring the stories of a young gay man who commits suicide and a young lesbian who accepts herself and is supported by her family. Available (with study guide) for sale from BANGLE (Bay Area Network of Gay and Lesbian Educators), c/o Wolfe Video, P.O. Box 64, New Almaden, CA, 95042; tel. (408) 268-6782. Price: $60, plus $6 for shipping and handling.

My Beautiful Laundrette (1985; 98 minutes; directed by Stephen Frears; stars Daniel Day Lewis and Gordon Warnecke). The story of two men, one a working-class white guy and the other a middle-class Pakistani, who take over a beat-up laundromat in London and become lovers.

Parting Glances (1986; 90 minutes; directed by Bill Sherwood; stars John Bolger, Steve Buscemi). Twenty-four hours in the lives of a young gay couple in New York City and their close friend who has AIDS. Funny, clever, and touching.

Personal Best (1982; 124 minutes; directed by Robert Towne; stars Mariel Hemingway and Patrice Donnelly). The story of two female athletes training for the 1980 Olympics who have a lesbian relationship.

The Times of Harvey Milk (1984; 87 minutes; directed by Robert Epstein). This Oscar-winning documentary tells the story of Harvey Milk, the first openly gay elected official in California, who was assassinated while in office. The film chronicles Milk's career and the dramatic impact that Milk's election and murder had on the gay community.

Torch Song Trilogy (1988, 117 minutes; directed by Paul Bogart; stars Harvey Fierstein, Matthew Broderick, Anne Bancroft). Film version of Fierstein's Broadway play about Arnold Beckoff, an aging drag queen searching for love and demanding acceptance from his mother.

Word Is Out (1977, 130 minutes; produced by the Mariposa Film Group). Compelling personal portraits of more than two dozen gay men and lesbians.

MAIL ORDER

Most of the books, magazines, and videos listed above—and a great deal of other material of interest to gay people—can be ordered through the following sources. Each of these bookstores also publishes its own catalogue of available publications and recommended titles:

A Different Light
548 Hudson Street, New York, NY 10014; tel. (800) 343-4002

Lambda Rising
1625 Connecticut Avenue, NW, Washington, D.C., 20009; tel. (800) 621-6969

Appendix 2: Resources

This appendix contains information on national and local hotlines that serve lesbian, gay, and bisexual youth; state-by-state listings of support groups for gay youth; and addresses for pen pal programs and scholarship opportunities for gay and lesbian young people.

Much of the information in this section is reprinted with permission from *You Are Not Alone: National Lesbian, Gay, and Bisexual Youth Organization Directory*, published by the Hetrick-Martin Institute of New York. The information was accurate as of the summer of 1993; since then, however, addresses, phone numbers, and meeting times may have changed. Copies of *You Are Not Alone* can be obtained through the Hetrick-Martin Institute, 401 West Street, New York, N.Y., 10014; tel. (212) 633-8920. A donation of five dollars is requested. Another helpful directory of information about lesbian, gay, and bisexual organizations, resources, and businesses in the U.S.A. and Canada is *Gayellow Pages*, available for ten dollars from Renaissance House, Box 292 Village Station, New York, N.Y., 10014-0292; tel. (212) 674-0120.

NATIONAL HOTLINES

Two hotlines for gay, lesbian, and bisexual youth have toll-free telephone numbers that can be reached from anywhere in the United States:

Gay, Lesbian, and Bisexual Youth Hotline
Toll-free number:
(800) 347-TEEN
Hours: Thursday through Sunday, 7:00 P.M.–11:45 P.M.

Central time. This hotline provides information about the gay, lesbian, and bisexual community, referrals, and emotional support to young adults.

Out Youth Austin Hotline
Toll-free number:
(800) 96-YOUTH
Local number: (512) 472-9246
Hours: daily, 5:30 P.M.–9:30

P.M. Central time. This hotline, based in Austin, Texas, welcomes calls from around the country. The hotline provides peer support and referrals to local resources for gay, lesbian, bisexual, and questioning youth.

Boston Alliance of Gay and Lesbian Youth (BAGLY) Information Line
Toll-free number:
(800) 42-BAGLY
Recorded information available 24 hours a day on AIDS issues, including safer sex, condom use, and HIV testing, as well as on services offered by BAGLY. BAGLY is a Boston-based youth-run social support group for lesbian, gay, and bisexual youth, age 22 and under.

Coalition for Lesbian and Gay Student Groups
P.O. Box 190712, Dallas, TX 75219; tel. (214) 621-6705
This group coordinates lesbian and gay student organizations on campuses in the South and Southwest. The coalition sponsors an annual conference and has established a lending library.

National HIV/AIDS Hotlines
Toll-free number for English-language hotline:
(800) 342-AIDS
Hours: daily, 24 hours a day.
Toll-free number for Spanish-language hotline:
(800) 344-7432
Hours: Monday through Sunday, 8:00 A.M.–2 A.M. Eastern time.
Toll-free number for TDD hotline for the hearing-impaired: (800) 243-7889
Hours: Monday through Friday, 10:00 A.M.–10:00 P.M. Eastern time.
These hotlines, operated by the Centers for Disease Control, provide education, information, and referrals on all issues related to AIDS and HIV infection, including guidelines for safer sex, location of HIV test sites, and names and addresses of local AIDS organizations. Literature available at no charge.

National Native American AIDS Prevention Center Hotline
Toll-free number:
(800) 283-AIDS
Hours: Monday through Friday, 8:30 A.M.–5:00 P.M. Pacific time. This Oakland (CA)-

based hotline provides information to people of any age concerning AIDS prevention and education as it relates to native Americans.

National Runaway Switchboard
Toll-free number:
(800) 621-4000
Hours: daily, 24 hours a day. Hotline for runaway and homeless youth of all sexual orientations and for their families. Provides crisis intervention on all issues facing runaways, including suicide. Also provides information, referrals, and message and conference services.

Parents and Friends of Lesbians and Gays (P-FLAG)
P.O. Box 27605, Washington, D.C., 20038; tel. (202) 638-4200
Hours: Monday through Friday, 9:00 A.M.–5:00 P.M. Eastern time. This national support group is designed to keep families in loving relationships and to support lesbians and gay men in their struggle for civil rights. P-FLAG operates 280 family groups and contacts nationwide. Call the office for the nearest available group in your area. P-FLAG publishes literature for men and women who are coming out; for parents of gay, lesbian, or bisexual children; for spouses of gay men, lesbians, or bisexuals; and on AIDS and safer sex. P-FLAG expects to have a 24-hour 800 or 900 number in effect in late 1993.

NATIONAL ORGANIZATIONS

These two organizations focus exclusively on the needs of lesbian, gay, and bisexual youth:

Lambda Youth Network
P.O. Box 7911, Culver City, CA 90233; tel. (310) 216-1312
Provides listings of talk lines, newsletters, pen pal programs, and bibliographies for lesbian, gay, and bisexual youth. Send a self-addressed, stamped envelope with your age to the above address. A donation of one dollar is requested.

National Gay Alliance for Young Adults (NGAYA)
P.O. Box 190712, Dallas, TX 75219; tel. (214) 701-3455
This organization tries to help

gay and lesbian youth understand their own feelings, as
well as to increase communication between the homosexual and heterosexual
communities. The Alliance
publishes *NGAYA News*.

**AIDS Coalition to Unleash
Power (ACT-UP)**
135 W. 29th Street (Suite 10),
New York, NY 10001; tel.
(212) 594-5441
Founded in 1987, ACT-UP is
a diverse, nonpartisan group
united in anger and committed
to direct action to end the
AIDS crisis. The New York
chapter can provide information on other groups around
the country.

**American Civil Liberties
Union—Lesbian and Gay
Rights Project**
132 W. 43rd Street, New
York, NY 10036; tel. (212)
944-9800
The ACLU works to secure
equal rights for lesbians and
gay men. If you are involved
in a legal case involving gay
rights, or if you have a question regarding gay people and
the law, the ACLU can help.
Contact the national office in

New York for referrals to local chapters.

**American Indian Gays and
Lesbians**
P.O. Box 10229, Minneapolis,
MN 55458-3229

**Asian/Pacific Lesbians and
Gays, Inc.**
Box 433, Suite 109, 7985
Santa Monica Boulevard,
West Hollywood, CA 90046-
5111

**Gay and Lesbian Alliance
Against Defamation
(GLAAD)**
150 W. 26th Street (Suite
503), New York, NY 10001;
tel. (212) 807-1700
GLAAD combats homophobia
in the media by organizing
grassroots responses to bigotry
and by fostering gay and lesbian visibility.

**Gay and Lesbian Arabic
Society**
Box 4971, Washington, D.C.,
20008
A support network for gays
and lesbians of Arabic de-
scent.

**Gay Games IV and Cultural
Festival**
19 W. 21st Street, New York
NY 10010; tel. (212) 633-9494

Organizers of a gay Olympics-style competition scheduled for 1994 in New York.

Gay, Lesbian, and Bisexual Veterans Association of America
1350 N. 37th Place, Milwaukee, WI 53208

The Gaylactic Network
Box 1051 Back Bay Annex, Boston, MA 02117-1051
An international organization for gay science fiction, fantasy, and horror fans and their friends.

Human Rights Campaign Fund (HRCF)
1012 14th Street, NW, Washington, D.C., 20005; tel. (202) 628-4160
National political organization for lesbians and gay men, devoted to civil rights, AIDS, and other health issues.

National Coalition for Black Lesbians and Gays
Box 19248, Washington, D.C., 20036
This national political and educational organization provides support and advocacy on issues affecting the black lesbian and gay community. The coalition combats racism, sexism, and homophobia; strives to create positive attitudes between and among black non-gays and black gays; and seeks to improve the working and social relationships between and among black lesbians and black gay men. The coalition works with local black organizations around the country and can provide referrals to those organizations.

National Coming Out Day (NCOD)
P.O. Box 8349, Santa Fe, NM 87504
National Coming Out Day, held yearly on October 11, is designed to heighten the visibility of gay men and lesbians across the country. Contact NCOD to learn about activities scheduled for your community.

National Gay and Lesbian Task Force (NGLTF)
1734 14th Street, NW, Washington, D.C., 20009-4309; tel. (202) 332-6483
NGLTF works to secure equal rights for gay men and lesbians and to create a society in which gay people can live openly without violence or discrimination. In addition to the Campus Project, which

provides resources to gay organizations on college and university campuses, NGLTF's focuses include reducing anti-gay violence, supporting lesbian and gay families, ensuring privacy and civil rights, and ending the military ban on gay people.

National Latino/a Lesbian and Gay Organization (LLEGO)
P.O. Box 44483, Washington, D.C., 20026; tel. (202) 544-0092

North American Multicultural Bisexual Network
584 Castro Street, Box 441, San Francisco, CA 94114-2558

Rainbow Alliance of the Deaf
P.O. Box 14182, Washington, D.C., 20044-4182
This national umbrella organization can provide referrals to local support organizations for the gay and lesbian deaf community.

Trikone: Gay and Lesbian South Asians
P.O. Box 21354, San Jose, CA 95151; tel. (408) 270-8776

LOCAL YOUTH SUPPORT GROUPS AND HOTLINES

In this section, community support groups specifically geared to young adults are listed on a state-by-state basis. In states where these groups do not exist (or where information on existing groups was not available at the time of publication), we have provided listings of general hotlines and/or support groups, many of which are open to both youth and adults. In addition, please note that we have not attempted to list organizations for gay, lesbian, and bisexual students on individual college campuses. As a growing number of colleges and universities do have such organizations, we urge college students to inquire about the existence of such groups on their campus. For information and advice on how to establish a new campus group, contact the Campus Project of the National Gay and Lesbian Task Force (listed above, under National Organizations).

Alabama

Birmingham
Gay and Lesbian Information Line
Lambda, Inc., P.O. Box 55913, Birmingham, AL 35255; tel. (205) 326-8600 (daily, 6:00–10:00 P.M.) Information, referrals, resources, and support on gay and lesbian issues. TDD service available for the deaf.

Alaska

Anchorage
Gay Helpline
Identity, Inc., P.O. Box 200070, Anchorage, AK 99520; tel. (907) 258-4777 Helpline available 24 hours a day; if no one is in the office to answer your call, you may leave a message and a representative will call you back.

Arizona

Phoenix
Phoenix Gay and Lesbian Youth Group
P.O. Box 80174, Phoenix, AZ 85060; tel. (602) 280-9927 Social/support group for gay and lesbian teens headed by professional counselors and a committee of group members. Meetings every Wednesday at 7:30 P.M.; call for location.

Also speakers on scheduled topics, social functions, and fundraising events.

Tucson
Wingspan Youth Group
Lesbian, Gay, Bisexual Community Center, 422 N. 4th Avenue, Tucson, AZ 85705; tel. (602) 624-1779 Community center for gays, lesbians, and bisexuals, offering a weekly support group for youth ages 23 and under.

Arkansas

Little Rock
Women's Project
2224 S. Main Street, Little Rock, AR 72206; tel. (501) 372-5113 Office hours: Monday through Friday, 8:30 A.M.–5:00 P.M.; Saturday, 11:00 A.M.–1:00 P.M. The Project offers a lesbian support group for young women "from late teens through twenties."

California

Berkeley
Pacific Center for Human Growth
2712 Telegraph Avenue, Berkeley, CA 94705; tel. (510) 548-2192 Office hours: Monday through Saturday, 10:00 A.M.–10:00

P.M.; Sunday, 10:00 A.M.–9:00 P.M. Funded by the United Way, this outreach group provides a Saturday-afternoon rap group for youth, various coming-out groups, and Saturday-evening table games.

Garden Grove
Young Adult Program
Gay and Lesbian Center of Orange County, 12832 Garden Grove Boulevard (Suite A), Garden Grove, CA 92463; tel. (714) 741-6501
Hotline: (714) 534-3261 (hotline hours vary)
Social and educational outreach to gay, lesbian, and bisexual youth ages 24 and under, as well as peer assistance and counseling. Meetings on Sunday evenings. No fees.

Long Beach
Young Adult Program of Long Beach
The Center—Long Beach, 2017 E. 4th Street, Long Beach, CA 90802; tel. (310) 434-4455
Hours: Monday through Friday, 10:00 A.M.–10:00 P.M.; Saturday, noon–6:00 P.M.
One-on-one peer counseling, structured and open discussion groups, monthly events, and

community services for gays and lesbians age 24 and under.

Los Angeles
Family Workshops
10861 Queensland Street, Los Angeles, CA 90034; tel. (310) 274-0219 (Barbara Bernstein, Ph.D.) and (310) 475-3225 (Marillyn Lebow, M.A.)
Information and support workshops for the parents of lesbian, gay, or bisexual children. Also support groups and workshops on coming out to families.

Gay and Lesbian Community Services Center
1625 N. Hudson Avenue, Los Angeles, CA 90028-9998, tel. (213) 993-7400
Mailing address: P.O. Box 197, Los Angeles, CA 90078
Hours: Monday through Friday, 9:00 A.M.–5:00 P.M. Services available at various locations throughout Los Angeles include Gay and Lesbian Youth Talkline (see below), rap groups, AIDS education, newsletter, pen pal program, training for professionals, crisis counseling, advocacy/referral, drug counseling, health care, food and clothing, street outreach, and transitional housing.

Gay and Lesbian Youth Talkline

Los Angeles, CA
(213) 993-7475 or (818) 508-1802 (Monday–Saturday, 7:00–10:00 P.M.)
This hotline for people under age 23 provides information about the gay and lesbian community, resources, referrals, and emotional support. Monday night is Women's Night, for female callers who wish to speak to women only.

Project 10

7850 Melrose Avenue, Los Angeles, CA 90046; tel. (818) 441-3382
Hours: Monday through Friday, 8:00 A.M.–4:00 P.M. Information and support for lesbian and gay teens, as well as resources for teachers, guidance counselors, and parents.

Pleasant Hill
NEAT Family Project (New Experiences in Affection and Trust)

391 Taylor Boulevard (Suite 120), Pleasant Hill, CA 94523; tel. (510) 687-8980
Hours: Monday through Friday, 8:30 A.M.–5:00 P.M. Support groups for gay and lesbian youth, ages 12 to 18, at risk for substance abuse.

Various locations; call office for information. No fees.

Sacramento
Lambda Community Center

1931 L Street, Sacramento, CA 95814; tel. (916) 442-0185
Hours: Monday through Friday, 10:00 A.M.–6:00 P.M.; Saturday, noon–4:00 P.M. Lambda Youth Group, a rap group (with occasional speakers), meets on Fridays and also offers Saturday dances, movies, and socials; lesbian youth movie night held the last Wednesday of the month. A peer counseling program is being established.

San Diego
Gay Youth Alliance San Diego

P.O. Box 83022, San Diego, CA 92138; tel. (619) 233-9309 (24-hour information line). Social support group for young gays, lesbians, bisexuals, and people exploring their sexuality who are 24 years old or younger. Biweekly discussion meetings.

San Francisco
Eighteenth Street Services

217 Church Street, San Francisco, CA 94114; tel. (415) 861-4898 (English) or (415) 861-8803 (Spanish)

Hours: Monday through Friday, 9:00 A.M.–7:00 P.M. Outpatient drug and alcohol counseling for gay and bisexual men, including homeless and runaway youth. Services include free support groups for youth, bilingual counseling, and street-based HIV/substance abuse/STD prevention.

Bay Area Sexual Minority Youth Network (BASMYN)
P.O. Box 460268, San Francisco, CA 94146-0268
Organization for bisexual, lesbian, gay, transgenderal, and questioning youth. Services include *Inside/Out* newsletter, information and referrals on youth groups, and pen pal programs for high-school-age youth. Submissions for newsletter welcome. No fees; all inquiries confidential.

Lambda Youth and Family Empowerment (LYFE) Program
1748 Market Street (Suite 201), San Francisco, CA 94102; tel. (415) 565-7681
Multicultural substance abuse and prevention center for gay, lesbian, bisexual, and questioning youth and their families, providing support groups,

a theater-writing class for youth of color, and leadership and health training.

Lavender Youth Recreation and Information Center (LYRIC)
1853 Market Street, San Francisco, CA 94103; tel. (415) 703-6150
Weekly peer-led support group for young women and young men; HIV prevention and education project focusing on gay and bisexual males; lesbian support project; coed softball teams; women's basketball; hiking and camping; quarterly clean-and-sober dances; and talkline (see below). Spanish speaker on staff and TTY available for the hearing-impaired.

LYRIC Youth Talkline and Infoline
Talkline: (415) 863-3636 (Thursday–Sunday, 6:30–11:30 P.M.)
Infoline: (800) 246-PRIDE (outside San Francisco but within the Bay Area; daily, 24 hours)
The Talkline is a confidential hotline that allows gay, lesbian, bisexual, transgender, and questioning youth to talk to other young people about

whatever is on their mind. The Infoline provides recorded information about being young and gay, coming out, stereotypes and basic facts about homosexuality, and information on upcoming activities at LYRIC.

San Francisco Suicide Prevention / Youth Line

3940 Geary Boulevard, San Francisco, CA 94118; tel. (415) 752-4866
Office hours: Monday through Friday, 9:00 A.M.–5:00 P.M. Youth Line: (415) 752-2000 (Monday–Thursday, 5:00–11:00 P.M.; Friday and Saturday, 7:00 P.M.–2:00 A.M.)
The Youth Line receives calls from gay, lesbian, bisexual, and questioning youth, ages 13 to 24, and provides peer counseling, crisis intervention, support information, and referral. The line is staffed by high-school and college-age youth.

Voice and Vision: Lutheran Lesbian and Gay Ministry

152 Church Street, San Francisco, CA 94114; (415) 553-4026
Hours: Monday through Friday, 9:00 A.M.–5:00 P.M. Of-

fers Voice of Pride youth project, a support program for sexual minority youth in Oakland consisting of group meetings for social and spiritual support, chemical-free social events, resource referrals, and counseling.

San Jose
The Billy DeFrank Lesbian and Gay Community Center

175 Stockton Avenue, San Jose, CA 95216; tel. (408) 293-2429
Hours: Monday, Tuesday, Thursday, Friday: 6:00–9:00 P.M.; Wednesday, 3:00–9:00 P.M.; Saturday, noon–6:00 P.M.; Sunday, 10:00 A.M.–6:00 P.M. A support group for youth 17 and under meets on Thursdays at 4:00 P.M.; social groups for youth 25 and under meet on Sundays at 1:30 P.M.

San Mateo
Peninsula Family YMCA– Project FOCYS

1710 S. Amphlett (Suite 216), San Mateo, CA 94402; (415) 349-7969
Hours: Monday through Thursday, 10:00 A.M.–9:00 P.M.; Friday, 10:00 A.M.–5:00 P.M.; Saturday, 10:00 A.M.–3:00 P.M. Provides individual, group, and family counseling

for gay, lesbian, bisexual, and questioning youth, ages 23 and under, and their families; provides outreach and education in San Mateo County. No fees.

Youth and Family Assistance
Community Living Room, 28 W. 37th Avenue, San Mateo, CA 94403; tel. (415) 572-0535
Hours: Monday through Friday, 2:00 P.M.–8:00 P.M.; Saturday, 2:00 P.M.–6:00 P.M.
Sponsors Sexual Identity Forum, a weekly support group for gay and lesbian youth, ages 21 and under. Monthly social activities, speakers from gay and lesbian community, open topic nights for socializing and support, and individual counseling available. No fees.

Santa Barbara
Gay and Lesbian Resource Center Youth Project
126 East Haley (Suite A-17), Santa Barbara, CA 93101; tel. (805) 963-3636
Hours: Monday through Friday, 10:00 A.M.–4:00 P.M.; Wednesday, 10:00 A.M.–7:30 P.M. Center offers Lookout!, a weekly rap group for lesbian

and gay youth, ages 23 and younger. No fees.

Santa Cruz
Lesbian, Gay, and Bisexual Community Center
P.O. Box 8280, Santa Cruz, CA 90561-8280; tel. (408) 425-LGBC
Hours: seven days a week, evenings. Referrals for gay, lesbian, and bisexual youth services in Santa Cruz County and outlying areas.

Men's Network
903 Pacific Avenue (Suite 207A), Santa Cruz, CA 95060; tel. (408) 457-1441
AIDS Project: (408) 427-3900
Weekly support groups for gay and lesbian teens, ages 19 and under; for young men; and for gay, bisexual, and questioning men, ages 30 and under. Call for times.

Santa Rosa
Positive Images
1023 Fourth Street (Suite C), Santa Rosa, CA 95404; tel. (707) 579-4947 or (707) 433-5333
Hours: daily, 24 hours a day. Provides support/rap group meetings in a safe atmosphere for gay, lesbian, and bisexual youth, ages 14 to 27. A speak-

ers' panel is available for community outreach and education.

Colorado

Denver
Gay and Lesbian Community Center
P.O. Drawer E, Denver, CO 80218; tel. (303) 831-6268
Office hours: Monday through Saturday, 10:00 A.M.–10:00 P.M.
Youth Crisis Line: (303) 461-1650 (daily, 24 hours)
Anti-violence Hotline: (303) 324-4297 (daily, 24 hours)
Provides services for gay, lesbian, bisexual, and questioning youth, including Outright!, a group for gay and lesbian youth, ages 21 and under; a support group for gay men 25 and under; a young lesbians support group for women 25 and under; an after-school Drop-In Center for youth 21 and under, providing tutoring and GED preparation; Young and Positive, an HIV/AIDS support group for youth 25 and under, including heterosexual youth; a substance-abuse treatment program; and Youth to Youth, an HIV education and prevention program that uses improvisation.

Connecticut

Danbury
Danbury Gay, Lesbian, and Bisexual Youth Group
105 Garfield Avenue, Danbury, CT 06810; tel. (203) 798-0863
24-Hour Helpline: (203) 354-5170
Holds weekly social/support group meetings on Mondays at Western Connecticut State University (in Elgross Library). Group provides community outreach through presentations on gay and lesbian youth issues.

New Haven
AIDS Project New Haven
850 Grand Avenue (Suite 206), New Haven, CT 06510; tel. (203) 624-0947 (office)
Office hours: Monday through Friday, 9:00 A.M.–5:00 P.M.
Hotline: (203) 624-AIDS (Monday–Friday, 6:30–9:00 P.M.; Saturday, noon–2:00 P.M.)
Programs include Bisexual, Gay, and Lesbian Active Dialogue (B-GLAD), a social, recreational, and educational support group for bisexual, gay, and lesbian youth. The

group addresses coming out, AIDS, risk-reduction education, and gay and lesbian history. Individual counseling also available. No fees.

Delaware

Wilmington
Gay and Lesbian Alliance of Delaware
800 West Street, Wilmington, DE 19801-1526; tel. (302) 655-5280 (office)
Hotline: (800) 292-0429
Hours: Monday through Thursday, 10:00 A.M.–10:00 P.M.; Friday, 10:00 A.M.–7:00 P.M.

District of Columbia

Washington
Sexual Minority Youth Assistance League (SMYAL)
333½ Pennsylvania Avenue SE (3rd floor), Washington, D.C., 20003-1148; tel. (202) 546-5940 (office)
Youth Helpline: (202) 546-5941 (Monday–Thursday, 7:00–10:00 P.M.)
Youth services and advocacy agency for gay, lesbian, and bisexual youth, ages 14 to 21. Programs include weekly youth support group, with meetings on Saturdays from 11:30 A.M. to 3:00 P.M.; a Youth Helpline; an after-

school program, on Wednesdays and Fridays from 3:30 P.M. to 7:30 P.M.; HIV prevention peer-led workshops; and community training and education.

Florida

Gainesville
Gainesville Gay Switchboard
P.O. Box 12002, Gainesville, FL 32604; tel. (904) 332-0700
Hours: daily, 6:00 P.M.–11:00 P.M.; recorded message other times. Peer counseling, information, and referrals for gay, lesbian, and bisexual community of Gainesville and north-central Florida. Call for information on Teen Closet, a local high-school organization.

Orlando
Delta Youth Alliance Your Turf
c/o Gay and Lesbian Community Services of Central Florida, P.O. Box 533446, Orlando, FL 32853-3446; tel. (407) THE-GAYS
Office hours: Monday through Friday, 1:00 P.M.–9:00 P.M.; Saturday, noon–5:00 P.M.
Hotline: (407) THE-GAYS
Hotline hours: 24 hours a day. The Youth Alliance offers

Monday-night rap group for gay, lesbian, and bisexual youth, ages 13 to 21, from 6:00 to 7:30. Social events include movies, beach trips, and outings to sports events and entertainment parks. Your Turf, a social/support group for gay, lesbian, and bisexual youth, ages 18 to 25, meets on Friday evenings at 7:00; call for location. Weekly raps on various topics, including coming out, family, relationships, HIV and AIDS, and religion.

Georgia

Atlanta
Young Adult Support Group
c/o Atlanta Gay and Lesbian Community Center, 63 12th Street, Atlanta, GA 30309
Center hours: Monday through Friday, noon–9:00 P.M.
Helpline: (404) 876-5372 (daily, 6:00–11:00 P.M.)
Multiracial support group for lesbian and gay youth, ages 24 and under. Meetings on Thursday evenings from 6:30 to 8:00 led by mental health facilitator. Various topics include safer sex education. No fees.

Hawaii

Honolulu
Youth Outreach Services
1154 Fort Street Mall (Room 415), Honolulu, HI 96813
Hours: Monday through Friday, 10:00 A.M.–7:00 P.M.
Weekly support group and information for gay and lesbian youth. Write or stop by for details.

Illinois

Chicago
Horizons Youth Services
961 W. Montana Street, Chicago, IL 60614; tel. (312) 472-6469 (office)
Office hours: Monday through Thursday, 9:00 A.M.–10:00 P.M.; Friday, 9:00 A.M.–5:00 P.M.
Helpline: (312) 929-HELP (daily, 6:00–10:00 P.M.)
AIDS Information Hotline: (800) AID-AIDS (daily, 10:00 A.M.–10:00 P.M.)
Social service agency for gay, lesbian, and bisexual youth, ages 14 to 23. Services include youth rap groups on coming out, family concerns, and other issues; AIDS and substance abuse prevention; a drop-in center for socializing; a newcomers' group; a Young

Adult Group for 18-to-23-year-olds; and other services.

Indiana

Indianapolis
Indianapolis Youth Group
P.O. Box 20716, Indianapolis, IN 46220; tel. (317) 541-8726
Hotline: (800) 347-TEEN
(Thursday–Sunday, 7:00–11:45 P.M.)
Social support and education group for gay and lesbian youth under the age of 21. Services include biweekly meetings, dances, retreats, support groups, and peer counseling hotline. They also run the Lesbian and Gay Youth Network, an under-21 national pen pal program to reduce isolation. Write for an application.

Iowa

Des Moines
Gay and Lesbian Resource Center
4211 Grand Avenue, Des Moines, IA 50312; tel. (515) 279-2110 (office)
Information Line: (515) 277-1454 (Monday–Friday, 4:00–10:00 P.M.)
Information and referrals for the gay and lesbian community.

Kansas

Topeka
Gay Rap Telephone Line
P.O. Box 223, Topeka, KS 66601–0223
Rap Line: (913) 233-6558
(daily, 9:00 P.M.–midnight; recorded message at other times)

Wichita
Land of Oz Information Service
P.O. Box 16782, Wichita, KS 67216
Info Line: (316) 269-0913
(daily, 6:00–10:00 P.M.)

Kentucky

Lexington
Gay/Lesbian Services Organization
(606) 231-0335

Maine

Portland
Outright—Maine
P.O. Box 5028, Portland, ME 04101; tel. (207) 774-HELP
Support group for gay, lesbian, bisexual youth, and those questioning their sexuality under the age of 22. Provides support and information in a safe and social environment. Meetings on Friday evenings.

Maryland

Baltimore
Gay and Lesbian Community Center of Baltimore
241 W. Chase Street, Baltimore, MD 21201; tel. (410) 837-5445 (office)
Hotline: (410) 837-8888 (daily, 7:00–10:00 P.M.)
Provides support and social opportunities for gay and lesbian youth, ages 14 to 22, and their families. Offers a weekly support group led by adult facilitators, and social activities such as dances and field trips.

Massachusetts

Boston
Boston Alliance of Gay and Lesbian Youth (BAGLY)
P.O. Box 814, Boston, MA 02103
Hotline: (800) 42-BAGLY
Youth-run social support group for lesbian, gay, and bisexual youth, ages 22 and under. Offers Wednesday meetings for new members, separate men's and women's groups, and general meetings. Sunday afternoons are informal drop-in days for socializing. Also offers a peer counseling program. The toll-free hotline offers recorded information on upcoming events, women's issues, AIDS/HIV, as well as referrals to local groups and services for youth.

Framingham
Framingham Regional Alliance of Gay and Lesbian Youth (FRAGLY)
P.O. Box 426, Framingham, MA 01701
Support/social group for gays and lesbians, ages 23 and under. Discussions and participation in community events. Meetings held on Tuesday evenings. Write for location.

Worcester
Supporters of Worcester Area Gay and Lesbian Youth
P.O. Box 592, Westside Station, Worcester, MA 01602; tel. (508) 755-0005
Recorded information available 24 hours a day. Youth-run support group with adult advisers open to all youth, ages 22 and under. Meetings held on Wednesdays at 7:00 P.M. at the United Congregational Church, 6 Institute Road, Worcester.

Yarmouth Port
Cape and Islands Gay and Lesbian Youth Group
Drawer 78, Yarmouth Port, MA 02675; tel. (508) 362-

7606; in surrounding area (800) 421-7874
Phone hours: 8:00 A.M.–11:00 P.M. daily. Social and support group for gay and lesbian youth, under age 22. Group meetings on Sunday evenings from 5:00 to 7:00. No fees.

Michigan

Ann Arbor
Ozone House Gay and Lesbian Youth Group
608 N. Main Street, Ann Arbor, MI 48104; tel. (313) 662-2222
Hours: 11:00 A.M.–11:00 P.M.; 24-hour phone line. Crisis intervention and counseling for runaways, homeless teens, and families. Support group for lesbian and gay youth. No fees.

Ferndale
Affirmations Lesbian and Gay Community Center
195 W. Nine Mile Road (Suite 106–110), Ferndale, MI 48220; tel. (313) 398-7105
Hotline: (313) 398-GAYS (Monday–Friday and Sunday, 4:30–11:00 P.M.)
Social and support group for lesbian and gay youth, ages 21 and under. Services include a hotline, AIDS prevention, education, and peer support. Meetings every Saturday from 1:00 to 3:00 P.M. at Wellness Networks, 845 Livernois, in Ferndale.

Grand Rapids
Windfire—Grand Rapids
c/o Lesbian and Gay Community Network of Western Michigan
909 Cherry SE, Grand Rapids, MI 49506; tel. (616) 459-5900
Weekly support group meetings on Thursdays at 7:00 P.M. for gay, lesbian, bisexual, and questioning youth, ages 22 and under. Anonymous HIV testing and counseling offered semiannually, free of charge. Network offers lending library.

Kalamazoo
Windfire—Kalamazoo
c/o WMU Alliance for Lesbian and Gay Support, Faunce Student Services, Kalamazoo, MI 49008; tel. (616) 387-2134
Friday-night support group for high-school-age and older youth. Call for location.

Traverse City
Windfire—Traverse City
P.O. Box 562, Traverse City, MI 49685; tel. (616) 922-4800

Thursday-night support group open to gay, lesbian, bisexual, and questioning young people. Call for location.

Minnesota

Minneapolis
District 202
2524 Nicollet Avenue South, Minneapolis, MN 55403; tel. (612) 871-5559
Storefront resource center, performance and gallery space, and meeting place for lesbian, gay, bisexual, and transgender youth and their friends.

Gay and Lesbian Community Action Council
310 E. 38th Street (Suite 204), Minneapolis, MN 55409; tel. (612) 822-0127 (office)
Hotline: (612) 822-8661; in upper Midwest (800) 800-0907 (daily, noon to midnight)
In addition to the hotline, the council provides services to address hate crimes, domestic violence, legal advocacy, community education, and media.

So What If I Am?
2200 Emerson Avenue, Minneapolis, MN 55405; tel. (612) 377-8800
Education and support group for gay, lesbian, and bisexual youth, ages 10 to 17. Meets Thursday evenings; call for time.

South High School's Lesbian, Gay, and Bisexual Student Support Group
South High School, 3131 19th Avenue South, Minneapolis, MN 55410; tel. (612) 627-2510
Weekly support group for students at South High. A safe, confidential place for lesbian, gay, and bisexual students to meet and discuss issues of personal or common concern. No fees.

University of Minnesota Youth and AIDS Project (YAP)
428 Oak Grove Street, Minneapolis, MN 55403
Hours: Monday through Friday, 8:30 A.M.–4:30 P.M.
AIDS prevention program for gay and bisexual males, ages 14 to 21. Services include risk assessment interviews, peer education, and referrals to medical, mental health, housing, educational, and chemical health resources. No fees.

St. Paul
Gay, Lesbian, and Bisexual Support Group
Central High School, 275 N.

Lexington Parkway, St. Paul, MN 55104; tel. (612) 293-8700 Weekly student-directed support group for gay, lesbian, and bisexual students at Central High School and their friends, and for students who have gay, lesbian, or bisexual parents or family.

Lesbian and Gay Youth Together (LGYT)
Mailing address: Wingspan Ministry of St. Paul-Reformation Lutheran Church, 100 N. Oxford Street, St. Paul, MN 55104; tel. (612) 224-3371 Weekly social support group provides a safe and supportive environment for gay, lesbian, bisexual, and transgender youth, ages 15 to 21. Meetings are on Sundays, 4:30 to 6:30 P.M. at 428 Oak Grove Street, Minneapolis. Provides referrals and information on support groups in high schools and elsewhere in Minnesota. Also provides resources for families, outdoor activities, and information on scholarships.

Lutheran Social Services Street Program
1299 Arcade Street, St. Paul, MN 55416; tel. (612) 774-9507 Support and advocacy for homeless youth and youth involved in prostitution.

Missouri

Columbia
Gay and Lesbian Helpline
(314) 449-4477 (Friday, Saturday, Sunday, 7:00–11:00 P.M.)

St. Louis
In Our Twenties
(314) 231-9100 Social and support group for gay men, lesbians, and bisexuals, ages 20 to 29, meets the second and last Fridays of each month at the Metropolitan Community Church, 1120 Dolmen Avenue.

Montana

Missoula
Lambda Alliance
P.O. Box 7611, Missoula, MT 59807 Western Montana's gay, lesbian, and bisexual support group. Write for meeting times and locations.

Nebraska

Lincoln
Gay and Lesbian Youth Talkline
P.O. Box 94882, Lincoln, NE 68502 (402) 473-7932 (Fridays and Saturdays, 7:00 P.M.–midnight)

Provides support, active listening, referrals, safer sex information, pamphlets, and a caring phone connection for youth, ages 13 to 23.

Nevada

Las Vegas
Gay Switchboard
c/o Metropolitan Community Church, 1119 S. Main Street, Las Vegas, NV 89104
(702) 733-9990 (daily, 6:00–11:00 P.M.)

New Hampshire

Concord
Gay Info Line of New Hampshire
(603) 224-1686 (daily, 5:00–8:00 P.M.)
In addition to providing information on gay, lesbian, and bisexual issues, the Info Line also offers dances and workshops as fundraising events in a safe environment.

New Jersey

Convent Station
Gay and Lesbian Youth in New Jersey
P.O. Box 137, Convent Station, NJ 07961-0137; tel. (201) 285-1595
Hours: 7:30–10:30 P.M. daily. Social and support group for gay, lesbian, and bisexual youth, ages 16 to 21. Meetings on selected Saturdays from 1:30 to 4:30 P.M. in South Orange, New Brunswick, and Trenton.

New Brunswick
Rutgers University Peer Counseling and Info Line
(908) 932-7886 (Monday–Thursday, 7:00–11:00 P.M.)

New Mexico

Albuquerque
One in Ten
c/o Common Bond YES, 4013 Silver SE, Albuquerque, NM 87106
Helpline: (505) 266-8041 (Monday–Friday, 7:00–10:00 P.M.)
Youth support group providing information, counseling, and social activities for gay and lesbian youth under age 21 meets every Friday at 7:00 P.M.

New York

Albany
Gay and Lesbian Young Adult Support Group (GLYA)
c/o Capital District Gay and Lesbian Community Council
P.O. Box 131, Albany, NY 12201; tel. (518) 462-6138
Support group facilitated by counselors and teachers to

provide an opportunity for
young people under age 21 to
explore their concerns about
their sexual identity. Meetings
are on Thursday, from 7:30 to
9:00 P.M.

Buffalo
**Gay and Lesbian Youth of
Buffalo (GLYB)**
190 Franklin Street, Buffalo,
NY 14202
Hours: Monday, Thursday,
and Friday, 6:30 P.M.–9:00
P.M.; Saturday, 1:30 P.M.–4:30
P.M. Support services for gay
and lesbian youth in western
New York State in a safe and
positive environment.

New York City
**Bisexual, Gay, and Lesbian
Youth of New York
(BI-GLYNY)**
c/o Gay and Lesbian Community Center, 208 W. 13th
Street, New York, NY 10011;
tel. (212) 777-1800
Peer-run support group. General meetings are on Saturdays, from 3:00 to 6:00 P.M.
Office hours for new and pro-
spective members are on
Wednesdays, from 4:30 to
6:00 P.M.

**The Hetrick-Martin
Institute**
401 West Street, New York,

NY 10014; tel. (212) 633-8920;
TTY: (212) 633-8926
This is a social service, education, and advocacy agency for
lesbian, gay, bisexual, and
homeless/runaway youth and
all young people, ages 12 to
21, who are exploring their
sexuality. Services include individual, group, and family
counseling; referrals to medical, legal, employment, and
shelter services; an after-school
Drop-In Center; the alternative Harvey Milk School;
Project First Step (see listing
below); and national advocacy.
All services free and confidential.

The Neutral Zone
162 Christopher Street, New
York, NY 10014; tel. (212)
924-3294
Hours: structured activities:
Monday through Thursday,
4:30 P.M.–7:30 P.M.; the Drop-
In Center: Monday through
Thursday, 8:00 P.M.–mid-
night; Friday and Saturday,
8:00 P.M.–2:00 A.M.; Sunday,
8:00 P.M.–midnight.
The volunteer- and youth-run
Drop-In Center provides a safe,
alcohol- and drug-free environment for lesbian, gay, and
bisexual youth, ages 14 to 21.
Services include peer counsel-

ing for substance abuse; HIV/ AIDS education; job fairs; creative and vocational workshops; and referrals.

Ninety-Second Street Y, Teen Division
1395 Lexington Avenue, New York, NY 10128; tel. (212) 415-5615
Hours: Monday through Friday, 9:00 A.M.–6:00 P.M. Social/support group for gay, lesbian, bisexual, and questioning youth, ages 15 to 19. Free and confidential.

Project First Step
338 W. 4th Street/24 Horatio Street, New York, NY 10014; tel. (212) 633-0887
Hours: Monday through Friday, noon–8:00 P.M. Provides support services for homeless and transitional youth. Services include showers, clothing, and food; information and intervention on HIV and safer sex; counseling; referrals; job training; GED program; and street outreach.

Project Reach Anti-Discrimination Space (ProRADS)
1 Orchard Street (2nd floor), New York, NY 10022; tel. (212) 966-4227
Community-based drop-in

center for young people; open Monday through Friday, 3:00 P.M.–6:30 P.M. Weekly support group for lesbian, gay, and bisexual youth meets on Thursdays from 4:30 P.M. to 6:00 P.M.

Youth Enrichment Services
208 W. 13th Street, New York, NY 10011; tel. (212) 620-7310
Hours for youth program: Tuesday through Friday, 9:00 A.M.–12:00 P.M.; Saturday, 9:00 A.M.–6:30 P.M. An alcohol- and drug-abuse prevention program for lesbian, gay, bisexual, and transgender youth, ages 13 to 22. Other weekly programs include creative writing, theater, video, and other visual arts. Also offers: *Out Youth*, magazine by and for lesbian and gay youth; a youth mentor program; and a leadership development program with youth from Bisexual, Gay, and Lesbian Youth of New York (BI-GLYNY), listed above.

Rochester
Lighthouse
Downtown United Presbyterian Church, 121 N. Fitzhugh Street (Room 441), Rochester, NY 14614; tel. (716) 251-9604

Social/support group for gay, lesbian, and bisexual youth, ages 14 to 21. Meets the first and third Sundays of the month.

Gay Source Infoline
(716) 244-8640 (Monday–Friday, 6:00–9:30 P.M.)

Selden
Long Island Gay and Lesbian Youth
P.O. Box 704, Selden, NY 11784; tel. (516) 579-0117
Peer-run support group, including "20 Something LI," for gay men and lesbians to meet people, share ideas, and learn more about gay and lesbian issues. Meetings are the first and third Sundays of each month.

Syracuse
Lesbian and Gay Youth Program of Central New York
Echo Center, 826 Euclid Avenue, Syracuse, NY 13210; tel. (315) 422-9741
Support groups, information referrals, and counseling services. No fees.

Syracuse Lesbian and Gay Youth Program
c/o Lambda Youth Services, P.O. Box 6103, Syracuse, NY 13217; tel. (315) 422-9741

Services for gay, lesbian, and bisexual youth, ages 14 to 21, include a support group, one-on-one and group counseling, a lending library, and community education.

North Carolina

Durham
Outright—Triangle Gay, Lesbian, and Bisexual Youth
P.O. Box 3203, Durham, NC 27715; tel. (919) 286-2396 in Durham; (800) 879-2300 from surrounding area
Hours: Sunday through Thursday, 6:00 P.M.–9:00 P.M.
Nonexploitative drug- and alcohol-free environment for gays, lesbians, and bisexuals under age 22, as well as educational and referral services.

Ohio

Cleveland
Lesbian And Gay Community Service Center
1418 W. 29th Street, Cleveland, OH 44113; tel. (216) 522-1999
Hotline: (216) 781-6736 (Monday–Friday, 7:00–11:00 P.M.; Saturday, 3:00–11:00 P.M.; Sunday, 7:00–11:00 P.M.)
Weekly discussion and support group for gay and lesbian youth, ages 22 and under. Social events such as sports,

dances, parties, and other group activities. Community outreach to schools, colleges, and social service organizations.

Dayton
Serenity, Inc.
tel. (513) 274-1616
Support group for sexual minority youth, ages 21 and under, serving central and southern Ohio. Call for more information.

Toledo
Central United Methodist Church
701 W. Central Avenue, Toledo, OH 43610; tel (419) 241-7729
Gay and lesbian youth organization sponsored by Central United Methodist Church. Discussion and education group for peer support, HIV education, and socialization. Meetings are on Thursdays from 7:00 to 9:00 P.M.

Oregon

Eugene
Metropolitan Community Church of Eugene
The Koinonia Center, 1414 Kincaid Street, Eugene, OR 97440; tel. (503) 345-5963
Mailing address: P.O. Box 10091, Eugene, OR 97400
Hours for drop-in center: Wednesdays, 1:00 P.M.–5:00 P.M. This Christian-affirmative church for gays, lesbians, and bisexuals provides educational and social activities, support groups, and community networking. Worship services are held Sunday at 4:00 P.M. at First Congregational Church, 23rd Street and Harris in Eugene.

Portland
Park Avenue Social Club
P.O. Box 2294, Portland, OR 97208; tel. (503) 238-0334
Social support group for gay men 18 to 29 years old. Meets Tuesday from 7:30 to 11:00 P.M. Call for meeting place.

Phoenix Rising
620 SW 5th Avenue (Suite 710), Portland, OR 97204; tel. (503) 223-8299
Educational and referral organization for the sexual minority community. Offers two weekly youth groups: Windfire, for youth living at home; and Voices, for homeless youth. All gay, lesbian, and bisexual youth under age 21 are welcome.

Pennsylvania

Harrisburg
Eagles Perch
Box 11543, Harrisburg, PA 17108; tel. (717) 236-7387
Lesbian and gay youth organization serving central Pennsylvania.

Lancaster
Gay and Lesbian Youth Alliance
P.O. Box 31, Lancaster, PA 17603-0031; tel. (717) 397-0691
Hours: Sunday, Wednesday, and Thursday, 7:00 P.M.–10:00 P.M. Services include counseling, referrals, social events, and fund-raisers. Open to gay and lesbian youth, ages 14 to 23, and to young people who have not determined their sexual orientation; encourages racial and ethnic diversity. Meetings are held on the first and third Tuesdays of each month, from 7:30 to 9:30 P.M.

Philadelphia
Penguin Place Youth Group
201 S. Camac Street, Philadelphia, PA 19107
Helpline: (215) 732-2220 (daily, 24 hours)
Social/support group for lesbian and gay youth, ages 21 and under. Youth group meets at Penguin Place Community Center on the first and third Saturdays of the month. Weekly activities include discussions and social events.

Pittsburgh
Growing Alternative Youth (GAY)
4120 Brownsville Road (Suite 16-1416), Pittsburgh, PA 15229
A youth-run education and support group for lesbian, gay, and bisexual youth, ages 23 and under. Weekly activities include speakers, HIV/AIDS education and prevention workshops, and social events (such as dancing and trips) on Tuesday evenings. Regular meetings are held on Sunday evenings at 6:30.

Rhode Island

Providence
Rhode Island Gay/Lesbian Youth
P.O. Box 50 Annex Station, Providence, RI 02903; tel. (401) 751-3322
This organization also operates a hotline for gay, lesbian, and bisexual youth at the phone number listed above.

Texas

Austin
Gay Student Network
P.O. Box 2585, Austin, TX
78768; tel. (512) 445-7270
Hours: Monday through Friday, 1:00 P.M.–5:00 P.M. Information, support, and
roommate referrals. No fees.

Out Youth Austin
c/o University YWCA, 2330
Guadalupe Street, Austin, TX
78705; tel. (512) 472-9264
Hotline: (800) 96-YOUTH
(daily, 5:30–9:30 P.M.)
Peer support for gay, lesbian,
bisexual, and questioning
youth. Also provides community education, including
workshops, Friday-evening
recreation, and Sunday-night
rap groups. No fees.

Dallas
**Gay and Lesbian Young
Adults**
P.O. Box 197012, Dallas, TX
75219; (214) 528-4233 (office)
Info Line: (214) 621-7440
A support group for gay, lesbian, bisexual, and questioning young adults under age 25
meets on Thursday evenings
at 7:30 at the Gay and Lesbian Community Center, 2701
Reagon Street, Dallas. General membership is free.

El Paso
**Lambda Services—Youth
Network**
P.O. Box 30321, El Paso, TX
79931-0321
Information line/hotline: (915)
562-GAYS (daily, 24 hours)
Serving all gay, lesbian, bisexual, or questioning youth between ages 15 and 21, with
peer support groups, special
presentations, and social
events. Group meetings are
held biweekly.

Houston
**Houston Area Teen Coalition for Homosexuals
(HATCH)**
P.O. Box 66574, Houston,
TX 77266-6574
Peer support group for gay
and lesbian youth between 16
and 21. Counseling on self-image, parents, school, and
career. Meetings are held on
Fridays, 7:30–10:30 P.M., and
Sundays, 6:30–9:30 P.M.

Utah

Salt Lake City
The Youth Group
770 South 300 West, Salt
Lake City, UT 84102
(801) 539-8800
A support group for gay, lesbian, and bisexual youth, ages
14 to 23, meets weekly on

Wednesday nights at 7:00 at the Stonewall Center.

Vermont

Burlington
Outright Vermont
P.O. Box 5235, Burlington, VT 05402; tel. (802) 865-9677 Hotline (in Vermont only): (800) GLB-CHAT (Monday, Wednesday, and Friday, 10:00 A.M.–4:00 P.M.)
Offers a weekly support group for gay, lesbian, and bisexual youth under age 22.

Virginia

Arlington
Whitman-Walker Clinic—Northern Virginia
3426 Washington Boulevard (Suite 102), Arlington, VA 22201
Information and hotline: (703) 358-9550 (Monday–Friday, 9:00 A.M.–6:00 P.M.; answering machine at other times).
Offers support groups, peer education, HIV case management, and volunteer opportunities.

Richmond
Richmond Organization for Sexual Minority Youth (ROSMY)
P.O. Box 5542, Richmond, VA 23220; tel. (804) 648-5241

Hours: Monday through Friday, 9:00 A.M.–5:00 P.M.
Youth Support Line (reachable through above number): Wednesday, 3:00–8:00 P.M.; recorded message at other hours. Serves lesbian, gay, bisexual, and questioning youth, ages 14 to 21, with meetings every Saturday from 1:00 to 3:00 P.M. and a Youth Support Line.

Washington

Bellevue
Youth Eastside Services
Bisexual, Gay, and Lesbian Adolescent Drop-In Group (B-GLAD)
16150 NE 8th, Bellevue, WA 98008; tel. (206) 747-4937
A drop-in support group for high-school youth, ages 15 to 18, meets on Thursday evenings at 7:30. Regular coming-out group for gay, lesbian, bisexual, and questioning youth.

Olympia
Stonewall Youth
P.O. Box 7383, Olympia, WA 98507
Peer support group providing information and a safe social space for bisexual, gay, lesbian, and questioning youth, ages 21 and under. Youth

group meets weekly and holds social functions throughout the year. No fees.

Seattle
Gay, Lesbian, and Bisexual Youth Program
American Friends Service Committee
814 NE 40th, Seattle, WA 98105; tel. (206) 632-0500
Youth Infoline: (206) 332-7900 (daily, 24 hours)
Provides support groups and other direct services to lesbian, gay, and bisexual youth at Lambert House, including a Youth of Color Discussion Group, film festivals, and social and recreational activities.

Gay and Lesbian Youth Rap Group
c/o Gay Community Social Services, Box 22228, Seattle, WA 98122; tel. (206) 292-5144
Gay and lesbian youth group run by Gay Community Social Services. No fees. Call for details.

Lambert House Gay, Lesbian, and Bisexual Youth Center
1818 15th Avenue, Seattle, WA 98122; tel. (206) 322-2735
Drop-in hours: Monday through Thursday, 4:00 P.M.–10:00 P.M.; Friday, 4:00 P.M.–midnight; Saturday, 3:00 P.M.–midnight. Social, recreational, cultural, educational, counseling, and recovery programs for gay, lesbian, and bisexual youth, ages 15 to 24.

Lesbian Resource Center
1208 E. Pine Street, Seattle, WA 98122; tel. (206) 322-3953
Hours: Monday through Friday, 2:00 P.M.–7:00 P.M. Provides services for the lesbian community, including a drop-in center, referrals for housing and other services, and a support group for women, ages 24 and under. Extensive library and monthly newspaper.

Seattle Counseling Service for Sexual Minorities
200 W. Mercer (Suite 300), Seattle, WA 98119; tel. (206) 282-9314 (office)
Hotline: (206) 282-9307 (Monday–Friday, noon–9:00 P.M.)
General services include drop-in center for sexual minority youth, outpatient therapy, domestic violence group, case management, AIDS crisis intervention,

and long-term therapy. No
fees.

Spokane
Odyssey
Spokane County Health District AIDS Program, 1101 W.
College Avenue (Room 401),
Spokane, WA 99201; tel. (509)
324-1547
AIDS Hotline in surrounding
area: (800) 456-3236
Rap and support group for
gay, lesbian, bisexual, and
questioning youth, ages
21 and under. Weekly
meetings.

Tacoma
Oasis Gay, Lesbian, and Bisexual Youth Association
3629 South D Street, Tacoma, WA 98408; tel. (206)
596-2860
Rap and support groups for
gay, lesbian, bisexual, or
questioning young adults
age 25 and under. Meetings
are held on Thursdays from
6:00 to 7:30 P.M. Also sponsors retreats and a speakers'
bureau.

West Virginia

Charleston
Young, Gay, and Proud
P.O. Box 3642, Charleston,
WV 25336-3642

Information and hotline: (304)
340-3690 (Wednesday, 5:00–
9:00 P.M.)
Peer support and counseling for gay, lesbian, and bisexual youth, ages 16 to 21.
No fees.

Wisconsin

Madison
Madison Community United
P.O. Box 310, Madison, WI
54701; tel. (608) 255-8582
Gay Line: (608) 255-4297
Lesbian Line: (608) 255-0743
Hours: Monday through
Friday, noon–4:00 P.M. and
7:00 P.M.–10:00 P.M. This
social service agency for
gay and lesbian youth provides counseling, referrals,
information, and advocacy.
No fees.

Milwaukee
Gay Youth Milwaukee
P.O. Box 09441, Milwaukee,
WI 53209
24-hour tel.: (414) 265-8500
This rap and support group
for lesbian, gay, and bisexual
youth, ages 18 and under, offers opportunities for young
people to meet in a comfortable environment to discuss
concerns about school, family,
and friends. Meetings are held
on the first and third Satur-

days of each month from 1:00
to 3:00 P.M.

Wyoming

Laramie
United Gays and Lesbians of

Wyoming
P.O. Box 2037, Laramie, WY
82070; tel. (307) 635-4301
Call for information on upcoming programs and social
events.

PEN PAL PROGRAMS

Pen pal programs can be an
effective way for gay and lesbian teenagers to reduce isolation and exchange ideas. For
information on corresponding
with a gay or lesbian pen pal,
send a self-addressed, stamped
envelope to one or more of the
following organizations. (If it's
not possible for you to receive
mail at your home address,
check at your post office about
renting a post office box or
about having mail sent to you
General Delivery and held for
you at the post office.)

Alyson Publications
Letter Exchange, 40 Plympton
Street, Boston, MA 02118

**Bay Area Sexual Minority
Youth Network (BASMYN)**
P.O. Box 460268, San Fran-
cisco, CA 94146-0268

**Gay and Lesbian Commu-
nity Services Center**
P.O. Box 197, Los Angeles,
CA 90028-9998

Indianapolis Youth Group
P.O. Box 20716, Indianapolis,
IN 46220

Lambda Youth Network
P.O. Box 7911, Culver City,
CA 90233

SCHOLARSHIPS

A growing number of organizations now offer scholarships
for gay and lesbian students.
Write for details and application materials.

**Dallas Gay and Lesbian
Community Scholarship
Fund**
P.O. Box 190712, Dallas, TX
75219
This fund offers Lambda

Scholarships to college juniors, seniors, and graduate students studying in Texas, Oklahoma, New Mexico, Arkansas, or Louisiana. Eligibility requirements include financial need, academic record, and community service.

The Markowski-Leach Scholarship

San Francisco State University, 1600 Holloway Avenue, San Francisco, CA 94132; tel. (415) 338-7129
This scholarship fund awards approximately ten scholarships of between $1,000 and $2,500 per year to gay and lesbian college juniors, seniors, and graduate students at San Francisco State, University of California at Berkeley, and Stanford University. Applicants must demonstrate "commitment to excellence through service, activities, employment or scholarship and dedication to making a contribution to society." Applications are available through the financial aid offices of the three schools mentioned above at the end of

January and are due by mid-March.

Minnesota Task Force for Gay and Lesbian Youth

c/o Minnesota P-FLAG, P.O. Box 8588, Minneapolis, MN 55408; tel. (612) 451-7996
An eleven-member board sponsors and secures tuition scholarships for gay youth, ages 16 to 23, who are residents of Minnesota or students at a college or university in Minnesota.

The Teachers' Group

Gays and Lesbians Working in Education, P.O. Box 280346, Lakewood, CO 80228; tel. (303) 232-3789
Annual $1,000 education scholarship to a gay or lesbian youth studying in Colorado.

The Wingspan Ministry of St. Paul-Reformation Lutheran Church

100 N. Oxford Street, St. Paul, MN 55404, tel. (612) 224-3371
Contact: Leo Treadway
Write for information on scholarships.

Permissions Acknowledgments

Excerpt from "My Brother on the Shoulder of the Road" by Clifford Chase. Copyright © 1992 by Clifford Chase. Reprinted by permission of the author.

"my brother" by Pat Parker. From *Jonestown & Other Madness* by Pat Parker. Copyright © 1985 by Pat Parker. Reprinted by permission of Firebrand Books, Ithaca, New York.

"Growing Up Gay in Little Havana" by Jesse G. Monteagudo. Copyright © 1992 by Jesse G. Monteagudo. Reprinted by permission of the author.

Excerpt from *Oranges Are Not the Only Fruit* by Jeanette Winterson. Copyright © 1985 by Jeanette Winterson. Used with the permission of Grove/Atlantic Monthly Press.

"Dawn" by James Purdy. Copyright © James Purdy 1984, 1987, 1993. Reprinted by permission of the author.

"A Chinese Banquet" by Kitty Tsui. From *The Words of a Woman Who Breathes Fire*. Copyright © 1983 by Kitty Tsui. By permission of the author and Spinsters/Aunt Lute.

"Commitments" by Essex Hemphill. From *Ceremonies* by Essex Hemphill. Copyright © 1992 by Essex Hemphill. Used by permission of the publisher, Dutton, an imprint of New American Library, a division of Penguin Books USA Inc.

Excerpt from *Gun-Shy* by Sean Mills. Copyright © 1993 by Sean Mills. Printed by permission of the author.

Excerpt from *Night Kites* by M. E. Kerr. Copyright © 1986 by M.E. Kerr. Reprinted by permission of HarperCollins Publishers.

"A Whisper in the Veins" by Terry Wolverton. Previously published in *Glimmer Train Stories*, Issue 4, Fall 1992. Used by permission of the author.

"Mother and Child." Excerpt from *Making History* by Eric Marcus. Copyright © 1992 by Eric Marcus. Reprinted by permission of HarperCollins Publishers Inc.

"A Lesbian in Class!" by Beth Harrison. From *Young, Gay, and Proud*. Copyright © 1980 by Alyson Publications. Used with permission of the publisher.

Also published by The New Press:

Lesbians, Gay Men, and the Law: A Reader, edited by William B. Rubenstein.
A pathbreaking documentary reader and casebook on the ways this country has attempted to legislate sexuality. "A wonderful anthology—one of the best compilations of writing by and about gay men and lesbians I've ever come across." —Larry Kramer (592 pages: Hardcover, $45.00; Paperback, $30.00)

AIDS Agenda: Emerging Issues in Civil Rights, edited by Nan D. Hunter and William B. Rubenstein.
Nine essays edited by the former and current director of the AIDS Project of the ACLU. "The most comprehensive analysis to date of the shifting features of the epidemic HIV/AIDS, the often misguided public reactions to it, and the inadequate responses of established institutions."—Mathilde Kim, American Foundation for AIDS Research (320 pages: Hardcover, $27.95)

WAC Stats: The Facts About Women by The Women's Action Coalition.
An invaluable handbook of statistics about the realities of women's lives today. "Factual firepower."—Susan Faludi, "Verbal Karate."—Robin Morgan (64 pages: Paperback, $5.00)

Gay & Lesbian Stats: A Pocket Guide of Facts and Figures, edited by Bennett L. Singer and David Deschamps.
An enlightening and provocative set of statistics about the state of gay and lesbian America on the twenty-fifth anniversary of Stonewall. (80 pages: Paperback, $5.95)